INTERNATIONAL ECONOMIC AND TRADE LAW

DE KOOPMAN.

(THE MERCHANT)

from Jan Luyken, Het Menselijk Bedrijf, 1694

M.e. cat.

International Economic and Trade Law

Universal and Regional Integration

edited by

a.e. + shelves

CLIVE M. SCHMITTHOFF
professor of international business law
City University and University of Kent

and

KENNETH R. SIMMONDS
professor of international law
Queen Mary College, University of London

director of The British Institute of
International and Comparative Law

A. W. Sijthoff - Leyden - 1976

ISBN 90 286 0076 0

Printed in The Netherlands.

TABLE OF CONTENTS

Part II: International Trade Law

PREFACE

An examination of the macro and micro aspects of the legal regulation of international economic relations has long been overdue. The central problem is here the relationship between universalism and regionalism.

On the macro level, economic regions have been constituted in many parts of the world and by countries of free market economy and of socialist planning. The relationship of these regional bodies to world-wide international organisations and to each other forms an important part of international economic law.

The situation is similar on the micro level. Bodies such as UNCITRAL and Unidroit strive for the regulation of international trade law on a universal basis, but other organisations, such as the European Economic Communities and the Council for Mutual Economic Assistance, pursue regional policies, and some countries, including the United States and Czechoslovakia, have even regulated international trade law on a national basis.

In this volume an attempt is made to examine the universal and regional tendencies in international economic and trade law. The volume consists of a number of essays contributed by an international team of specialists. They have selected certain key subjects which indicate the tension between universalism and regionalism and the possibility of accommodating these apparently conflicting trends in the emerging pattern of modern economic life.

The book is divided into two Parts. Part I deals with International Economic Law. Here there are covered problems pertaining to the European Economic Communities, Central and Latin-American regional integration, and the East African Economic Community in its relationship to the EEC. Part II treats the relationship between universalism and regionalism in International Trade Law. Here the following topics are considered: universal and regional organisations, international sales, international carriage by sea, international commercial arbitration, and international trade law and world peace. The Introduction is intended to make the substance of the essays contained in the two Parts of the work easily accessible.

The essays reproduced in this volume are founded on papers presented by the authors to the Oxford International Symposium on Universalism and Regionalism in International Economic and Trade Law, held at Christ Church, Oxford, in October 1973. For the publication in this volume, the essays have been revised and brought up-to-date. The Symposium, which we had the honour of organizing, was arranged under the auspices of the Board of Management of the Foster-Wills and Theodor Heuss Scholarships, Oxford University, and the German Academic Exchange Service. We wish to express our gratitude to these organisations and also to acknowledge the generous support provided by the Kulturabteilung des Auswärtigen Amtes der Bundesrepublik Deutschland and by the Stifterverband für die Deutsche Wissenschaft. Our special thanks are due to Dr. Martin Mruck, B. A. (Oxon.), then Director of the London Branch of the German Academic Exchange Service, who attended to the administration of the Symposium with exceptional skill and tact.

We further wish to record our sincere thanks to Dr. Katrin Cutbush, Lecturer in European and International Business Law at the Graduate Business Centre of the City University, who assisted us skilfully and conscientiously in the difficult task of editing the contributions for the press and who provided the tables and the index.

London, 17th July 1976

Clive M. Schmitthoff
Kenneth R. Simmonds

TABLE OF INTERNATIONAL CONVENTIONS AND OTHER INTERNATIONAL FORMULATIONS

TABLE OF NATIONAL LEGISLATIONS AND OTHER NATIONAL FORMULATIONS

TABLE OF CASES

TABLE OF ABBREVIATIONS

ABBREVIATIONS OF TITLES OF INSTITUTIONS AND ORGANS[1]

AAA	American Arbitration Association
AASM States	Associated and Associable States and the Malagasy Republic
A.C.P.	African, Caribbean and Pacific countries, signatories to the Lomé Convention of February 28, 1975.
BIMCO	Combiconbill by the Baltic and International Maritime Conference
CACM	Central American Common Market
CAFTA	Central American Free Trade Association
CARICOM	Caribbean Community and Common Market
CARIFTA	Caribbean Free Trade Association
CECLA	Special Committee on Latin American Co-ordination
CITEJA	Comité International Technique d'Experts Juridiques Aériens (so-called International Technical Committee of Legal Experts on Air Questions)
COMECON	see CMEA
CMEA	Council for Mutual Economic Assistance
CMI	Comité Maritime International; see IMC
ECA	United Nations Economic Commission for Africa
ECAFE	United Nations Economic Commission for Asia and the Far East
ECE	United Nations Economic Commission for Europe
ECLA	United Nations Economic Commission for Latin America
EEC	European Economic Communities
EFTA	Free Trade Association
FAO	United Nations Food and Agricultural Organisation

1. Abbreviations of names of international organisations are quoted in accordance with the *Yearbook of International Organizations*, 15th edition 1974, which is a reference publication produced by the Union of International Associations, publication No 226; UDC 061 (100) (058).

FIATA	Fédération Internationale des Associations de Transitaires et Assimilés (the International Federation of Forwarding Agents Associations)
FOSFA	Federation of Oils, Seeds and Fats Associations (London)
GAFTA	Grain and Feed Trade Association (London)
GATT	General Agreement on Tariffs and Trade
HMG	Her Majesty's Government in the United Kingdom
IBRD	International Bank for Reconstruction and Development
ICAO	International Civil Aviation Organisation
ICC	International Chamber of Commerce
IMC	International Maritime Committee
IMCO	Inter-Governmental Maritime Consultative Organisation
IMF	International Monetary Fund
LAFTA	Latin American Free Trade Association
NATO	North Atlantic Treaty Organisation
OAS	Organisation of American States
OAU	Organisation for African Unity
ODECA	Organisation of Central American States
OPEC	Organisation of Petroleum Exporting Countries
SIECA	Secretariat of Central American Economic Integration
SMGS	Russian initials for the Railway Convention for Eastern Europe (i.e. the Agreement Concerning the International Rail Transport of Goods)
UNCITRAL	United Nations Commission on International Trade Law
UNCTAD	United Nations Conference on Trade and Development
UNIDROIT	The International Institute for the Unification of Private Law
UNO	United Nations Organisation

II. OTHER ABBREVIATIONS

AGB	Allgemeine Geschäftsbedingungen
AWD	Außenwirtschaftsdienst des Betriebsberaters, Recht der internationalen Wirtschaft
CITC	Czechoslovak International Trade Code
CMLR	Common Market Law Reports
C.M.L.Rev.	Common Market Law Review
CMR	Convention on the Contract for the International Carriage of Goods by Road
CTO	Combined Transport Operator (see Draft Convention on Combined Transport of Goods (TCM) 1972)
E.C.R.	Reports of cases before the European Court of Justice in Luxembourg published since January 1, 1973. Reports covering the years 1962-1972 are now in the process of being published in English by the Court. The years 1954-1961 will follow.

GNP	Gross National Product
INCOTERMS	International Rules for the Interpretation of Trade Terms 1953, supplemented in 1967 (ICC)
ICLQ	International and Comparative Law Quarterly
J.B.L.	Journal of Business Law
J.O.	Journal Officiel
LDCs	"less-developed countries"
MDCs	"more-developed countries"
MFN Clause	Most Favoured Nation Clause
Stabex	Stabilisation of Export Earnings
TCM	Draft Convention on Combined Transport of Goods
u.a.	Units of Account (EEC)
UCC	The American Uniform Commercial Code
ULIS	The Hague Uniform Laws of International Sales

INTRODUCTION

PART I: INTERNATIONAL ECONOMIC LAW

The five contributions to the first part of this volume give a selective overview of the progress of regional economic integration movements in Western Europe, Central and Latin America, and the Caribbean and East Africa. The papers by Professor H. G. Schermers, Professor A. R. Brewer-Carías, Dr. F. V. García-Amador, Sir Hugh Wooding and Professor K. R. Simmonds, are concerned with the objectives, sources, techniques and implementation of the law of integration in the regional organisations surveyed. They seek to examine both the evolution and the impact of the disparate regional and sub-regional arrangements that have so radically transformed our attitudes toward the form and the competence of international institutions during the last twenty-five years. They do not purport to provide a comprehensive examination of world developments; for example, what Dr. W. E. Butler has recently called the "... curious, almost dialectical relationship between community-building in East and West..." [1] is not investigated in this part of the volume, although the unification and harmonisation activities of COMECON are discussed by Professor Jakubowski in a later chapter.[2] As has been indicated above, the contributions were originally prepared for consideration at a conference which was primarily concerned with the often uneasy relationships between regional and universal arrangements. They can, therefore, only attempt to give a critical, but interim, progress report.

Professor Schermers' paper on *The Role of the European Court of Justice in the Harmonization and Unification of European Law* [3]

1. W. E. Butler, "Legal Configurations of Integration in Eastern Europe", in 51 (1975) *International Affairs*, pp. 518-530, at 518.
2. See pp. 105 *et seq.*
3. See pp. 3 *et seq.*

stresses that this institution, the most sophisticated and innovative tribunal of its kind yet evolved, has both become an essential instrument of integration within the European Communities and is also largely responsible for the development, in furtherance of the objectives and policies of the Communities, of a "European Judicial Power'. The direct, and complementary, relationships that have been established between the Community legal order and the domestic legal orders of the Member States have done much to make the Western European system of regional integration both coherent and dynamic.

Professor Brewer-Carías, in his paper on *Regional Integration in Central and Latin America: A Progress Report,*[4] contributes a wide-ranging review of the long history of confrontation between regionalism and universalism in the international legal relationships between states in Central and Latin America. His paper draws particular attention to the most recent sub-regional integration movement sponsored by the "Andean Group" countries since the Pact of Cartagena in 1969.[5] This movement provides, for the first time in South America, an institutional scheme of integration with supranational organs. Although initiated within the overall framework of the Latin American Free Trade Association (LAFTA), it clearly reflects many of the disappointments felt at the performance of the "parent" organization since its own establishment by the Treaty of Montevideo in 1960.[6]

Dr. García-Amador's study of *Universalism and Regionalism in International Economic and Trade Law: The Experience of Latin America*[7] also underlines the dissatisfaction of many Latin American developing states with the principles and mechanisms of traditional international economic relationships, whether universal or regional

4. See pp. 13 *et seq.*

5. For text see *Instruments for Economic Integration in Latin America and in the Caribbean* (Inter-American Institute of International Legal Studies, 1975), Volume I, at p. 175.

6. See K. R. Simmonds, "International Economic Organisations in Central and Latin America and the Caribbean: Regionalism and Sub-Regionalism in the Integration Process", in 19 (1970) *International and Comparative Law Quarterly,* pp. 376-397.

7. See pp. 35 *et seq.*

in origin and character. These sentiments were, of course, strongly expressed by delegates from a number of these countries in the debates which preceded, and inspired, the controversial 1974 U.N. General Assembly Declaration on the Establishment of a New International Economic Order,[8] the ensuing Programme of Action on the Establishment of a New International Economic Order,[9] and the Charter of Economic Rights and Duties of States.[10]

The contribution by the late *Sir Hugh Wooding,* formerly Chief Justice of Trinidad and Tobago, whose death was announced on July 26, 1974, examines *Regional Integration in the Caribbean and the Commonwealth* [11] with particular regard to the emergence of the Caribbean Economic Community.[12] His analysis of the Compatibility of the CARICOM Treaty with art. xxiv of GATT is of particular relevance at a time when criticisms of regional arrangements are being revived within both GATT and UNCTAD in consequence of the conclusion of the Lomé Convention.

Finally, the paper by *Professor K. R. Simmonds* on *The East African Economic Community and the European Economic Communities* [13] traces the evolution of another of the interesting experiments in regional integration being implemented in the "new" Commonwealth. New relationships between the Member States of this Community (Kenya, Tanzania and Uganda), forty-three other African, Caribbean and Pacific developing countries, and the nine Member States of the enlarged EEC have been established within the framework of the Lomé Convention, signed on February 28, 1975. The writer suggests that the Lomé Convention, with many unprecedented

8. Resolution 3201 (S-VI), adopted without vote on May 1, 1974.
9. Resolution 3202 (S-VI), adopted without vote on May 1, 1974.
10. Resolution 3281 (xxix), adopted by a vote of 120 in favour, with 6 against and 10 abstentions, on December 12, 1974. Belgium, Denmark, the Federal Republic of Germany, Luxembourg, the United Kingdom and the United States voted against the Resolution. Austria, Canada, France, Ireland, Israel, Italy, Japan, the Netherlands, Norway and Spain abstained. The Maldive Islands and Spain were not represented.
11. See pp. 45 *et seq.*
12. Cf. K. R. Simmonds, "The Caribbean Economic Community: A New Venture in Regional Integration", in 23 (1974) *International and Comparative Law Quarterly,* pp. 453-458.
13. See pp. 59 *et seq.*

and unique features, moves away from some of the weaknesses of traditional forms of regional and intra-regional economic co-operation agreements. It may mark, for the EEC, a transition from a conventional commercial policy towards a new development-oriented external economic policy and could, more generally, create an influential new pattern for relationships between industrialized and developing countries.

PART II: INTERNATIONAL TRADE LAW

The thirteen contributions which form the second part of this work deal with the following problems of International Trade Law: Universal and Regional Organisations, International Sales, International Carriage by Sea, International Commercial Arbitration, and International Trade Law and World Peace.

A. Universal and Regional Organisations

Professor *John Honnold* who, at the time when he wrote his contribution, was the Chief of the United Nations Commission on International Trade Law (UNCITRAL), in his paper on *The Reconciliation of International and National Codifications of International Trade Law* [14] deals in particular with the relationship of the efforts of UNCITRAL to the regional approaches in this field. He points out that the special mission given to UNCITRAL by the General Assembly of the United Nations is the unification in those fields of international trade law where a world-wide approach is possible. He refers to the four topics which are included in the present work programme of UNCITRAL: (1) international sale of goods; (2) international payments, with special attention to a Uniform Law on International Bills of Exchange and Promissory Notes; (3) international commercial arbitration; and (4) international legislation on shipping. About the relationship between world-wide and regional unification, Professor Honnold observes: [15] "Certainly, in the Commission's work, I have seen no indication that regional economic or

14. See pp. 77 *et seq.*
15. On p. 78.

legal integration has reduced the need for unification, on a world-wide scale, of the basic rules of law applicable to international trade. Even the most intensive and successful regional arrangements are not designed to limit trade to that region." Professor Honnold comments on the rich variety of competing legal ideas which one meets in the work of unification. In his view, it is an over-simplication to refer to the civil law and the common law or the law of Eastern Europe. He examines two controversial questions which have to be answered in a pragmatic manner, viz. whether a Uniform Law shall apply unless the parties exclude it or whether it shall apply only if they adopt it; and whether a Uniform Law shall be applied by the courts generally or only in transactions that have a prescribed contact with a state that has adopted the Uniform Law. These problems are of fundamental importance to the world-wide unification of international trade law.

Mr. *Mario Matteucci,* the present President of the International Institute for the Unification of Private Law in Rome (Unidroit), in his paper on *The Contribution of Universal and Regional Organisations to the Development of International Trade Law,*[16] puts forward an eloquent plea for world-wide unification, where possible, in preference to regional unification. Mr. Matteucci refers to the unifying activities of various international organisations, such as the League of Nations; Unidroit, which advanced the Uniform Laws on International Contracts of Sale and on the Formation of such Contracts, of agency, of the law of transportation and other topics; of the United Nations Economic Commission for Europe; the Council of Europe; the Benelux countries; the Nordic countries; the Council for Mutual Economic Assistance; the Asian-African Legal Consultative Committee; and the Organisation of American States. He expresses the view that UNCITRAL is the proper channel through which such unifying provisions should be presented to a larger forum of countries. He then examines the difficult question whether a pragmatic approach to individual problems should be the sole avenue of approach of unification or whether the time has come also to attempt a systematic approach to the whole field of international trading contracts. In his view, time is not yet ripe for a systematic codification "but attempts should be made to look to the future." For these reasons

16. See pp. 85 *et seq.*

Unidroit is now studying the possibility of achieving a Uniform Law which will represent a code of international relations. In conclusion, Mr. Matteucci warns against attempting a regional or continental solution without having first tried to obtain an agreement on a universal level. He concludes: [17] "... with regard to the general principles of the law of commerce, it would be advisable to pursue universal unification. Only if universal unification is not feasible, should one be satisfied with regional unification. To insist primarily on separate regional unifications without a link between the different continents, would be a great mistake."

Dr. *Hans Claudius Ficker,* an official of the Commission of the European Communities, but speaking in his personal capacity and not for the Commission, in his paper on *The Contribution of the European Economic Community to the Development of International Trade Law,* [18] reviews first the machinery of EEC legislation, viz. Regulations and Directives, and discusses its enforcement under Community law. In his view the transnational character of the Community serves as a model for other regional organisations in their formative stages. He illustrates this statement by referring to the proposed harmonisation of company law and, in the sale of goods, the introduction of uniform standards for liability for defective goods.

Professor *E. Allan Farnsworth,* in his article on *The Uniform Commercial Code and the Global Unification of International Trade Law,*[19] compares the Uniform Commercial Code (UCC) of the United States with the Uniform Law on the International Sale of Goods (ULIS) and the work carried out by UNCITRAL in revising ULIS. He lists four ways in which the UCC may advance international codification, viz. by reducing the traditional common law resistance to codification, by presenting many common law principles in a statutory form, by formulating novel solutions to many troublesome problems in international trade law, and by serving as an example for a successful unification of the laws of many jurisdictions. Professor Farnsworth then lists the ways in which the UCC may

17. On pp. 91 and 92.
18. See pp. 93 *et seq.*
19. See pp. 97 *et seq.*

retard international codification. The most important of them are by affording American jurists an advanced set of norms, and by setting a standard of comprehensiveness and detail. Professor Farnsworth's study confirms the view expressed by Mr. Matteucci [20] that a successful regional or national codification may operate as an obstacle to eventual world-wide unification.

Professor *Jerzy Jakubowski,* in his paper on *The Unification Measures of the Council for Mutual Economic Assistance and the National Regulation of International Trade Law by its Members,*[21] refers to the limitation imposed by the community law of the Council for Mutual Economic Assistance (CMEA) to the regulation of international situations. He compares the application of unified law in CMEA and the EEC. He notes that, as a rule, relations of purely internal character are not affected by the community law of CMEA, whilst the harmonisation of law in the EEC involves also internal relations. Professor Jakubowski emphasises that it is a firm principle of socialist integration, which is the aim of CMEA, that it can be reconciled with world-wide co-operation. He mentions that the adoption of CMEA community law by the member states of CMEA is a measure of international character; it is either done by an international convention which requires ratification or by acceptance of a recommendation of CMEA by the member states and its implementation in the territories of those member states. In the countries of CMEA, the principles of party autonomy and applicability of commercial customs, especially those of international character, play a dominant role as superior principles of international trade law.

The contribution by *Professor Pavel Kalenský* on *The International Trade Code of Czechoslovakia* [22] (CITC) is devoted to the explanation of this important enactment, its origin, its relationship to the General Conditions for the Delivery of Goods of 1968 of the CMEA countries, the Hague Uniform Laws on International Sales (ULIS and ULFIS), and the American UCC, and to the exposition of the main provisions of the CITC. Professor Kalensky points out that the CITC is a municipal codification which forms part of the Czechoslovak legal

20. On p. 91.
21. See pp. 105 *et seq.*
22. See pp. 111 *et seq.*

order. The central concept of the CITC is the definition of the legal relationship arising in international trade. Unlike the definition in ULIS, it is not made dependent on the personal quality of the parties as criterion for its application. The CITC forms the subsidiary law in the application of the General Conditions for the Delivery of Goods 1968, issued by CMEA, which apply to legal relations arising between the foreign trade corporations of the member states of CMEA. In other words, if a matter is not regulated by the General Conditions and a Czechoslovak enterprise is the seller, the CITC applies as the law of the seller. Beyond that, the CITC applies to transactions between Czechoslovak trade corporations and corporations in other countries, particulary those of the Western world, if Czechoslovak law is the law governing the contract.

B. International Sales

Professor *André Tunc,* in his contribution on *The Need for Universal Unification of the Law of International Sales* [23] considers the present position of the Uniform Laws on International Sales, adopted at The Hague in 1964, and their future. He does not share the view expressed in some quarters that regional unification is an absolute pre-requisite to global unification. In his view the tremendous increase in international trade requires a world-wide unification of the law of international sales without prior regional unification because the need for global unification is more widely and more strongly felt every year. The great weakness of the Uniform Laws, as adopted at The Hague, is that the preparing commission was, in fact, a West-European commission. There were represented some socialist countries, yet the commission was without the Soviet Union, and there were only a few Latin American countries, no African countries, no Asian countries, not even Japan. For that reason the revision of the Uniform Laws at present undertaken by UNCITRAL is highly important. It enables the approximation of the Uniform Laws to the Uniform Commercial Code of the United States, to the General Conditions of Delivery of the CMEA countries, to the laws of the African and Asian countries. However, as regards the revision of the Uniform Laws on International Sales, Professor Tunc expresses some

23. See pp. 127 *et seq.*

misgivings but he expects considerable advantages from such a revision. He expresses the hope that many nations will accept a revised version of the Uniform Laws but he fears that at the end a great profusion and resulting confusion of uniform laws may result. Some nations may accept the Uniform Laws on International Sales in their original form, others in their revised version, the United States may continue to adhere to the Uniform Commercial Code, and the CMEA countries to the General Conditions of Delivery. In conclusion, Professor Tunc expresses the hope that he is not unduly pessimistic without serious justification.

Professor *Freiherr Wolfgang Marschall von Bieberstein*, in his contribution on *The Hague Uniform Laws of International Sales*,[24] considers that a universal unification of the law of international sales is possible, since no basic differences exist as to the public policies of the various countries in the field of international sales. In his view, the differences between various legal systems are not as great as they may appear at first sight, even in such a question as specific performance, which in the common law countries is admitted less easily than in the countries which found their law on the Roman system; the reason for this experience is that in the field of international sales the enforcement of judgments for specific performance is, in any event, rare. The real problem of universal unification in the law of international sales is not one of substance, but rather one of procedure and drafting techniques. In order to avoid conflicts with the desired universal unification, new regional projects should not be restricted to international sales. Considerable difficulty is here created by so-called back-to-back contracts because the international contract between the exporter and his customer abroad and the supply contract between the exporter and his supplier at home may be governed by different legal régimes, the former by the Uniform Laws on International Sales and the latter by the municipal law relating to sales. If in such a situation the exporter excludes the application of the Uniform Laws and gives preference, in his export contract, to his own or another national law, this could be a serious obstacle to the desired unification. It will, concludes Professor Marschall von Bieberstein,

24. See pp. 137 *et seq.*

"be a great task for all desiring unification to 'sell' their idea and to develop new contract forms and general conditions which are based on the new unified law."

C. International Carriage by Sea

Professor *Kurt Grönfors* contributes an essay on *Universalism and Regionalism in the Law of Carriage by Sea.*[25] He refers to the fact that transportation is international by nature. This applies particularly to maritime and air transportation, and although carriage by rail, road and inland waterways are geographically less extensive activities, often regional only, as parts of combined transports they still bear the hallmark of universality. Universal activities require universal legal rules. In international maritime and air transport, the traditional technique of universal law-making is by making an international convention. Such a convention was drafted first by a small group of persons but as it took firmer form, a wider circle of persons and bodies was consulted until the final version emerged. This pattern of international law-making was surprisingly successful in the past. However, a changing world demands changing methods of international legislation. The countries in the course of development do not wish to entrust the main part of the preparatory work to small groups but wish to be concerned with it from the beginning. The golden days of the traditional conventions, aiming directly at global acceptance, have, in the opinion of Professor Grönfors, come to an end. New procedural means must be devised to achieve uniformity of maritime law. First, one should concentrate on adopting regional conventions. Regionalism does not necessarily imply that countries co-operating and forming a region must also be neighbours in the geographical sense of the word. A number of geographically divided countries could have a "regionally" common interest to accept such a convention. Secondly, there is the method of the model law; and thirdly, another method is to leave it to the organisations of commercial life to create standard rules that can be incorporated in contracts by reference, as e.g. is done by Incoterms sponsored by the International Chamber of Commerce. No doubt these modern methods, which are not based on the traditional concept of the international convention,

25. See pp. 147 *et seq.*

have their drawbacks, since there will be no guarantee for real uniformity. But, as Professor Grönfors observes,[26] "one condition for future success is to look in an unconventional way at the tools available for the harmonisation of law."

Mr. *Thomas A. Mensah* entitles his contribution *Universalism and Regionalism in the Law of Carriage by Sea: The IMCO Experience.*[27] He describes the activities and experience of the Inter-Governmental Maritime Consultative Organisation (IMCO). Mr. Mensah points out, at the risk of over-simplification, that the work of IMCO has been principally concerned with the tort law in the field of shipping, i.e. the liability of the shipowner, vis à vis third parties, as the result of the operation of law, rather than with the law of contract in the field of shipping, although IMCO was concerned in producing a convention on the combined transport contract. Nevertheless, the lessons to be drawn from the work of IMCO are valuable because IMCO was the first body of global participation and orientation to be engaged in the work of developing international shipping law. As with most United Nations organisations, IMCO likewise experienced a grouping of nations. That grouping was not by geographical regions but it was determined by the state of economic development of the states concerned and their political organisation. Essentially there are three of these groupings, viz. the states in the course of development, the developed industrial states, and the socialist countries. The developed maritime states, including the developed maritime states of the Eastern European Socialist block, favour the extension of the scope of existing maritime law régimes and a modification only where necessary. The developing countries, on the other hand, tend to demand the adoption of entirely new régimes. The former group tends to be in favour of self-regulation, whilst the latter prefers state action at national level and inter-governmental agreement at the international level. It is remarkable that in matters of shipping law the attitude of the socialist countries of Eastern Europe is, in general, barely distinguishable from that of the developed countries of market economy. Whilst the developing countries suggest generally solutions appropriate to their own requirements, they normally try to persuade

26. On p. 154.
27. See pp. 155 *et seq.*

the other countries to accept the preferred solutions for application on a universal basis. Mr. Mensah is a strong supporter of the universalist approach to questions of maritime law. He observes [28] that "the regional or sectional movements have, at least in the field of maritime carriage of goods, been aimed at infusing sectional objectives into world-wide régimes, with a view to making these régimes universally acceptable." He concludes that, if this trend continues, there will be no reason for pessimism about the attainment, in time, of uniformity.

D. International Commercial Arbitration

Professor *Clive M. Schmitthoff,* in his contribution on *Universalism and Regionalism in International Commercial Arbitration,*[29] states that the main reason for the popularity of arbitration in international business transactions is that it is the only means of settling disputes in a manner appropriate to the international character of the transaction. He notes that in view of the inherently international character of international commercial arbitration it is not appropriate to arrange the subject in geographical regions but it is better to refer to four great areas of international commercial arbitration. They are the area which consists of the countries of free market economy, in which the Rules of Conciliation and Arbitration of the International Chamber of Commerce (ICC) have special significance; the area in which the Commercial Arbitration Rules of the American Arbitration Association (AAA) apply; the area covered by the arbitration rules of the Council for Mutual Economic Assistance (CMEA), and the area covered by the arbitration rules of the great commodity associations. Whilst commodity arbitrations are in a special category, the areas covered by ICC, AAA and CMEA are, generally speaking, self-contained. Fortunately, however, there exist also some attempts at an arbitration regulation on an international level. This category includes four arrangements: the Protocol on Arbitration Clauses of 1923 and the Convention on the Execution of Foreign Arbitral Awards of 1927, the United Nations Convention on the Recognition and Enforcement of Foreign Arbitral Awards of 1958, the European

28. On p. 168.
29. See pp. 171 *et seq.*

Convention on International Commercial Arbitration of 1961, and the UNCITRAL Arbitration Rules, first published in 1974. Professor Schmitthoff then considers the various attempts at bridging the gulf which divides the great areas of arbitration. He concludes that the idea to establish a world-wide network of arbitration tribunals, culminating in an obligatory arbitration appeal tribunal, is not only utopian and impracticable but, even as a final goal, undesirable. "The strength of international commercial arbitration lies in its multitudinous form." [30] He advocates the creation of a world-wide, universally applicable code of arbitral conduct and expresses the hope that the UNCITRAL Arbitration Rules may, in due course, become such a code. Further, as a result of the progressive complication of arbitral disputes, it is desirable for the parties in arbitrations involving difficult questions of law or questions of general interest to adopt a two-instances procedure, i.e. to admit an appeal from the arbitration tribunal to an arbitration appeal tribunal or a court. It will, in the end, be necessary to establish an international appeal tribunal to which the parties, by agreement, can have resort if they so desire and have not made other arrangements for the review of the award by way of appeal. Such an international arbitration appeal tribunal could operate as a stand-in and "could make a valuable contribution to the internationalisation of commercial arbitration and the development of a modern international law merchant".[31]

Professor *Aleksandar Goldštajn* deals with *Permanent and ad hoc Arbitration.*[32] Professor Goldštajn points out that differences in the social structures and legal systems are by no means an unsurmountable obstacle to the evolution of uniform rules. There are, in the contributor's view, no essential differences between arbitration in the socialist and many other countries regarding the agreement to arbitrate, the selection of foreign arbitrators for ad hoc arbitration, the qualification of arbitrators, the choice of law, and the enforcement of foreign trade arbitration awards. Indeed, differences are sometimes greater between the arbitration systems of the Western countries than between systems of socialist and other countries. Professor Goldštajn

30. On p. 180.
31. On p. 181.
32. See pp. 183 *et seq.*

then examines in detail the merits and drawbacks of ad hoc and institutional arbitration. He supports the view expressed by Professor Ion Nestor[33] that there does not exist a substantial difference between these two types of arbitration. He considers the choice of forum of arbitration and mentions that Yugoslav enterprises most frequently stipulate the competence of the Court of Arbitration of the International Chamber of Commerce with the proviso that the seat of the arbitration tribunal shall be in Zürich (ad hoc arbitration in Zürich, as well as the Arbitral Tribunal of the Zürich Chamber of Commerce). In his general conclusions Professor Goldštajn makes the following points. He suggests that it should be generally accepted that international arbitration should, on principle, be separated from domestic commercial arbitration. There are, in his view, no doctrinaire differences that would hinder the establishment of a world-wide system of international commercial arbitration and we should, therefore, look with hope at UNCITRAL's suggestions to establish uniform rules on international commercial arbitration which, however, in his view, should not be restricted to ad hoc arbitration but should also deal with institutional arbitration. Professor Goldštajn then makes some suggestions for the improvement of ICC arbitration and expresses the view that the trend towards improving international commercial arbitration in general is justified.

E. International Trade Law and World Peace

Professor *Fritz Fabricius* in his contribution on *The Universal and Regional Harmonisation of International Trade Law as a means of maintaining World Peace*[34] approaches the subject from a wider angle. He first refers to the division of the world into capitalist, socialist and communist states, into rich and poor nations, but there are also nations having a mixed racial composition, and often serious conflicts of interest and ideology occur between states. World trade must be taken into consideration as a means of promoting international peace. Professor Fabricius then enters into a detailed examination of the relationship between law, power and state authority. He considers the classical liberal concept of a world economy and

33. United Nations General Assembly, Doc.A/CN 9/64, 1 March 1972.
34. See pp. 201 *et seq.*

examines the possibility of creating an international economic law and international trade law on a universal basis. He also pays attention to regional economic and trade law and refers, in this connection, to the differences between the structure of the EEC and CMEA. The former is a supranational institution, the nucleus of which is the formation of a common market and consequently the intention to co-ordinate the economic policies of the member states. The latter is not supranational but has the function of co-ordinating the efforts of the member states represented in the Council and to develop the national economies of their peoples according to plan. In the view of Professor Fabricius, the principle of a democratic welfare state is capable of bridging the ideological differences between the two power blocks. Professor Fabricius concludes that, if it is possible to achieve a harmonisation of international trade law and international economic law on a universal basis, that would be a great contribution to the cause of world peace. He adds that regional systems of economic and trade law may help to fulfil this function if they can assist developing regions towards an appropriate degree of economic, social and political parity with the rest of the world. They may also be of value insofar as they may lead to the realisation of the principles of a democratic welfare state.

F. Conclusions

The great majority of contributors, if not all, expresses the view that the approximation and unification of the law of international trade must proceed on a universal basis, in spite of the obstacles which the economic and ideological division of the world places in the path of that trend. That must be the aim, notwithstanding the fact that the unification of international trade law on a universal basis can only be advanced step by step and will take a long time to achieve. As regards unification on a regional basis, the opinion of the contributors is divided. Some consider it a retarding element on the way towards universal unification. Others take the view that it represents a useful intermediary stage. All contributors emphasise the economic background of the movement to unification of the law of international trade and indicate that the ideological division of the world is of minor importance in this connection. The contribution which that movement can make to the maintenance of world peace is fully acknowledged by the contributors.

Part I

International Economic Law

1

THE ROLE OF THE EUROPEAN COURT OF JUSTICE IN THE HARMONISATION AND UNIFICATION OF EUROPEAN LAW

*Henry G. Schermers**

This contribution will be devoted to the method of making and developing international economic and trade laws. How do we achieve uniform rules of law in several nations, how do we develop such a law and how do we keep its application uniform? In the European Communities uniform rules of law can be made in three different ways:

a) The community may issue *regulations* containing rules of law directly binding on every citizen within the member states. These rules come directly from the Community to the citizens, and national governments play no role in their formulation.
b) The community may instruct governments of member states to incorporate particular rules of law into their national legal systems. For this purpose the EEC Treaty provides in article 189 for *directives* which are binding as to the result to be achieved, but leave the choice of form and method to the national authorities. The degree of discretion left to national governments varies; either a general purpose may be given, such as a particular system of turnover tax – and here governments may be entirely free to draft the necessary legislation – or detailed rules of law may have to be drafted, which the governments are to incorporate into their national legal order. Often, the Community may obtain the same result as that, which is achieved through a directive, by addressing binding *decisions* to the governments of the member states in which

* Professor of Law, Director of the Europa Instituut of the University of Amsterdam, The Netherlands.

these governments are ordered to take particular legislative measures.

c) Most other international organisations draft *multilateral treaties* to create uniform rules of law. The Communities may use this method as well (art. 220 of the EEC Treaty).

As a rule, the Communities are not free to choose from the above mentioned systems. The EEC Treaty usually indicates which particular methods may be chosen.

No rule of law is complete and we shall discuss the important role played by the Court of Justice of the European Communities in further clarifying the law by its authentic interpretation later. Does this role apply to all three ways of making uniform rules of law? According to the EEC Treaty (article 164) the Court "shall ensure that, in the interpretation and application of this Treaty, the law is observed". There is no doubt that "this Treaty" includes the regulations, directives and decisions made under the Treaty, but it could be disputed to what extent the Court of Justice can play a role in the interpretation and application of further treaties, made within the scope of the common market. So far, only two such treaties have been concluded [1] and in both cases, jurisdiction was conferred upon the Court of Justice by special protocol,[2] though not exactly in the same way as under the EEC Treaty itself, and we may also expect that express provisions on the role of the Court of Justice will be made in other separate conventions. When there are no such special provisions, the power of the court to interpret the text, probably depends on the question of whether Community institutions have participated in drafting the particular convention. This stand seems to have been taken by the court when interpreting the association treaty between the EEC and Greece. When asked about an interpretation of this treaty, the court held: [3]

The Athens Agreement was concluded by the Council under articles 228

1. The Convention of February 29, 1968 on the Mutual Recognition of Companies and Legal Persons and the Convention of September 27, 1968 on the Jurisdiction and the Enforcement of Civil and Commercial Judgments.

2. Protocols of June 3, 1971, 8 *C.M.L.Rev.* (1971), pp. 491-494.

3. In the *Second Haegeman Case*, 181/73, d.d. April 30, 1974, considerations 3-6, [1974] *ECR*, pp. 459-460; [1975] 1 CMLR 515.

and 238 of the Treaty, as appears from the terms of the decision dated September 25, 1961. This Agreement is, therefore, in so far as it concerns the Community, an act of one of the institutions of the Community within the meaning of subparagraph (b) of the first paragraph of article 177. The provisions of the Agreement, on coming into force, form an integral part of Community law. Consequently, within the framework of this law, the Court has jurisdiction to give preliminary rulings on the interpretation of this Agreement.

What is the role of the Luxembourg Court of Justice in promoting uniform laws within the European Communities? We may distinguish three ways in which the court exercises its influence:
1. The fact that a common law exists, is of an importance which cannot easily be underestimated. The court renders nearly up to a hundred decisions a year, creating thereby a body of case law which necessarily influences individual national jurisdictions. The court decisions are read, criticised and discussed within the member states and that has, though indirectly, an effect on the future development of legal thinking, an effect, which is very difficult to measure and even more difficult to quantify, but certainly of great importance. Here, a uniform development of law is promoted by a common court which develops not only a system of mainly administrative law, but also of general principles of law.
2. A second way, in which the Court of Justice does promote further uniformity of law within the common market, is by interpretation of community law. The Court of Justice does not play this role alone. It is one of the basic features of the common market judiciary system that we do not have a special court, where international cases can be directly brought (and I refer here to the different practice within the member states of the Council for Mutual Economic Assistance (CMEA), where national cases are dealt with by national courts and international cases by international tribunals). In the common market, all disputes between individuals or between an individual and a state, are brought before the national courts first. There is no possibility of two parties, arguing on an EEC rule, to bring their own case directly before the common market court. It is an accepted basic principle of the legal system of the Community that common market law is incorporated into national legal systems. When a case does contain a problem related to the EEC besides a purely national law

problem, or even, when disputes relate entirely to an EEC problem, the case goes always first to the particular national court, the advantage being, that in cases, which cover national as well as community law, community law is not separated from national law. Of course, this situation creates a risk of divergent interpretation. If a national court, e.g. of the Netherlands, considers an item differently from another national court, e.g. of Germany, the uniformity of the legal rule would be affected.

Professor Honnold, in his contribution, has mentioned such notions as *tort* and *trust* [4], which are of great importance in some legal systems, but of a lesser impact in others. Other notions, like *public order* and *force majeure* are well known in all European legal systems, but their meaning diverges from one legal system to another. Therefore, a national court in the Netherlands, interpreting the notion *public order*, will undoubtably come to an entirely different solution than a national court in Luxembourg or in France. Furthermore, the general outlook of courts differs. By tradition, some legal systems are based on the principle of freedom of contract and courts will stress this principle or pay at least great attention to it, while in other legal systems, the freedom of contract plays a much lesser role and more stress is put on equity or on other general principles.

All these national differences could lead to divergent interpretations of the common legal rule; this has been foreseen by the treaty makers and lead to the introduction of the, by now famous, article 177 which makes it obligatory for the highest national court to bring all questions of community law to the Court of Justice by way of, what we call, the preliminary ruling, meaning that even though a national court decides the case, questions concerning community law are singled out and referred separately to the Court of Justice. Therefore the Court of Justice may, for example, be asked by a national court: "How should article 12 of the EEC Treaty be interpreted in this or that respect? Is the article one, which can be invoked by private parties or not?" It is then the task of the Court of Justice to rule on that question and this ruling is binding on the national court which decides its case in accordance with the binding interpretation given by the Court of Justice. As I pointed out, the highest national

4. See Chapter 6, p. 80, *post*.

courts are obliged to ask for such a preliminary ruling, whenever they encounter a question of community law, while the lower national courts are entitled to do the same, but are not obliged to do so. This system of application of the international rule by the national court and referring international law problems to the international court, has worked extremely well. An ever-increasing number of references are made to the Court of Justice under article 177 and the subsequent applications of rulings present usually very little problems to a national legal order.

The Court of Justice, in its role as interpreter of the law, performs necessarily a function which comes close to that inherent to a legislator. All international harmonisation and unification efforts lead to a legislation which is rather general. Thus, the Uniform Laws on International Sales (ULIS) go much less into detail than the provisions of the Uniform Commercial Code (UCC), because ULIS is a compromise between different legal systems and different legal thinking, which cannot pay great attention to finer details. We encounter exactly the same situation within the common market. Here we make uniform rules through the organs of the Community, but these rules are rather general, broad outlines in need of refinement. Like any other rules of law, also international rules need increasingly to be refined, because of the fast development which takes place in the respective subject areas. If new methods of trade are developed or new products invented, legal rules may have to be adopted, refined or extended. International organs are usually slow in performing their legislative functions and may not be able to make the necessary adaptations in time. In addition, courts may have to adapt the rules subsequently, when applying them. The refinement and adaptation needed, can be obtained in different ways. The CMEA, for instance, leaves it to the national tribunal to make these further refinements in the law. The organisation accepts that one tribunal will achieve this aim differently from another, and that uniformity of law will, therefore, gradually diminish. If then, after a long time, the variant national legal refinements grow too far apart, the Council itself will discuss the problem again and will make new rules. In the common market, the Court of Justice will make the necessary refinements of the existing legal rules through its preliminary rulings. In performing this function, the Court of Justice sometimes comes close to legislating. To some extent, all courts refine the law by interpreting it, but this task is vaster, when there are no detailed legal rules than as if a legislator introduces all detailed provisions. There are, for example, different import duties on "edible offal of poultry" and on "turkeys, or parts of turkeys", but, there were no legislative provisions on the demarcation of the two groups, so that the Court of Justice had to decide, whether turkey tails belong to the one classification or the other.[5] In other subject areas, however, there is a total lack of legislation and all rules must, therefore, be deduced from the case law as developed by the Court of Justice.

Examples can be seen in the rules on temporary validity of competition agreements which have been notified to the Commission and those on the relationship between anti-trust law and the laws on industrial property as well as those on enterprises obtaining a dominant market position.[6]

3. A third role of the Court of Justice, which may affect the harmonisation and unification of European law, is that of a supervising body of the community legal system. When a member state has been accused of violating its obligations under the EEC Treaty, the Commission will first try to remedy the situation through consultations, but if this approach proves to be impossible, the question will be brought before the Court of Justice. If the court finds that the member state has indeed failed to fulfil an obligation under the Treaty, that state must take the necessary measures to comply with the judgment of the court.[7] Under these articles, unilateral alterations in harmonized or unified laws may be prevented or annulled. If a member state would make a new law, clearly in conflict with a harmonized or unified rule, the supervision procedure lead the court to order that member state not to adopt the law or to render it inoperative. Obviously, this would only happen in cases of clear conflict which are, fortunately, very rare indeed. It is far more likely that national law may conflict with unified rules of community law in a hidden and unexpected way. Any national law on social security,

5. *Turkey Tail Case*, 40/69, February 18, 1970, [1970] ECR, pp. 69-84; [1970] CMLR 141.

6. See the *Continental Can Case*, 6/72, February 21, 1973, [1973] CMLR 199.

7. EEC articles 169, 171. See also article 170 which has never been applied.

for example, may contain a provision which conflicts with community provisions on free movement of labour or on social security for migrating workers. In such cases, the procedure under articles 169 and 170 on treaty violation will then not be applied, because there is no clear case of treaty violations *per se*. Instead, it is much more likely for national courts to solve such problems by themselves. In such a case, a national court has then actually two questions to solve. First, the court has to decide whether there is a conflict between national and community legislation, and secondly, if there is a conflict, to decide, how to solve it. The first question can be put to the Court of Justice under article 177 and may be answered by way of a preliminary ruling. However, the Court of Justice is not entitled to give a ruling on a national rule of law, its only function lies in the interpretation of community law. Therefore, a national court cannot ask for a ruling on the validity of a particular national law. But, when a national court thinks there may be a conflict between national law and community law, it can ask for an interpretation on the rule of community law; the court can ask, "should this rule be interpreted in such a way that it permits further national legislation or should it be interpreted in a way that it does not permit further national legislation?" And when the court receives the answer to that question, it knows whether to implement new national legislation or not. Such questions have been presented to the Court of Justice a number of times and the Court of Justice has always given clear answers to them. As to the other question, i.e. on priority in case of conflict, the Court of Justice has also been absolutely clear: whenever there is a conflict between a national rule of law and a rule of community law, the latter should prevail. However, here we are confronted with another problem and have to ask, if the Court of Justice had sufficient competence to decide such a question? If two legal systems conflict, is then the court of one of these legal systems entitled to settle the dispute? One may also approach the question from a more practical point of view: what will actually happen? Will the national court which actually decides the case, follow the Court of Justice in its view that community law prevails or will it follow its national legal system, which may be interpreted differently? A final solution to the problem of conflict will only be reached if, apart from the community legal system, also the national legal systems will make provisions to grant priority to community rule. Here, the small countries have taken the lead, and understandably so. The Netherlands, in particular, is such a small country without real power, but with immense commercial interests all over the world. Since these interests cannot be defended by power, they must be defended by rules of law. It is not by accident that the Netherlands have always advocated that all states should strictly obey the rules of international law. It is not by accident either that the constitution of the Netherlands (articles 65-67) sets a good example by providing that all national rules of law, even the constitution, give way to binding provisions of international law. Belgium and Luxembourg have no similar constitutional provisions, but their legal system is the same through the case-law developed by their supreme courts. For the courts of these countries, the problem of priority in case of conflict has been settled: both their national legal system and the community legal system grant priority to the latter. The French constitution contains the same rule, though the French legal system, in particular the prohibition to question the legality of laws, offers some difficulty in practice.[8] The Italian supreme court originally took another view, but accepted the supremacy of community law in 1973.[9] The German constitutional court went far in the same direction, but recently refused to accept priority of community law in cases concerning human rights.[10]

The problem of priority will present more difficulties to the new member states of the Community, particularly, when an international rule conflicts with a later national law. Traditionally British courts have never accepted that international rules could have priority over national ones. Quite recently Lord Diplock said in the case of *Salmon v. Commissioners of Custom:*[11] "if the terms of the legislation are clear and unambiguous, they must be given effect to, whether or not they

8. Manfred Simon, "Enforcement by French Courts of European Community Law" in the *Law Quarterly Review,* October 1974, pp. 467-485.

9. Gerhard Bebr, "How Supreme is Community Law in the National Courts?" in 11 *C.M.L.Rev.* (1974), pp. 17-24.

10. Internationale Handelsgesellschaft mbH v. Einfuhr- & Vorratsstelle für Getreide & Futtermittel, *Bundesverfassungsgericht* May 29, 1974, AWD 1974, pp. 551-553; [1974] 2 CMLR 540.

11. [1967] 2 QB 116.

carry out Her Majesty's treaty obligations, for the sovereign power of the Queen in Parliament extends to breaking treaties."

This quotation illustrates the traditional great power contempt for rules of international law which are seen as a hindrance rather than a help. It needs no comment that such an attitude is unacceptable to the community legal system and that it must be changed, but it is equally clear that a necessary change of outlook takes time. The influence of education on the law is strong. This may be illustrated by the fact that a completely British educated community court (that of the East African Community) upheld a court decision of a member state (High Court of Kenya) in which priority was granted to the national law in the case of a conflict with community law.[12]

The question of priority raises a more fundamental question i.e. *in whose service does a court operate?* Is a court the servant of the "law", whatever the attitude of the court's national government or is it the servant of the national state? Both attitudes have clear advantages and, certainly, clear dangers.

To see the court, like perhaps a Dutch court regards itself, as a servant of the "law", irrespective of national legislation, creates, of course, the problem that a court acts above the national legislator, leaving aside rules of law which have been democratically agreed upon by a national Parliament. On the other hand, when we regard the functions of courts to be, that they are merely the servants of their national states, we sacrifice almost all judicial control on the application of law and justice by the national state itself, not only with regard to its citizens but also with regard to its international obligations. There are very few international courts and most of them have little power, so that international law will often not be applied, if it is not applied by national courts and given priority over possibly conflicting national rules.

12. See 21 *ICLQ* (1972), p. 363 and 9 *Int. Legal Materials* (1970), pp. 561-566.

2

REGIONAL INTEGRATION IN CENTRAL AND LATIN AMERICA: A PROGRESS REPORT

*Allan R. Brewer-Carías**

I. Inter-American regionalism

There is no doubt that Latin America has had a long history of confrontation between regionalism and universalism in its international relations. If we look at the political side, the first regional international organisation came on the American continent with the Pan-American Union, which was transformed in 1948 into the Organisation of the American States. This does not mean, however that the system usually referred to as the Inter-American System [1] is of recent origin, for its precedents and constitution date back to the nineteenth century, and originate ultimately in the ideas of Bolivar on continental solidarity. This does not mean that the regional political set-up has remained static in its organisation, functions and manner of working: on the contrary, since the Pan-American Union was transformed into the Organisation of American States (OAS) [2] it has not ceased changing and adapting itself to the new demands made on it by Latin American social and economic development, above all since the beginning of the sixties. This can be seen particularly in the Reform of the Charter of the OAS which was established by the protocol signed in Buenos Aires on February 27, 1967, and which

* Professor of Law, Central University of Venezuela, Caracas; Visiting Fellow, Clare Hall and Member, Trinity College, Cambridge, England (1972-1974).

1. See in general, Inter-American Institute of International Legal Studies, *The Inter-American System: Its Development and Strengthening* (New York, 1966), 530 pp.
2. See: The 1948 Charter of the OAS; *idem*, p. 331 ff.

came into force in 1970.[3] This affected not only the institutional side of the Organisation, but what is more important, it assigned to it new and more closely defined responsibilities in economic, social and cultural matters, and among these, there were certain aims related to Latin American economic integration. The reform of the Charter of the OAS in 1967 is still however, a reflection of the strong influence the United States has attempted to wield over Latin America, for the Organisation has in fact been one of its instruments, to the extent that the economic and social content of the reforms of the Charter of the OAS in 1967 are merely a reflection of the change in political attitude of North America to Latin America – a change brought about by the Kennedy Administration. One should take into account as an important precedent for this reform the Charter of *Punta del Este* of 1961 [4] and its concrete result: the Alliance for Progress [5]; and also the Social and Economic Act of Rio de Janeiro adopted in 1965 by the Rio Conference.[6]

But while the sixties bring awarness to social and economic questions within the OAS, the beginning of the seventies shows the first radical change in the polical notion of the Organisation. For the first time Latin American countries have attempted to take up an independent political position vis-à-vis the United States, especially in economic matters. Since April 1973 the member countries of the OAS have been committed to a radical reform of the Organisation. This was agreed on by the Conference of Ministers of Foreign Affairs in 1973, and their resolutions for a complete reform of the Organisation are being effected at the moment. Last July saw the first meeting of the Special Committee studying this reform, and even though

3. See: The Buenos Aires Protocol of 1967 and the Revised Charter of the OAS, in Inter-American Institute of International Legal Studies, *Instruments Relating to the Economic Integration of Latin America* (New York, 1968), p. 392 ff.; these instruments are also reproduced in *International Organisation and Integration* (Leyden, 1968), p. 1044 ff.

4. See: The Charter of Punta del Este, in *Instruments Relating to the Economic Integration of Latin America*, p. 369 ff.

5. See: Resolution on the Creation of the Inter-American Committee on the Alliance for Progress (CIAP - 1963), *ibid.*, p. 378 ff; also in *The Inter-American System*, p. 459 ff.

6. See: Economic and Social Act of Rio de Janeiro (1965), in *Instruments Relating to the Economic Integration of Latin America*, p. 391 ff.

collective working papers about its activities were not adopted, a feeling was evident that it was imperative for all the Inter-American System to adapt to the present conditions of the Latin American countries. What is interesting about the present process is that for the first time in the Assembly of Ministers of Foreign Affairs one heard Latin American voices speaking on the question of the "latinamericanisation" of the OAS and its redefinition, which included a redefinition vis-à-vis the United States. As far as Latin and Inter-American affairs are concerned, there is no doubt at all about the sixties having brought about a real revolution in the traditional relations between the United States and the countries of Latin America. Not only have some of them taken up socio-political positions which are radically different from those "permitted" by North American politics during past years, as in the cases of Cuba and Chile, but many countries have also adopted political ways which are progressively nationalistic in the face of North American interests, as in the cases of Peru and Venezuela, and more recently, Argentina.

II. Latin American regionalism: the economic perspective

The special influence of the United States on Inter-American politics up to the sixties has, without doubt, been one of the factors most conspiring against the formation of Latin American regionalism, both in the political and economic fields. One could say that Latin America had never, in any of its countries, heard any official discussion about the creation of a Latin American regional political organisation from which the United States would be absent. The first time such a subject was broached was in the Conference of OAS Ministers which took place in Washington in 1973. Nonetheless, even if the OAS were changing from an Inter-American organisation into a Latin American one, and it is not clear that this situation either does or should arise, it seems that until the sixties, the presence of the United States in the OAS clearly presented itself as a block to any notion of the setting up of Latin American regional organisations. There is one exception to this which should be indicated, and this is the constitution in 1951 by the Charter of San Salvador, of the Organisation of Central American States (ODECA). The remote precedent of this, of course, is the Central American Federal Republic which existed between 1824 and 1838, and which grouped together all the countries of the region.

The ODECA, which followed the lines set out by the OAS Charter of 1945 and which is, at present, governed by the Charter granted in Panama on December 12th, 1962,[7] was set up basically as an international political organisation. Its smooth working has been affected recently by the violent conflict between El Salvador and Honduras. If one can single out a positive achievement of the ODECA, it is the beginning of a process of economic integration in Latin America. In effect, one result of the meetings of the Committee for Economic Co-operation of the Central American Isthmus, of the Central American Council of the ODECA was the signing of the Multilateral Treaty of Free Trade and Central American Economic Integration at Tegucigalpa in 1958.[8] This represented the culmination of a long line of agreements and bi-lateral treaties between the Central American countries, many of them signed under the same heading (free trade and economic integration). The Treaty of Tegucigalpa was changed by the General Treaty of Central American Economic Integration signed at Managua in 1960,[9] which created the Secretariat of Central American Economic Integration (SIECA) as a permanent organisation with certain supranational powers. This event has been responsible for heading the process of economic integration in this region, by setting up a Central American Common Market. That this Common Market arose despite the difficulties of the ODECA, is a confirmation of the phenomenon observed in other attempts of political integration, which have resulted in processes of economic integration.[10]

7. See: Charter of the Organisation of Central American States (1962), in *The Inter-American System*, p. 480 ff; also in *International Organisation and Integration*, p. 1095 ff.

8. Reproduced in *Instruments Relating to the Economic Integration of Latin America*, p. 3 ff; also in *Multilateral Economic Co-operation in Latin America* (U.N., New York, 1962), Vol. 1, p. 17 ff.

9. See: *Instruments Relating to the Economic Integration of Latin America*, p. 23 ff.; also in *Multilateral Economic Co-operation in Latin America*, Vol. 1, p. 5 ff. and as appendix to Sydney Dell, *A Latin American Common Market*, (London, 1966), p. 256 ff.

10. Cf. D. W. Bowett, *The Law of International Institutions*, (London, 1975, Third Edn.), pp. 201-202.

However, the development of Central American integration, while showing a promising start,[11] has been suffering a severe setback since 1969. In that year, although the activities of the CACM had been subject to a process of revision, which led to the suspension of some immediate objectives [12] a final paralysis of the Organisation was produced by the violent conflict between El Salvador and Honduras which split the Common Market. It was necessary to establish a *modus operandi* which assured the SIECA in 1970 of the possibility of continuing to work towards integration. As a result, Central America is still faced with the problem of achieving normalisation of the Common Market, which has also been affected by unilateral acts of violation from Costa Rica [13] and by the earthquake which destroyed Managua in Nicaragua early in 1973; it is now necessary to bring the market up to date and to improve it.

Apart from the Central American experience which has shown attempts to form regional political organisations (leaving aside the East Indian Federation formed by some former British colonial island possession in the Caribbean, which ceased to exist in the sixties), all regionalism in the American area has had an economic purpose. This has been particularly so in the organisation of two free trade zones: one in South America and the other in the Caribbean.

Because of the activities put into motion by the United Nations Economic Commission for Latin America (ECLA), and the negotiations between various Latin American countries at the end of the fifties,[14] one could say that economic integration in Latin America

11. See the account of the speech of Roberto Mayorga Cortez, Secretary-General of SIECA, in *El Nacional*, Caracas, July 16, 1973, p. A-8.

12. In March, 1969, the Signatories agreed upon the following immediate objectives; (i) the establishment, by a gradual and progressive programme, of a customs union between the five countries, (ii) the co-ordination and harmonisation of national policies on industrial development, agricultural structure, finance and infrastructure, and (iii) the creation of a common capital market. See: *ibid.*

13. *Ibid.*

14. The most important documents relating to these negotiations are collected in *Multilateral Economic Co-operation in Latin America*, Vol. 1, p. 33 ff.

began in 1960 with the signing of the Treaty of Montevideo [15] which created the Latin American Free Trade Association (LAFTA).[16] One of the first objectives of this Treaty was to establish a free trade zone. This meant that customs duties and other restrictions on the trade of native products of the member countries of the zone were to be eliminated, but that each country retained customs rights with respect to countries outside the free trade zone. Like any zone of this type the LAFTA seeks to attain freedom of intrazonal trade without going so far as to set up a customs union. The process of completion of this free trade zone, which should have been established definitively in 1972, has, because of functional difficulties experienced by the LAFTA, been extended until 1980.[17] Difficulties have been produced by the excessive protection of national economies allowed by the Treaty, and by the fact that the organs of the association lacked supranational powers. Decisions of the LAFTA have been reached only after a laborious process of negotiation between the parties concerned. Nonetheless, twelve years after its foundation, the LAFTA, as an instrument for lowering duties in trade, has produced all the immediate results that could be expected. At the same time it has led to certain important repercussions. The Treaty of Montevideo, besides containing the immediate aims of the LAFTA connected with the Free Trade Zone, has also a series of indirect aims which have been slowly reaching success. These are linked to Latin American integration and to the setting up of a Latin American Common Market.[18] Thus, not

15. See: *Instruments Relating to the Economic Integration of Latin America,* p. 207 ff.; *The Inter-American System,* p. 485 ff.; Sydney Dell, *op. cit.,* p. 228 ff.; *Multilateral Co-operation in Latin America,* Vol. 1, p. 57 ff.; and *International Organisation and Integration,* p. 1073 ff.

16. The Treaty of Montevideo was ratified by Argentina and Bolivia in 1960; Brazil, Chile and Colombia in 1961; Ecuador in 1961; and by Mexico, Paraguay, Peru, Uruguay and Venezuela in 1966. The Latin American Free Trade Association (ALALC) is thus in size the largest regional economic integration area amongst developing countries, with a population of some 240 million inhabitants and a territory of some 19 million square kilometres.

17. Following the Protocol of Caracas of December 12, 1969, which modified the original provisions of the Treaty of Montevideo.

18. For example, Art. 54 of the Treaty of Montevideo provides expressly that:

only did the meeting of *Punta del Esta* in 1961 consider the LAFTA an adequate tool for the attainment of economic integration, but in the Declaration of the Presidents of America in 1967, signed also in Punta del Este,[19] it was stated that the Latin American Common Market, which, it had been decided, was to be created gradually from 1970 over a period of not more than fifteen years, should be based on the full development and the gradual convergence of the CACM and the LAFTA. These two organisations of integration were considered sufficient for the setting up of the future Latin American Common Market, which, since the reform of the Charter of the OAS in 1967, forms in some way a part and an aim of the Inter-American System.[20]

But the apparent momentum gained by the LAFTA in the political sphere made the less developed countries and those with insufficient trading outlets apprehensive that the grouping might prove to be decidedly advantageous for the more developed countries of the region (Argentina, Brazil and Mexico)[21] at their expense. As a result,

---

"The Contracting Parties shall make every effort to direct their policies with a view to creating conditions favorable to the establishment of a Latin American Common Market. To that end, the Committee (Standing Executive Committee) shall undertake studies and consider projects and plans designed to achieve this purpose and shall endeavor to co-ordinate its work with that of other international organisations' (see: *Instruments Relating to the Economic Integration of Latin America*, p. 219).

19. *Ibid.*, p. 395 ff.

20. In Art. 40 of the Protocol of Buenos Aires, by which the Charter of the OAS was revised, it its provided expressly that:

"The Member States recognise that integration of the developing countries of the Hemisphere is one of the objectives of the Inter American System and, therefore, shall orient their efforts and take the necessary measures to accelerate the integration process, with a view to establishing a Latin American Common Market in the shortest possible time" (see: *Instruments Relating to the Economic Integration of Latin America*, p. 392; also in *International Organisation and Integration*, p. 40).

21. Note the comments in Ernst B. Haas, "The Study of Regional Integration: Reflections on the Joy and Anguish of Pretheorising", in 24 (1970) *International Organisation*, p. 615, on the presence in a regional integration movement of more highly developed countries.

the Andean countries, which had internal conditions which were relatively similar or easily convertible, committed themselves to the formation of a subregional economic unity which would have an expanded market, a common external tariff and a co-ordinated industrial policy which would enable them to participate in a Latin American Common Market on fair and equal terms. The formula of the Sub-regional Agreement had already been put forward by the Declaration of Bogotá in 1966 which was adopted by the Presidents of the Andean countries and was ratified by the Declaration of the Presidents of America in 1967.[22] This led to the setting up of the Andean Group for subregional integration through the Agreement of Cartagena in 1968, which outlines what is clearly the most detailed and developed scheme for economic integration in Latin America.

In addition to the LAFTA formation, the Caribbean region has also developed into a free trade zone. On December 15, 1965, after unsuccessful attempts to reach political integration, the General Treaty of Antigua was signed between Antigua, Barbados and British Guiana. This established the Caribbean Free Trade Association (CARIFTA) which, by virtue of the revision of the Treaty in 1968, extended its application to all the Caribbean countries, most of them former British colonies. This agreement, as its name indicates, limited itself to the establishment of a free trade zone between the twelve Caribbean countries forming the Association.[23] Its objectives were

22. The Declaration of Bogota of 1966 was subscribed by the President of Colombia, Chile and Venezuela, and by the personal representatives of the Presidents of Ecuador and Peru, on August 16, 1966. Bolivia adhered to the Declaration in 1967. In the Declaration of the Presidents of the Americas of 1967, a recommendation was made for the promotion of the conclusion of temporary subregional agreements, with provision for reducing tariffs within the subregions and harmonising treatment towards third nations more rapidly than within the general agreement, in keeping with the objectives of regional integration. See: *Instruments Relating to the Economic Integration of Latin America,* p. 400.

23. In May, 1968, the Ministers of Commerce of Antigua, Barbados, Guyana, Trinidad and Tobago, subscribed to the Treaty of Dickenson Bay, which established a free trade area. In July, 1968, Grenada, St. Lucia, St. Vincent, Domenica, Montserrat and St. Kitts-Nevis-Anguilla subscribed, and, in August, 1968, Jamaica. Belize was later accepted as a member of the area.

the promotion, expansion and diversification of trade within the area, the assurance of fair competition, the stimulation of economic development, and the harmonious growth and increased flow of trade by the removal of inhibiting obstacles.

III. Subregionalism in Latin American economic integration: the Andean Group

On May 26, 1969, after a long period of negotiations and after the Council of Ministers for Foreign Affairs of the LAFTA had approved both the Resolution on Norms concerning the Subregional Agreements and the Resolution on the Bases of the Subregional Agreement of the Andean Group,[24] the signatory countries of the Declaration of Bogota of 1966,[25] with the exception of Venezuela, signed the Agreement of Cartagena, that is the Agreement of Subregional Integration of the Group of Andean Countries.[26] Thus the Andean Group was born, and represented above all a move to economic integration within the limits of the Treaty of Montevideo, and hence of the CAFTA. Consequently, one of the first decisions made after the signing of the Agreement was the LAFTA Resolution [27] which declared the "compatibility" of the Andean Pact with the Treaty of Montevideo, as it was required to do under the text of the Agreement of Cartagena.[27a] This does not mean, however that the Agreement of Cartagena was not independent, but that it was complementary to the

24. Resolutions 202 (CM-II/VI-E), 203 (CM-II/VI-E) of September 2, 1967, and 222 (VII) of December 17, 1967.

25. Bolivia, Chile, Colombia, Ecuador and Peru. The Agreement is open to adhesion by other contracting parties of the Treaty of Montevideo (Art. 109). Venezuela began the process of adhesion through the Declaration of Lima, of February 13, 1973; see also Decision No. 70 of the Pact Commission on "Conditions for the Admission of Venezuela into the Andean Group".

26. The text of the Agreement is reproduced in *El Pacto Andino* (Madrid, 1973), p. 303 ff.

27. See the Resolution of the Permanent Executive Committee of the Latin American Free Trade Association, No. 179 of July 9, 1969, which declared the compatibility of the two agreements.

27a. Art. 110 of the Agreement of Cartagena.

efforts within the LAFTA in developing the future Latin American Common Market.

The Agreement of Cartagena may, therefore, be considered as the only effective move towards integration in Latin America, which has led to the community adoption of decisions principally in the three following areas: the establishment of a customs union, the harmonisation of economic policies between member countries, and the setting up of a subregional industrial programme. But, before analysing the decisions adopted in relation to these mechanisms, it would be helpful to comment first on some legal problems created in Latin America by the Agreement.

First of all, one must admit that despite the word "agreement" and the fact that it may be considered as a legislative instrument derived from and interdependent with the Treaty of Montevideo, in the sense that it develops and perfects it, the Agreement of Cartagena is in its turn a Treaty and as such, is subject to the norms of admission into internal law established by each of the signatory countries. There is no norm in the text of the Treaty of Montevideo which foresees that Agreements of Subregional Integration may be signed without parliamentary approval; [28] thus it is not possible to sustain, as did the Caracas Round Table of 1970 on the Legal and Institutional Problems of the Andean Subregional Pact, that, given that the Agreement of Cartagena is derived from the Treaty of Montevideo, it "has not been necessary to subject it to parliamentary approval in certain of the member countries, since the original approval of the Treaty of Montevideo is enough to include its application and development as outlined in the Subregional Agreement".[28a] On the contrary, legal reality shows that all of the member countries of the Agreement of Cartagena with the sole exception of Chile, have through laws or acts of equal standing, approved the text of the Agreement, and in one of

28. See: Francisco Villagrán Kramer, "Sistematización de la estructura jurídica del Acuerdo de Cartagena", in *Derecho de la Integración*. No. 12, INTAL, Buenos Aires, 1973, p. 15.

28a. See: Round Table on "La Problemática Jurídica e Institucional del Acuerdo Subregional Andino", in *Revista de la Facultad de Derecho*, 1970, UCV, Caracas, p. 121.

the countries (Columbia), where it was originally approved by executive decision through the intervention of the constitutional judiciary, it has been necessary to obtain parliamentary approval afterwards.[29]

On the other hand, despite the derivative character of the Agreement of Cartagena, it is clear that it foresees an institutional scheme of integration which, for the first time, in South America gives rise to supranational organs. Thus the Agreement of Cartagena goes much further than the original scheme of the LAFTA, having envisaged not only the setting-up of a Commission as an intergovernmental organ, but also of a *Junta* as a regional organ. Both organs have, among their multiple functions, been endowed with the power to create secondary community law of immediate application in the member countries, except in those cases, where the Agreement itself demands that it should be incorporated into the internal legal system afterwards.[30]

But the setting up by the Agreement of Cartagena of these supranational institutions with power to adopt decisions with effect *erga omnes* and immediate application to internal law, inevitably brings with it other problems which derive from the constitutional power of internal legal systems to allow national matters (particularly legislative ones) to pass to a supranational organ, which results in a limitation in the spheres of influence of national organs. This prob-

29. This is the case of Colombia: the text of the Agreement was approved by Decree No. 1245 of August 8, 1969; the Supreme Court of Colombia, in a judgment of July 26, 1971, pronounced on the Decree; and Congress enacted the text of the Agreement in 1973. On this process, see Francisco Orrego Vicuña, "La Incorporación del ordenamiento jurídico subregional al derecho interno. Análisis de la práctica y jurisprudencia de Colombia", in *Derecho de la integracion,* No. 11 INTAL, Buenos Aires, 1972, p. 39 ff. On the case of Chile see Francisco Orrego Vicuña, "La Incorporación del ordenamiento jurídico subregional al derecho interno. Análisis de la práctica Chilena", in *Derecho de la Integración,* No. 7, INTAL, Buenos Aires, 1970, p. 42 ff.

30. The Agreement of Cartagena established, it is believed, a presumption in favour of the immediate application of the decisions of the Commission of the Member States, except in those cases where the internal legal order of the Member States concerned required an express adoption of the decision. See: Fdo. Villagrán Kramer, "*Sistematización de la estructura jurídica del Acuerdo de Cartagena*", *op. cit.*, pp. 27 ff. and 31 ff.

lem, which in Europe has been overcome either by a special constitutional provision as in Italy and Germany, that have an institutionalised constitutional judiciary or by the absence of such a control (by which it is converted into a political matter) as in the other member countries of the European Common Market,[31] this problem is still awaiting a solution in Latin America. All Latin American countries have institutionalised a control of the constitutionality of laws, in some cases in an extreme manner as in Venezuela,[32] by which the lasting nature of an integration scheme like the Andean Pact will require the Constitutions of member countries to be adjusted to suit the demands of the community.[33] This, for example, is what Colombia did in 1968 [34] and what was discussed in the Chilean Congress the same year.[35]

It should be pointed out, however that, while there is no doubt about the supranational and community nature of the organs created by the Agreement of Cartagena and of the law which they themselves may establish,[36] the supranational structure is still incomplete and deficient, since no supranational judicial control has as yet been

31. See: Nicola Catalano, "La posición del Derecho Comunitario dentro del Derecho de los Estados Membros", in *Relaciones entre el derecho comunitario y el derecho nacional* (Inter-American Institute of International Legal Studies, Washington, 1967), p. 187 ff.

32. See note 29 *supra.*

33. See, in general, A. R. Brewer-Carías, *Los Problemas Constitucionales de la Integración Económica Latinoamericana,* Caracas, 1968, p. 64 ff.

34. Art. 76 of the revised Constitution of 1968 provides specifically:

"... Por medio de Tratados o convenios aprobados por el Congreso podrá el Estado obligarse para que sobre bases de igualdad y reciprocidad, sean creadas instituciones supranacionales que tengan por objeto promover o consolidar la integración económica con otros Estados ...".

35. See: Emilio J. Cárdenas, "Hacia un derecho comunitario latinoamericano", in *Derecho de la Integración,* No. 1, INTAL, Buenos Aires, 1967, p. 49; and Alberto A. Natale, *La Integración Lationoamericana y el Problema Constitucional,* Rosario, 1967, pp. 11, 12.

36. Cf. Jerónimo Irala Burgos, "La Supranacionalidad en el Acuerdo de Integración Subregional Andina", in *Revista de la Facultad de Derecho,* No. 47, UCV, Caracas, 1970, p. 49 ff.

established over the decisions of the organs of the Agreement or over decisions taken by member countries which fall inside or outside its regulations. As a result, not only do individuals of the states find that they are truly in a vulnerable position in the face of actions by the Community organs,[37] but also that these actions, apart from the political control exercised, are not subject to any judicial control on behalf of the member states. Community law is, therefore, not subject to a uniform interpretation by the ordinary national tribunals or by administrative or constitutional courts of member states. One of the first demands of the Andean Group is then that a suitable independent and supranational judicial control of its actions should be set up. In the very establishment of such a control, however, the constitutional problems, as already indicated, would again be present.[38]

As I have said, subregional integration agreed to by the Andean countries and organised by the Agreement of Cartagena in 1968, lays the foundations for an Andean Common Market between Bolivia, Columbia, Chile, Ecuador, Peru and Venezuela. The Market covers an area of over 5,400 million sq. km., with a population of more than 68 million, and external trade worth more than 11,000 million dollars.[39] Three main objectives are sought through the scheme of Andean integration: to promote balanced and harmonious development of the member countries; to speed up their growth through economic integration, making it easier for them to participate in the process of integration envisaged in the Treaty of Montevideo and creating conditions which are favourable for the conversion of the LAFTA into a Common Market; and to achieve a fair distribution of benefits deriving from the integration of the countries of the subregion by reducing the differences between them.[40] The Agreement of

37. Cf. Francisco Orrego Vicuña, "Contemporary International Law and the Economic Integration of Latin America", in Académie de Droit International de la Haye, *Recueil des Cours,* Colloque, 1971.

38. Cf. A. R. Brewer-Carías, *op. cit.,* note 33 *supra,* at p. 61.

39. The statistics are drawn from *El Pacto Andino, op. cit.,* pp. 12, 13, 28 and 29.

40. Arts. 1 and 2 of the Agreement of Cartagena.

Cartagena evisages a number of measures for the realisation of these objectives, of which the following are most worthy of attention: the establishment of a customs union through a programme of reduction of duties, restrictions in trade and the creation of a common external tariff; the joint programming for industrial development in the subregion; the harmonisation of social and economic policies and rapprochement of legal systems; the setting up of bodies for financing subregional development.

The aspect which one should first single out about the establishment of a customs union between the six countries of the Andean Group, is the programme for increasing the flow of trade which aims at the elimination of all kinds of taxes and restrictions which affect the importation of goods originating in another member country.[41] The difference between the programme of the Andean Group and the free trade zone of the LAFTA is that in the former the programme is automatic and irreversible, and will include all products, reaching a total freedom of trade not later than December 31, 1980.[42] In the LAFTA, by contrast, the process of reduction of taxes and increasing the flow of trade is to be realised by a series of long and complicated negotiations.[43] Again, and this is perhaps the aspect in which the Andean Group differs most from the LAFTA, the aim is not just to try to increase the flow of trade, and through this to create and develop a free trade zone, but to set up a common external tariff for all countries

41. Art. 41, *do.*

42. Art. 45, *do.* On the conditions relating to the entry of Venezuela into the Andean Group, see Chap. I of Decision No. 70 of the Commission, of February 13, 1973 (in *El Pacto Andino, op. cit.,* p. 340 ff.). The Pact also provides (Art. 96 and following articles) a special regime, within the trade liberalisation programme, for products emanating from the two least developed countries within the sub-region – Bolivia and Ecuador.

43. These negotiations made for enormous difficulties in the establishment of both the national and the common lists provided for by Art. 4 of the Treaty of Montevideo. See: *Instruments Relating to the Economic Integration of Latin America, op. cit.,* p. 208; and *The Inter-American System, op. cit.,* p. 486. See also the account of these problems given in Michael J. McDermonth and William H. Weiland, "Latin American Experience with Economic Integration", in 10 (1970) *Virginia Journal of International Law,* p. 153 ff.

of the Group before December 31, 1980.[44] To facilitate this move, there has already been established a common minimum external tariff which has been inforce since 1972, seeking to provide adequate protection for subregional industry and to promote its productivity, while, at the same time, gradually creating a margin of subregional preference.[45]

Besides the establishment of a customs union before 1980, the Agreement of Cartagena defines precisely one of the characteristic aspects of this subregional economic integration process in providing that all member countries of the region should be obliged to undertake subregional industrial development, by means of a joint programme to achieve greater expansion, specialisation and diversification of industrial production, the highest utilisation of resources available in the area, the improvement of productivity and efficient use of means of production, the use of large-scale economies, and fair distribution of benefits.[46] This attempt at subregional planning for industrial development, already initiated by the Andean Group, goes much further than the complementation agreements of industrial sectors defined in the Treaty of Montevideo as a means to achieve the free trade programme.[47] As the Agreement of Cartagena envisaged, industrial planning of the subregion is to be realised through Sectorial Programmes of Industrial Development, which should cover the following aspects: new investment on a subregional scale and the measures to finance it; location of industrial plants in the countries of the subregion; harmonisation of policies which directly affect the programme; and a programme of special treatment of products

44. See Art. 61 of the Agreement of Cartagena.

45. See Art. 63, *do.* Venezuela must fully apply the common minimum external tariff in 1976; see Art. 8 of Decision No. 70 of the Commission, in *El Pacto Andino, op. cit.*, p. 343.

46. See Art. 32 of the Agreement of Cartagena.

47. See Art. 16(b) of the Treaty of Montevideo: in *Instruments Relating to the Economic Integration of Latin America, op. cit.*, p. 211, and *The Inter-American System, op. cit.*, p. 488. Note the Petrochemicals Agreement signed between Bolivia, Chile and Peru on July 25, 1968, and comments in *Revista de la Integración,* No. 3, INTAL, Buenos Aires, 1968.

resulting from the application of the Sectorial Programme.[48] In accordance with this policy, the Commission of the Agreement of Cartagena recently approved the First Sectorial Programme of Industrial Development which related to the light engineering industry,[49] by which it is intended to promote the industry in the territories by the introduction and consolidation of the basic technological infrastructure which is necessary.[50] Apart from the joint programming of industrial development of the subregion[51] the scheme of economic integration of the Andean Group also requires the co-ordination of economic development plans in the countries of the subregion in certain specific sectors, and the harmonisation of their political and social policies with the aim of reaching a joint planning system for the integrated development of the area.[52]

Besides the establishment of a customs union and the development of joint or co-ordinated planning of industrial development, one of the main mechanisms envisaged in the Agreement of Cartagena for the speeding up of economic integration is undoubtedly the harmonisation of economic and legislative policies in the specific field of foreign investment, industrial property and multi-national enterprises. The Commission of the Agreement of Cartagena, in its Decision No. 24 approved in 1970 the Common Regulation of Treatment for

48. See Art. 34 of the Agreement of Cartagena.

49. Approved by Decision No. 57 of August 20, 1972, of the Commission. See: *El Pacto Andino, op. cit.*, p. 389 ff., and *Derecho de la Integración,* No. 12, INTAL, Buenos Aires, 1973, p. 187 ff.

50. See Art. 1 of Decision No. 57, in *Derecho de la Integración,* No. 12, *op. cit. supra,* p. 187.

51. Note the comments on this programme by Mauricio Guerrero, "La programación conjunta del desarrollo industrial subregional y el primer programa sectorial de la industria metalmecánica", in *Derecho de la Integración,* No. 12, *op. cit. supra,* p. 35 ff.

52. This process of co-ordination and harmonisation will be realised in parallel and in co-ordination with the establishment of the subregional market, using the mechanisms outlined in Art. 26 of the Agreement of Cartagena. This has involved the Ministers of Planning of the Andean Group countries meeting together since 1973.

Foreign Investments and Brands, Patents, Licenses and Royalties,[53] thus regulating in a uniform manner the control of foreign investment in all the member countries of the Group.[54] The application of this text in the six countries of the Andean region represents an entirely new move in the uniform and coherent treatment of foreign investment in a group of countries, which does not even exist in the European Common Market.[55] This Common Regulation, besides setting up controls on foreign investment in the area [56] limiting the

53. See the text of Decision No. 24, of December 31, 1970, in *El Pacto Andino,* p. 353 ff. This Decision was modified with regard to certain industrial property rights by Decision No. 37 of June 24, 1971. By reason of the adhesion of Venezuela to the Andean Group, modifications to Arts. 1 and 13 of Decision No. 24 were subsequently made by Decision No. 70 of 1973 (see Arts. 33 and 34, and *El Pacto Andino, op. cit. supra.,* p. 346 ff.).

54. Decisions Nos. 24 and 37 were approved by Decree No. 482 of June 25, 1971, of President Allende of Chile; by Decree Law No. 09708 of June 30, 1971, by President Torres of Bolivia; by Decree Law No. 18900 of June 30, 1971, by President Velazo Alvarado of Peru; and by Decree No. 974 of June 30, 1971, by President Velazco Ibbarra of Ecuador. In Colombia they were approved by Decree No. 1299 of 1971 of President Pastrana, and then incorporated in Decree No. 2153 of November, 1971, of the same President; both these Decrees were declared to be incompetent by the Supreme Court of Colombia in a judgment of January 20, 1972. It was not until 1973 that the Colombian Congress approved in a Law the Agreement of Cartagena and conferred extraordinary authority upon the President of the Republic to approve Decisions Nos. 24 and 37. See the references in Francisco Orrega Vicuña, "La incorporación del ordenamiento jurídico subregional al derecho interno. Analisis de la práctica y jurisprudencia colombiana", *loc. cit.,* p. 49 ff. On the various instruments through which Decisions Nos. 24 and 37 were approved, see document JUN di 14, of September 7, 1971, on "Instrumentos por los cuales se pone en vigor en los paises miembros el Régimen Común de Tratamiento a los Capitales extranjeros y sobre Marcas, Patentes, Licencias y Regalias", Lima.

55. Cf. Covey T. Oliver, "The Andean Foreign Investment Code; A New Phase in the Quest for Normative Order as to Direct Foreign Investment" in 66 (1972) *American Journal of International Law,* p. 762 ff.

56. Arts. 2, 5 and ff. of Decision No. 24; see *El Pacto Andino, op. cit.,* p. 356 ff.

economic fields in which this may be allowed [57] and not permitting goods which originate entirely from foreign owned industries to have full enjoyment of the benefits of the free trade programme,[58] also makes it quite clear that the member countries may not give any more favourable treatment to foreign investors than the treatment they give to national investors.[59] By this any favourable treatment for foreign investment in the countries of the Andean Group is made impossible. The object of the Common Regulation of foreign investment is to channel a suitable flow of investment to the various priority sectors in subregional development, and likewise to restrict its participation in certain sectors such as banking, insurance and investment institutions, public services, internal transport, publicity, commercial radio stations, television stations, newspapers, magazines and enterprises devoted to the internal commercialisation of goods of any kind.[60]

Moves towards uniformity of legislation and the harmonisation of economic policies have also come about recently with the adoption in Decision No. 46 of December 1971 of the Uniform Regulation of Multi-National Enterprises,[61] which undoubtedly has a remote precedent in the "industries of a regional nature" referred to by Resolution No. 100 of the LAFTA of 1964 which adopted the Basic Directives of Economic Policies of the Association,[62] and in the Programme of Integrated Industries of the Central American Common Market.[63]

57. Art. 3 of Decision No. 24; see *El Pacto Andino, op. cit.*, p. 356.

58. Art. 27 ff. of Decision No. 24; see *El Pacto Andino, op. cit.*, p. 361 ff.

59. Art. 50 of Decision No. 24; see *El Pacto Andino, op cit.*, p. 366.

60. Art. 41 ff. of Deicision No. 24; see *El Pacto Andino, op. cit.*, pp. 364, 365.

61. See the text of Decision No. 46 which also establishes the rules relating to capital in the subregion, in *Derecho de la Integración,* No. 10, INTAL, Buenos Aires, 1972, p. 190 ff.; see also *El Pacto Andino, op. cit.*, p. 375 ff. Art. 3 of this Decision was modified by Decision No. 70 of February, 1973, which established the conditions for the adhesion of Venezuela to the Andean Group; see *El Pacto Andino, op. cit.*, p. 347.

62. See Resolution 100 (VI) of December 8, 1964, Part I, B.4 ff.

63. See the Agreement on the System of Central American Integrated Industries, signed at Tegucigalpa, Honduras, on June 10, 1958, and the Protocols to the same signed in El Salvador on January 29, 1963, and

The great difference is that in these cases no principle on the national or foreign character of the integrated industries was formulated. By contrast, in the terms of the Andean Group, multi-national enterprises are defined als follows: they are only those enterprises situated in the subregion, with majority subregional capital reflected in the Board of Directors of the enterprise; the capital must come from national investors of at least two member countries, and foreign investment is not allowed to exceed 40 percent; they have subregional interest, that is, they must take part in sectorial programmes of industrial development and infrastructural projects, in programmes for the rationalisation for production in existing industries or in joint programmes of agricultural development.[64] In this way, a multi-national enterprise is an essential piece in the whole context of integration of the Andean subregion, for the establishment within the subregion of centres of decision, concerned with the dynamic or strategic sectors of subregional economy,[65] and it resembles a national enterprise with regard to the effects of the special treatment envisaged in the Common Regulation for Treatment of Foreign Investment.[66] The text of Decision No. 46 sets up a general framework for the statutes to be adopted,[67] which allows us to speak of the legal regulation of a "Latin American enterprise": a multi-national enterprise should in fact be constituted like an anonymous society within any one of the member countries, according to its internal legal system.[67a] To be active in the other countries however it does not need

November 5, 1965; texts in *Instruments Relating to the Economic Integration of Latin America, op. cit.*, p. 89 ff, 94 ff., and 109 ff.

64. See Arts. 8 and 10 of Decision No. 46, in *El Pacto Andino, op. cit.*, pp. 377, 378.

65. Cf. Gustavo Fernandez Saavedra, "El Régimen Uniforme de la Empresa Multinational en el Grupo Andino", in *Derecho de la Integración*, No. 11, INTAL, Buenos Aires, 1972, p. 19.

66. See Chap. VI, Arts. 28 ff. of Decision No. 46, in *El Pacto Andino, op. cit.*, p. 381 ff.

67. See Art. 18 and Chap. VII, Art. 38 ff. of Decision No. 46, in *El Pacto Andino, op. cit.*, p. 382 ff.

67a. See Arts. 16 and 19 of Decision No. 46, in *El Pacto Andino, op. cit.*, p. 378-9.

to submit to the general regulations established there for the conduct and location of foreign enterprises. It is sufficient that a copy of the original registration be inscribed in the relevant member country, for the legal personality of the multi-national enterprise to be recognised there.[68] Concerning law applicable to the enterprise, while it is true that no real "Latin-American Company law" exists, the text of Decision No. 46 itself resolves potential legal conflicts by establishing the following order of application of texts: in the first place the company statues of the enterprise; in the second place the Uniform Regulation of Decision No. 46; and in third place the laws of the country where the company statutes were originally registered in the case of matters concerning the location and administration of the enterprise; or the laws of each country where a specific relationship is established, or where the acts of the enterprise will have effect, as established by the appropriate norms of private international law.[69]

Lastly, within the actions envisaged by the scheme of the Andean Group for the initiation of the programme of subregional economic integration, is the channelling of the flow of resources in and out of the subregion to finance the necessary investment.[70] For these purposes, even before the Agreement of Cartagena was signed, the countries of the Andean Group established the Andean Development Corporation,[71] which began to function in Caracas in June 1970. This Corporation, which operates as an international organisation of a financial nature, or as a "public multi-national enterprise" [72] is regulated neither by the uniform text for multinational enterprises mentioned before, nor by the national legal systems of the member countries, nor even by the legal system of Venezuela, where it has its

68. See Art. 23 of Decision No. 46, in *El Pacto Andino, op. cit.*, p. 380.

69. See Arts. 24 and 25 of Decision No. 46, in *El Pacto Andino, op. cit.*, p. 380.

70. See Art. 3 (f) of the Agreement of Cartagena, in *El Pacto Andino, op. cit.*, p. 304.

71. The Treaty or Constitutive Convention was signed on February 7, 1968, between Bolivia, Colombia, Chile, Ecuador, Peru and Venezuela; see *El Pacto Andino, op. cit.*, p. 415 ff.

72. See Marcos Kaplan, "El Grupo Andino: Balance y Perspectivas", in *Revista de la Facultad de Derecho*, No. 47, UCV, Caracas, 1970, p. 89.

seat. on the contrary, it is ruled by norms of an international character foreseen in its Act of Constitution, for it is a case of an international organisation whose aim it is to promote subregional integration. To this end it has been granted a very wide scale of functions of promotion, finance, investment and aid.

Clearly, within the moves towards economic integration in Latin America and in other groups of developing countries, the scheme of the Andean Group is at present the most complete of all. The recent adherence of Venezuela to the Agreement of Cartagena, and the succeeding integrationist measures adopted by the bodies charged with the execution of the Agreement allow us to believe that, as in any system of integration, the adoption and application of irreversible measures is starting a chain reaction of demands which will require new decisions, which will in turn strengthen the economic and political links between the participating countries. If, in the context of Latin America, one admits the thesis that economic integration is a necessary condition in the economic and social development of our countries, there is no doubt that the Andean Group's contribution is meeting those objectives.

3

UNIVERSALISM AND REGIONALISM IN INTERNATIONAL ECONOMIC AND TRADE LAW: THE EXPERIENCE OF LATIN AMERICA

*F. V. García-Amador**

An examination of the experience of Latin America in matters of international economic law reveals interesting perspectives with regard to the functioning of the principles and juridical institutions that have in the past or present guided the grand schemes of international trade. In that experience, universal and regional approaches have been joined together, in a constant search for solutions and objectives that would satisfy the interests of the region in the light of its different historical needs.

The scheme of classic economic liberalism

The first period embracing this Latin American experience extends from the independence years to post-World War II. During this long period international trade schemes were based on the principles of economic liberalism, which had reached its highest expression in Mancunian thought. The theory of comparative advantages and the international division of labor conveyed a concept of a world market without barriers, in which the international distribution of resources would be guided by supply and demand, and in which all nations would benefit by virtue of their equal opportunity to participate. The approach clearly corresponded to a universalist criterion.

This scheme was translated, from the juridical viewpoint, into the principle of the most-favoured-nation (MFN) treatment which was

* Doctor of Law, Director, Department of Legal Affairs, Organisation of American States (OAS), Washington D.C., The United States of America.

intended to ensure equality and nondiscrimination in trade between nations, which were the basic premises of economic liberalism. The great number of treaties of commerce that included the MFN clause attest to the primary role that it played within this approach. Latin America, in reacting against the commercial ties that had bound it to the Spanish metropolis during the colonial period, quickly attached itself to the new scheme of universal participation which the liberal system offered.

However, the premises of the scheme never actually took shape. The political and economic power of the countries, varied as it was, determined that equality would be a rather formal structure, lacking real content, and as a consequence of this the principle of nondiscrimination in practice took on little meaning. The juridical equality assumed by the MFN clause, when applied to a relationship between economically unequal countries, inevitably led to the stronger country receiving the greater benefits. It follows that Latin America would continue to be limited to its role of provider of raw materials and purchaser of industrial products, just as had happened under the trade system of the Spanish colonies. Thus, the liberal system of the clause, far from achieving an equitable international distribution of the resources that it theoretically postulated, stressed the concentration of those resources in the great industrialized nations of the period.

Corrective effort of the MFN clause: the Bello clause

When in the practical application of the MFN clause the adverse effects that resulted from this relationship of economic inequality were observed, an interesting corrective mechanism was thought of: *the Bello clause,* by virtue of which the privileges granted to the Latin American countries through their reciprocal trade would not be extended to other countries benefiting from the MFN clause. The purpose of such an exception to the application of this clause was to create regional preferences in Latin America that would contribute to strengthening the economic capacity of these countries and, on this basis, permit them to participate competitively in the international system. In this way a regional approach was introduced as a way of ensuring effective participation in the prevalent universalist approach. At the same time, the need was recognized, for the first time, of adopting special measures in favor of the countries that had a lower level of economic development, as a result of which the formal equality of the MFN clause was somewhat tempered.

In spite of the corrective action taken through the *Bello clause*, it failed to impose its authority due to a lack of reciprocity between the Latin American countries, in that they did not rigorously observe the preferences that were not extensible, by virtue of the clause, to third countries. Moreover, each of them eventually continued to be governed in their trade relations by the general system of the MFN clause within the world scheme. This panorama was maintained practically without change until after World War II. It should also be noted that during this long period the United States, in securing its position as a world economic power in the decade of the 1920s, shifted its strategy from the conditional most-favoured-nation clause to the unconditional clause, therefore maintaining the same juridic-economic scheme on which the international trade policy of Great Britain had been based.

Multilateralisation of the MFN clause

Following the second world war, the system of bilateral relationships based on the MFN clause was replaced by a multilateral system, based on the same principle and with the same aspirations of universality. The new system is the one that originally let to the creation of the General Agreement on Tariffs and Trade (GATT). Although GATT admits free trade zones and customs unions as an exception to the MFN clause, which presumes recognition of the need for special treatment for certain groups of countries, in essence the basic disequilibrium of the classic scheme is not change: the developing countries continue to be subject to a relationship that is juridically equal but economically unequal, without obtaining the preferential treatment that would permit them to overcome their disadvantage.

As a result, participation of the developing countries in the GATT framework has generally been marginal. In effect, on the one hand, their influence in negotiations is minimal due to their meager contribution to the great international trade flows, and, on the other hand, their *locus standi* is also very limited because they have no real capacity to adopt trade reprisals, which are an effective dissuasive tool within that organisation. Part IV (Trade and Development) was included in the General Agreement to counterbalance that inequality but its contribution has been more theoretical than practical.

Search for new alternatives; economic integration and preferences

Faced with the reality of this negative panorama of the universal scheme, which continued to be based on the principles of economic liberalism, Latin America is beginning to seek new alternatives which will enable it to overcome the drawbacks of that scheme. This marks the second important stage of its experience in the field of international economic law. One of the principal characteristics of this second stage stems from the fact that, for the most part, the alternatives mentioned above propose to introduce elements into the international scheme that reflect some type of social function, thus departing from the traditional individualism of international trade. Another characteristic is that, to a large extent, the Latin American position is already appearing within a strategy common to other developing countries, either general or sectoral.

The first alternative worthy of mention within this new stage is economic integration. The creation of the Latin American Free Trade Association, the Central American Common Market, and the Andean Group, as well as the Caribbean Free Trade Association and the more recent Caribbean Community and Common Markets reveals that the member countries of these regional and subregional associations understand the urgency of economic support among themselves and, as a consequence thereof, the strengthening of their competitive capacity in international markets. Economic integration schemes of developing countries are no longer based on the principles of free competition in order to stimulate trade and development, but rather on principles of well-balanced development designed to guarantee real equality of opportunity to the less developed countries that participate in each process, thus averting within the region the reproduction of the same vices that affect the region in its trade relations with industrialized countries. It is true that these principles of well-balanced development have not yet reached, in practice, the level of perfection that would be desirable, but they do constitute an evident evolution if they are compared with the classic postulates.

The second alternative of fundamental interest to the developing countries is the system of trade preferences. These preferences constitute *par excellence* the mechanism that ensures special treatment to developing countries in the markets of industrialized countries by placing them in a more advantageous and competitive position than that which they had attained under a scheme of equal treatment such as the MFN clause. This system is perhaps the best demonstration of how, in the field of international trade, economic inequality of the parties in the relationship requires juridical treatment that is also unequal, for the benefit of the weakest party, which in this way could bring that party to a situation of real economic equality.

With respect to the system of trade preferences, there always arises the problem of whether there should be a generalized application or a regional one. The protection of Latin American interests requires a generalized application, for in this way segmentation of the world into economic blocs is avoided, as well as the discriminatory effects on their exports generated by regional preferences between the European Economic Community and the African countries. This signifies, if you will, a new universalist approach but based on principles entirely different from those of the classic scheme of international trade.

Commodity agreements and producers' organisations

Another significant development consists in the basic commodity agreements, in which Latin America had had particular interest as a result of being an important producer of such products. The principles on which some of these agreements rest, as in the case of coffee and wheat, also depart considerably from the traditional liberal scheme. In fact, the interchange of products is no longer guided by the law of supply and demand but by a certain level of planning, which is variable in each case, and the purpose of which is to protect both the interests of the producer as well as the interests of the consumer. For this purpose prices and production must be regulated, thus guaranteeing their stability and minimum levels, which would be impossible to do merely by playing with the laws of the market.

However, in practice this new scheme has not solved all problems since economic trends continue to be those of overproduction and underconsumption, which has provoked conflicts between developing producer countries and developed consumer countries. At the same time, it has often been difficult to agree on the interests of the producers. For these reasons, the regulation of the market that is proposed by the agreements has not brought entirely satisfactory results for the developing countries. Furthermore, from the viewpoint of the scope of application of this scheme, it should be noted that it is typically sectoral, departing from universalism and regionalism. On the other hand, it has the characteristics of bringing together both the producer countries and the consumer countries.

Producers' organisations also reveal new trends in the development of international economic law. The most important of these organisations up to now is the Organisation of Petroleum Exporting Countries (OPEC), although efforts have also been made in the case of copper and other products. These organisations are formed exclusively by producer and developing countries, excluding the developed countries that are producers of the same raw material and, of course, the consumer countries, which also are developed countries with high consumption. Their objectives are to maximize the power of negotiation of the developing countries in the trading of certain basic products, based chiefly on the matter of controlling their supply. In comparison with the classic structure of international trade, perhaps these organisations are not introducing a new juridical principle since they continue to be guided by the law of supply and demand; but what they do represent is a different economic situation in which the control of the supply is concentrated in developing countries, which can arrange for a common strategy and a common policy. Furthermore, unlike what occurs in the case of commodity agreements, the economic trends in this case are underproduction and overconsumption, placing the consumer countries in a position of disadvantage. Also, this too, involves a sectoral structure, which departs from the universal and the regional, but only with the participation of developing countries.

State trading

Another of the alternatives to which reference is being made is state trading, which has been in practice since the beginning of the century, either under the form of partial intervention in foreign trade or in the form of complete state control. As is known, state trade virtually nullifies the effects of the most-favoured-nation clause in matters concerning customs tariffs, since they cease to constitute a stimulus or a discouragement to imports. From this point of view there is a complete innovation with respect to the juridical mechanism and the basic economic principles of the clause. However, as to its practical effects state trading does not manage to overcome the situation of disadvantage in which the developing countries find themselves. The *quid pro quo* principle, on which state trading is based, exacts equal reciprocal contributions, often adopting the form of barter. This means that the parties are placed in a situation of absolute equality, regardless of their different levels of development. Not even by this way does a developing country receive the preferential treatment it requires to overcome its disadvantages. From this other point of view its effects are very similar to the effects of the clause: juridical equality, which does not consider the differences in economic development of the parties in the relationship.

Notwithstanding the above considerations, partial state intervention in trade can produce some advantages, depending on the nature of the intervention, especially in strengthening the capacity of negotiation of a developing country and the use of its purchasing power. It is for these reasons that the Latin American countries practice some form of partial intervention in their foreign trade.

Multinational enterprises

Finally, reference should be made to a phenomenon which, to a large extent, breaks away from the traditional scheme of international trade. In fact, in the case of the multinational enterprise the buyer and the seller, even though located in different countries, often are not necessarily subjects apart in the trade relationship, since the operation is carried out within the structure of the enterprise itself and of the relationships between the home office and its subsidiaries or between the subsidiaries themselves. However, commercial operations do not necessarily presuppose an interchange of products across a physical border, since the enterprise is in a position to invest and produce in different consumer markets if it is in its own interest to do so. This phenomenon affects even the traditional trade relationship between developing countries and industrialized countries since in many cases the exporting entity located in the developing country is an integral part of the importing entity located in the industrialized country.

The impact produced in the developing countries by the phenomenon of the multinational enterprise is a strong one, as the experience of Latin America well demonstrates. While the contribution of capital and technology resulting from operations of the enterprise is a factor that merits consideration, the possibility of restrictive practices and eventual control of the international market is a negative aspect that must be corrected. For that purpose, thought is being given to multiple forms of control, both at the national as well as the regional and international levels. In this idea, the new approach to national laws on foreign investments that place special emphasis on the elimination of restrictive practices, the transfer of technology, and the prohibition of investment in certain sectors, as well as solutions of a regional nature, such as Decision 24 on foreign capital in the Andean group, have a leading role to play.

Future trends

From the above considerations one can see that, as regards international economic law, Latin America follows pragmatic criteria, regardless of whether they are concerned with universal or regional approaches. Thus, for example, as regards trade preferences, a generalized system of a universal character is aspired to. It is possible to develop the same trend with respect to the control of multinational enterprises. However, on the economic integration plane, the solutions sought are typically regional ones. But in other cases a sectoral and functional criterion has been followed, either by grouping developing countries or developing and developed countries. The Organisation of Petroleum Exporting Countries is an example of the former; the commodity agreements are an example of the latter.

This multiple trend is clearly explained by the fact that Latin America is essentially in pursuit of those economic mechanisms and their corresponding juridical principles that will ensure it: (a) special treatment adequate to its lesser level of economic development, which will permit it, in turn, to strengthen its competitive capacity; (b) non-discriminatory treatment in the markets of the developed countries as regards the treatment received by other developing countries; and (c) no demand for reciprocity in favor of the developed countries.

None of the above is possible under the classic system of the most-favoured-nation clause. Hence, the need for the development and establishment of those principles that are capable of ensuring some type of "international social justice", which means a departure from traditional economic liberalism. In this process international institutions play a fundamental role because through them those principles of social justice can be established, and because in any case some type of international control will be required to ensure the application and operation of that justice in practice. Also on this plane, mechanisms such as CECLA, (that is, the Special Committee on Latin American Coordination), and the United Nations Conference on Trade and Development (UNCTAD) are clearly representative of the trend to strengthen the capacity of the developing countries to put pressure to bear on their economic recovery through institutional means. In spite of the many differences that still separate the developing countries, it can be seen that a common strategy is in the process of being formed, at least with respect to the basic postulates.

In conclusion, the guidelines of this complex panorama seem to be oriented towards the establishment of a mechanism for the redistribution of income and international resources. On the domestic plane the simple operation of the laws of the market has been incapable of ensuring a fair redistribution; and the creation of mechanisms and institutions that can perform that function, such as the tax system, has been necessary; so, too, on the international plane it becomes necessary to proceed with institutionalized redistribution that provides a measure of justice while contributing to the peaceful relations between the developed world and the developing world.

4

REGIONAL INTEGRATION IN THE CARIBBEAN AND THE COMMONWEALTH

*Sir Hugh Wooding**

Like Professor Brewer-Carias,[1] I believe that the issue in the developing countries, of which there are so many, has less to do with the universal law than with socio-politico-economic conditions. That I think is, why the new world which is emerging from the past and seeking a foothold in the present, tends to see almost every subject in terms of its own needs. So, as a non-academic from that new world, I too look upon the questions from the point of those needs more so than of what is internationally desirable. Nevertheless, I do bear in mind that, whether we like it or not, we all live together in a tight, little, interdependent world.

The history and lack of development of the Caribbean area are too well known to require any exposition. I need only say that the challenges of the post-war world bestirred its people to examine, perhaps for the first time, what means they could best devise to achieve their own salvation. They adopted a functional approach to try and resolve their regional problems and were encouraged to set up The West Indies Federation. It failed, mainly I think, because of its inability to evolve an economic policy acceptable by all its constituent units. But out of that very failure emerged a recognition that without some plan for regional economic integration their chances of survival were negligible if not nil.

It was thus that the Caribbean Free Trade Association (CARIFTA) came into being.

The CARIFTA agreement, signed at a Heads of Government conference in October 1967, became operative from May 1, 1968. It

* Sometime Chancellor of the University of the West Indies.
1. See p. 13.

began with four adherents.[2] Five more members[3] acceded two months later, and a further two[4] after another month. Yet another[5] applied to join and was admitted to membership in May 1971. Altogether, therefore, there were twelve members: four[6] which had gained their independence since the failure of the federation, six[7] which had been given the status of "Associated States", and two colonies.[8] For certain purposes of the agreement, the four independents were designated as "more-developed countries" (MDCs), and the other eight member territories as "less-developed countries" (LDCs).

CARIFTA was created to comprise a free-trade area having as its central aims the economic development of its member territories and ultimately their economic independence.

Their *modus* was intended, at first, to stimulate development and as soon as practicable thereafter to move towards integration. Hence, after a brief five years CARIFTA is in the process of giving way to a Caribbean Community and Common Market (CARICOM).

Because CARIFTA was establishing a free-trade area, it was necessary to prescribe criteria for determining the origin qualification of goods for area tariff treatment. Three were prescribed.[9] I shall refer to one of them later.

Simultaneously with the efforts to establish CARIFTA, the LDCs in the Eastern Caribbean (that is, all except Belize) were working to create a common market among themselves. Endorsing this objective, paragraph 8 of Annex B to the CARIFTA agreement stipulated that none of its provisions should preclude any agreement made between the LDCs, and notified to the CARIFTA Council, for dismantling tariffs on trade among themselves at a faster rate than on their trade with other CARIFTA countries. An agreement so providing was

2. Antigua, Barbados, Guyana and Trinidad and Tobago.
3. Dominica, Grenada, St. Kitts-Nevis-Anguilla, St. Lucia and St. Vincent.
4. Jamaica and Montserrat.
5. Belize.
6. Barbados, Guyana, Jamaica and Trinidad and Tobago.
7. Antigua, Dominica, Grenada, St. Kitts-Nevis-Anguilla, St. Lucia and St. Vincent.
8. Belize and Montserrat.
9. q.v. article 5 of Carifta Agreement.

concluded on June 11, 1968 and was duly notified. But it should be noted that while Montserrat could (and did) participate as a member of the free-trade area under the *inter se* doctrine of Commonwealth relations, it did not join in the agreement for a common external tariff and, therefore, was not *stricto sensu* a member of the Eastern Caribbean common market.

In effect, then, the CARIFTA agreement permitted a mini common market within a larger free-trade area. Also, recognizing the more urgent revenue needs of all the LDCs, it included in a Reserve List, in the same Annex B, two sets of commodities – one on which the MDCs were to remove area tariffs immediately whereas the LDCs were permitted to phase them out during a five-year period, and the other on which the MDCs were to phase out area tariffs over a period of five years whereas the LDCs were allowed to phase them out over ten.

The creation of their mini common market and the facilities for phasing out area tariffs were not the only concessions that the MDCs made to the LDCs. Far from it. As I see it, they were assiduously applying what I discern to be a principle of compensation, whereby territories, which have remained economically more or less static during their colonial administration, should be given special advantages to accelerate their development. Let me mention other instances of its application.

Article 39 of the CARIFTA agreement provided an element of compensation which is probably without precedent in a free-trade area. It conceded that in the event of its being proposed to set up an industry in any of the LDCs which was already established in one or more of the MDCs, that LDC could invite a combined LDC application to the CARIFTA Council of Ministers to authorise them to suspend area tariff treatment of imports from the MDCs of that industry's products for such time as might be necessary to promote its development in the LDC. In effect, therefore, the provision permitted the LDCs to erect within the larger free-trade area tariff barriers such as would afford protection to one of their number against the MDCs.

Again, among resolutions adopted by the Heads of Government Conference and incorporated in Annex A to the CARIFTA agreement was one recognising the need to intensify industrial development throughout the area. It was, therefore, further resolved *inter alia* to invite the assistance of the ECLA Secretariat to work out a regional policy on incentives, to identify industries which might conveniently and successfully be located in the LDCs and to devise special measures to promote their establishment.

In the resulting study on incentives two guidelines were kept firmly in mind: (i) the need to relate the value of any grantable concessions to what the enterprise might be expected to contribute to the domestic economy, and (ii) the expediency of allowing the LDCs, in view of their relative lack of development, to grant to an enterprise more generous incentives for its given level of contribution than would be permissible for the MDCs. Hence the CARIFTA Secretariat has very pointedly observed that "incentives are being harmonised, not equalised".[10]

Yet another instance of applying the principle of compensation may be seen in the Agricultural Marketing Protocol which the Conference resolved should come into force at the same time as the CARIFTA agreement. The protocol listed twenty-two commodities produced in the region, not already the subject of bilateral or multilateral marketing agreements, and required each member territory to declare an annual forecast of its surpluses and deficits of each, to inform the Secretariat if and so soon as for any reason it should become apparent that any forecast might prove inaccurate and to route its selling and buying of the listed commodities through the Secretariat. And, further to the aim to accelerate their economic development, the LDCs were given priority in the regional market for the disposal of their surpluses.

One last illustration – the decision to establish the Caribbean Development Bank. Though not a part of the CARIFTA agreement, it ensued from the same discussions and was conceived as complementary to it. And it was prescribed as a major purpose of the bank that it should make soft loans available to the LDCs (but *not* to the MDCs) for investment in agriculture, industry and tourism – in that order of priority.

The aims and purposes of CARIFTA have been carried forward and entrenched in the CARICOM treaties. Among the objectives specified in article 4 of the Community treaty is the economic in-

10. See "Carifta and the New Caribbean" published by the Carifta Secretariat (1971) at p. 36.

tegration of the member states by the establishment of a common market with the following aims:

> "(i) the strengthening, co-ordination and regulation of the economic and trade relations among Member States in order to promote their accelerated harmonious and balanced development;
> (ii) the sustained expansion and continuing integration of economic activities, the benefits of which shall be equitably shared taking into account the need to provide special opportunities for the Less Developed Countries;
> (iii) the achievement of a greater measure of economic independence and effectiveness of its Member States in dealing with states, groups of states and entities of whatever description".

Perhaps I should say a bit more here about CARICOM. The agreement which led to the treaties for establishing a Caribbean Community and Common Market was concluded in Georgetown, Guyana in April 1973 and is referred to as the Georgetown Accord. Two of the LDCs, Antigua and Montserrat, declined to sign the Accord and, as at present minded, will opt out of joining either the Community or the Caribbean Common Market.

Although not a party to the Accord, the Bahamas Government has declared an interest in joining the Community but not the Common Market, presumably because having a tourist-based economy with no immediate or foreseeable future prospect of producing goods for sale in the market, the compensation for the resulting loss of much-needed tariff revenues would be practically nil. However, both treaties leave the door open to "any other State of the Caribbean Region that is in the opinion of the Conference (of Heads of Member Governments) able and willing to exercise the rights and assume the obligations of membership". The language used is I think significant. It is not anticipated that CARICOM will remain a Commonwealth Caribbean institution as CARIFTA was. Rather, it is confidently believed that as a regional association it will attract non-Commonwealth member territories such as Surinam, Haiti, Cuba and Colombia, some of which have already evinced an interest in participating.

The Georgetown Accord provided [11] that CARICOM should replace CARIFTA "which shall cease to exist on May 1, 1974 and which, prior thereto, shall cease to apply" as between the contracting

11. q.v. clause 2(1).

parties to CARICOM. It has been questioned [12] whether this provision is by itself effective since the CARIFTA agreement does not provide for its termination but only for withdrawal by any member territory on giving twelve months notice in writing. Termination would of course have been effective if, as contemplated, *all* the member territories had been parties to the Georgetown Accord, and it *is* contractually effective as between those which were.

But, while Antigua and Montserrat, who were not, could have maintained the continuing existence of CARIFTA, the MDCs gave them due notice of their withdrawal, as they were contractually entitled to do, effective on May 1, 1974. Their withdrawal has effectively knocked out the whole bottom from the CARIFTA agreement and thereby terminated it, but it leaves the LDCs with the option of joining CARICOM and/or of preserving their own mini common market.

Thus far, only the four MDCs have signed [13] and ratified the CARICOM Treaties. They are independent and accordingly have the required capacity. The LDCs subscribing to the Georgetown Accord undertook [14] to sign and ratify them so as to become contracting parties on May 1, 1974, the date on which CARIFTA factually ceased to exist. What of their capacity so to do?

In retaining responsibility for the defence and external affairs of the Associated States, the status accorded to all the LDCs except Montserrat and Belize, Her Majesty's Government in the United Kingdom (HMG) undertook to,[15] and did,[16] delegate to the governments of those states executive authority with respect to certain external relations which they might have with other countries, subject, in most instances, to their informing HMG in advance of any proposal to conduct negotiations to that end and subject also to their keeping HMG informed of the progress of the negotiations.

12. By Professor Hans Geiser in a letter published at p. 21 of *The (Trinidad) Express* of September 10, 1973.

13. On July 4, 1973 at Convention Centre, Chaguaramas, Trinidad.

14. q.v. clause 1 (4) of the Georgetown Accord.

15. See, e.g., paragraph 20 of the *St. Kitts-Nevis and Anguilla Constitutional Conference Report* 1966 (Cmnd 3031).

16. See e.g. letter from HMG to Administrator, St. Kitts dated February 16, 1967.

This general delegation included authority to negotiate and conclude

i. "trade agreements with other countries, whether bilateral or multilateral, relating solely to the treatment of goods;
ii. "agreements of purely local concern with any independent member of the Commonwealth in the Caribbean area or any other Associated States or any British colony in the Caribbean area or with such authorities in other neighbouring islands as the Government of (the Associated State) may request and Her Majesty's Government approve".[17]

Further, although in respect of the first of the abovementioned delegations of authority it was specifically stipulated that "agreements relating to establishment matters, i.e. agreements affecting the rights of persons and companies of the contracting parties, will continue to be dealt with in commercial treaties negotiated with Her Majesty's Government", the express assurance was given that HMG would "be prepared, in appropriate circumstances, to delegate to the government of (the Associated State) *ad hoc* authority to conclude individual trade agreements in which establishment matters are included". It was in pursuance of the authorities thus generally delegated that, after informing and keeping HMG informed of the proposal and the progress of the negotiations, the Associated States were competent to sign the mini common market and CARIFTA agreements.

In its general delegation of executive authority to conduct certain external affairs as specified, HMG also undertook [18] to "give sympathetic consideration to any request" by any of the Governments of the Associated States for authority to take action on individual questions of external relations not covered by the general delegation.

The Associated States accordingly requested HMG to confer authority on them, as well as on Montserrat, to negotiate, sign and ratify the treaty for establishing the Caribbean Community to which the treaty for establishing a Caribbean Common Market is an annex. The request is still under consideration, but HMG have intimated [19]

17. q.v. paragraphs 3 (c), 3 (e) and 5 of the letter referred to in note 16.
18. See paragraph 4 of the letter referred to in note 16.
19. By letter dated March 22, 1973 from the Deputy British Government

that in principle "they view with favour the proposed Community and wish to do everything possible to facilitate its formation", but that it will be necessary to study the implications of the treaty before further delegations of HMG's responsibilities can be determined upon. Now that the text of the treaty has been settled, it is expected that a decision will be had before May 1, 1974. But it is right to add that HMG have pointed out that "the participation of Montserrat, which is not an Associated State, presents some difficulties" which will need to be specially considered.

Because it provides for a common external tariff, Belize and Montserrat may encounter difficulty in joining the Caribbean Common Market. But it is certain they will do so if they should finally wish to join the Caribbean Community. To a lesser extent perhaps, the Associated States will be faced with a similar difficulty. This is because article 8 of the Community treaty provides *inter alia* that the conference of the heads of government of member states shall determine the policy of the Community, may establish (and designate as such) Community institutions in addition to those already established by the treaty, and shall be the final authority for the conclusion of treaties on behalf of the Community and for entering into relationships between the Community and international organisations and states.

Such powers and responsibilities may well conflict with HMG's responsibilities for or reservation of the direction and control of the external affairs of Belize and Montserrat and of all the Associated States, so that some special formula may need to be found. However, Grenada is scheduled to attain Independence in February 1974 and Belize should follow if and so soon as the Guatemala threat is dissolved.

In the treaty for establishing the Caribbean Common Market the principle of compensation has received further recognition. For instance, the criterion to which I said I would refer for determining the origin qualification of goods for area tariff treatment under the CARIFTA agreement was that a minimum of 50 per cent of the f.o.b. export price of the product must be constituted by local activity and local materials, but under the Caribbean Common Market treaty the

Representative in St. Vincent to the Hon. J. F. Mitchell, Premier of St. Vincent.

percentage of value added so to qualify goods produced in the LDCs has been reduced from 50 per cent to 40 per cent.[20] Also, the LDCs have been allowed greater latitude for phasing into the common external tariff in that for determining an appropriate plan and schedule of rates annual reviews are provided for, as well as a longer period for their introduction and for the completion of the phasing-in by the LDCs.[21]

Further, the MDCs have sponsored the establishment of a Caribbean Investment Corporation financed in part by their governments and in part by the private sector. Its objects include investigating and establishing appropriate industries in the LDCs, including agricultural industries, and thereby serving the LDCs in areas of development complementary to those of special interest to the Caribbean Development Bank.

I have recounted what I have about the structure of CARIFTA and CARICOM in order to make plain their essential aim and purpose. It was not, or certainly not primarily, that the member territories should be able to play a part in achieving, in the words of Professor Dam, "the most efficient allocation of resources for the world as a whole".[22] In my view, the Heads of Caribbean Governments have proceeded on the footing that compensation must precede equivalence if the development gap between the MDCs and the LDCs is to be effectively narrowed.

It is with such thoughts in mind that I look briefly at the provisions of the General Agreement on Tariffs and Trade (GATT) permitting the establishment of customs unions and free-trade areas. Its article 24 recognises "the desirability of increasing freedom of trade by the development, through voluntary agreements, of closer integration between the economies of the countries parties to such agreements"; also, that "the purpose of a customs union or free-trade area *should be* to facilitate trade between the parties and not to raise barriers to the trade of other member countries with such parties". Was this statement of purpose precatory or obligatory? The question remains as yet unresolved, but I think it was precatory.

Perhaps I should recall that it was the United States Government

20. See article 14 (1).
21. See article 31.
22. See note 29 infra.

which spearheaded the negotiations which led to the GATT. They were against preferences of any kind since, in their view, preferences were bad economically, but they saw no significant danger in customs unions.

The rationale for the distinction between them appears to have rested on the concept that a customs union creates for trading purposes what may be regarded as a single customs country, so that the members of the union cannot be said to discriminate in favour of one another against non-members. They merely free what is, in effect, an internal or domestic trade in accordance with the terms of their agreement for union, while, at the same time, maintaining the most-favoured-nation principle, which the GATT entrenched, in their trading relationships with all other states. Free-trade areas and interim agreements necessary for the formation of a customs union or a free-trade area were exempted on the same footing from the prohibitions of the most-favoured-nation principle.

CARIFTA and CARICOM fall within the exemptions, and it seems to me now too late for anyone to contend otherwise. However, in an article on "Regional Economic Arrangements and the GATT: The Legacy of a Misconception",[23] Professor Dam has argued that GATT "has two grand designs: That free trade be promoted through multilateral tariff negotiations, and that discriminations be eliminated by means of the most-favoured-nation principle".[24] But he appreciated that "for the draftsmen of the General Agreement, customs unions and free-trade areas produced a conflict between those two goals".[25] He explained that "such regional groupings seemed to be movements towards free trade to the extent that tariffs were lowered between member countries, but they also seemed to involve discrimination against non-member countries".[26]

And he went on to add, but on this point I find it difficult to agree, that "what may not have been appreciated at the time of the drafting of the General Agreement was that customs unions and free-trade areas need not involve movements towards free trade". On the other

23. Published in Vol. 30 of the *University of Chicago Law Review*, Summer 1963, No. 4, pp. 615/665.
24. At p. 622.
25. At p. 622.
26. At p. 622.

hand, I agree that "they may just as easily be, and perhaps in view of the widespread propensity towards protectionism are more likely to be, movements away from free trade".[27] Indeed, that seems to me obvious.

Starting, however, from the premise such as he did, it is not surprising that Professor Dam regards the GATT article 24 as "deceptive, so much so that no customs union or free-trade area agreement presented for review has complied with (its conditions) and yet every agreement has been approved by a tacit or explicit waiver".[28] In his view, "the fundamental justification for the free trade position ... is that the most efficient allocation of resources for the world as a whole will be achieved by the elimination of tariffs and other arbitrary barriers to trade".[29] Hence he stressed the importance of bearing in mind "the elementary distinction between the wealth of the world as a whole and the wealth of the member countries of a customs union or free-trade area".[30] So, appreciating that "it is possible ... for a group of countries, through creation of a customs union or free-trade area, to improve their own lot at the expense of the rest of the world",[31] he warned that "it is precisely the danger of such action which requires some rule on the subject in the General Agreement".[32]

That, I believe, is the point at issue in all regional movements for the development of trade. And, since the GATT is currently under review, that is the issue to which I seek to call attention. Should the concern be for "the wealth of the world as a whole" which, in the view of the developing and underdeveloped countries, really means the ever-increasing wealth of the world's economic giants and the ever-worsening deprivation of the economically depressed? Or should the concern be for the units in the regional grouping which look upon their economic integration as their only hope of survival? Or may the conflict be reconciled by working out a new rule founded on a world-wide application of what I have called "the principle of compensation"?

27. At p. 622/623.
28. At p. 619.
29. At p. 623.
30. See the note 22 at p. 623.
31. See the note 22 at p. 623.
32. See the note 22 at p. 623.

Concern for the wealth of the world as a whole? The three UNCTAD conferences that have so far been held, have not inspired the developing and underdeveloped countries with either confidence or hope. Nor do the harsh realities of the contemporary international scene or, more relevantly, of the international monetary system.

Concern for the regional grouping and its units? A Soviet writer, Genkin, is quoted as having observed in 1958 that "the inclusion in customs unions of important groups of states would lead to an essential limiting of the operation of the most-favoured-nation principle, and even in essence to its renunciation".[33] In so saying, he plainly anticipated the current fear that the trading world is being fractionated into discriminatory regional groupings.

Is this really satisfactory? Can it be commended? Especially as regards groupings as powerful as the European Economic Community (EEC)?

Perhaps, then, the compensation principle should be generally accepted and universally applied. That was the thinking behind the Commonwealth Caribbean's recent rejection of a Yaounde-type association with the EEC. As their delegate[34] said at the recent Brussels Conference, Commonwealth Caribbean countries can see no rational basis on which the EEC may demand reciprocity for granting them tariff-free entry when the concession is being sought as "a chance of redressing the economic imbalances that have been the heritage of (their) relationship with Europe". Further, he maintained, "reciprocity between those who are unequal in economic strength is a contradiction in economic terms". Hence, he insisted, if their development is to become a reality, they need *inter alia* (a) access to the European Development Bank, to the European Investment Bank and to other sources, both public and private, of EEC development finance on terms which do not compromise their national dignity and self-respect; and (b) a wider and more adequate protected regional market in which to co-ordinate the development of their natural

33. From Genkin's "The Principle of the Most-Favoured-Nation in Trade Agreements among States" (1958) 9 *Soventskoye Consudarstvo: Pravo* 22, at page 28, quoted in an unpublished paper by Dean Ryan of the Law School of the University of Queensland.

34. Hon. S. S. Ramphal, Attorney-General and Minister of External Affairs, Guyana.

resources and to promote the economic advancement of each of their countries as well as of the region as a whole.

This assertion of their claims parallels what the MDCs have so readily granted the LDCs in the conviction that by conceding to them means whereby they may redress the imbalances that have been the heritage of their history they will promote the development of the region of which each group forms a part.

So, too, I submit for your consideration that by a like application of the principle of compensation the dominant trading nations may redress the imbalances stemming from a similar heritage and, thereby, promote the welfare and progress of the world of which each of the developed, developing and underdeveloped countries is an integral part.

5

THE EAST AFRICAN ECONOMIC COMMUNITY AND THE EUROPEAN ECONOMIC COMMUNITIES (EEC)

*Kenneth R. Simmonds**

Both the objectives and the techniques of the forms of relationship open to negotiation between regional integration movements are at the present time under re-examination. The East African Economic Community was established by the Treaty for East African Co-operation, signed on June 6, 1967, by Kenya, Tanzania and Uganda, and which came into force on December 1, 1967.[1] Although this is, at least in its potential, one of the most interesting experiments in regional integration being carried on in the "new" Commonwealth, its progress since 1967 has been inhibited by a variety of political and economic tensions within the territories of the signatories and it is now faced with the very considerable task of coming to terms with the new relationships with other developing states, and with the member states of the enlarged EEC, presaged by the new 1975 Lomé Convention.

The East African Community is the heir to a complex history of administrative, legal, communications and fiscal co-operation which stretches over the half-century before these three countries achieved independence.[2] The principal stages in this evolution were marked by

* Professor of International Law, Queen Mary College, University of London, England; Director of the British Institute of International and Comparative Law; President of the International Association of Legal Science.

1. As amended 1969, 1970, 1971. Printed by the East African Community Printer, Nairobi 1972.

2. A good general account of the historical background is given in Delupis, "The East African Community and the Common Market" (Stockholm 1969), 19-50.

the work of the partial customs unions of the territories of 1917 and 1927, the "settlers federation movement" beginning in 1924, the operation of the East African High Commission from 1947 to 1961, and, finally, the development of the East African Common Services Organisation, which was set up at the London Conference of 1961. After independence and the failure of some attempts to move toward political federation, a joint review of the Common Services Agreement served as a basis for negotiating the 1967 Treaty for East African Co-operation, which had as its central purpose and aim "... to strengthen and regulate the industrial, commercial and other relations of the partner states to the end that there shall be *accelerated, harmonious* and *balanced development* and sustained expansion of economic activities *the benefits of which shall be equitably shared"*.[3]

The 1967 Treaty set out (i) to establish a regional common market, (ii) to ensure an equitable distribution between the signatories of the benefits of balanced industrial development, (iii) to secure the maintenance of common customs and excise tariffs, (iv) to provide a framework for the progressive harmonisation of regional economic and monetary policies, and (v) to provide for the establishment, at a later stage, of common agricultural and transport policies. The most controversial and difficult provisions of the Treaty are undoubtedly those which relate to the transfer tax system [4] – itself one of three key measures designed to assist balanced industrial development within the territories.[5] The Treaty provides that a state which is in deficit in its total trade in manufactured goods with the other two states may impose a transfer tax upon such goods originating from the other two states up to a value of goods equivalent in each case to its deficit with that country. The deficit is to be shown in the annual trade statistics

3. *Treaty for East African Co-operation* ("Treaty"), preamble and articles 1-4; see esp. article 2(1).

4. *Treaty,* article 20 (and cf. Annexes 4, 5 and 6).

5. The other measures include the harmonisation of fiscal measures offered by each country toward industrial development and the establishment of an East African Development Bank, one of the prime functions of which is to give priority to the provision of technical and financial assistance to industrial development projects in "... the relatively less developed partner states, thereby endeavouring to reduce the substantial industrial imbalances between them" *(Treaty,* Annex 6, Charter of the East African Development Bank, article 1 (1) (a) and (c)).

produced by the Customs and Excise Department and the list of manufactured goods to which the system applies is a very comprehensive one.[6] Transfer taxes can only be imposed if goods of a similar description to those taxed are being manufactured, or are reasonably expected to be manufactured within three months from the date of imposition of the tax, in the tax imposing country. Moreover, the industry to be protected by the tax must have a productive capacity equivalent to at least 15 per cent of the total domestic consumption of such products in the tax-imposing state (or to a value of £100,000 per year, whichever is less) and the maximum rate of any transfer tax is limited to 50 per cent of the equivalent external customs tariff imposed on such goods coming from outside East Africa.

In practice, this "transfer tax" system has related to the imposition of duties on Kenyan goods by Tanzania and Uganda, and on Ugandan goods by Tanzania. It has led to complaints from the Kenyan business community that the other two states could over-use their rights to impose transfer taxes, and that, taken together with the powers of the East African Development Bank to switch foreign investment from Kenya to the other two states, Kenya would be asked to make a disproportionate contribution to the benefits accruing to the East African Community as a whole. In addition, there have been complaints over the exercise of rights under the Treaty to impose restrictions on inter-territorial trade in basic foodstuffs, and over uncertainties in the industrial licensing system which might provoke the withholding of investment capital. In the early years of operation of the Treaty there were also difficulties over the over-ambitious fiscal, customs and excise integration provisions, over the dependance upon a dispensible external customs barrier, and over the total absence of a *lex fori* for the Common Market Tribunal.[7] The delay in establishing

6. *Treaty,* Annex 4.

7. *Treaty,* articles 32-42. The Common Market Tribunal is a body composed of a "judicial" Chairman and four members "of impartiality and independence", one each being chosen by each state and the fourth by the other three members and the Chairman acting in common agreement. Only partner states may make references to the Tribunal, although the Community Council (*Treaty,* articles 30-31) may request advisory opinions. The decisions of the Tribunal are to be reached by a majority and no dissenting opinions are permitted. Under article 41 each partner state agrees to accept the decisions of the Tribunal.

that Tribunal as an operative institution was regarded as symptomatic of a widespread reluctance within the territories to delegate "sovereign" jurisdictional powers and of an inability on the part of the signatories to face the political consequences of the imposition of sanctions in cases where a signatory fails to implement decisions of Community institutions.[8]

These early difficulties were aggravated by the severe political tensions following upon the Ugandan coup d'Etat of January 1971, which resulted in a rupture of relations between Uganda and Tanzania, and a tenmonth crisis during which the Community on several occasions came close to breaking up. In spite of this the East African Authority, which exercises the principal executive powers of the Community, was enabled to carry on its functions without the necessity of meetings of the Heads of State. In more recent years, other shortcomings of the founding Treaty have come to the fore. In particular, although the Treaty shows that the signatories have conferred upon the East African Economic Community the legal capacity and juridical personality required for the performance of its functions,[9] there is no doubt that the primacy of the law of the Community has not been secured. In the case of *East African Community v. The Republic of Kenya,*[10] the Court of Appeal of East Africa (itself a continuation of the court established under the earlier East African Common Services Organisation and a judicial organ of the East African Economic Community) declared that:

> "... the Constitution of Kenya is paramount, and any law, whether it be of Kenya, of the Community or of any other country which has been applied in Kenya, which is in conflict with the Constitution is void to the extent of the conflict." [11]

The jurisdiction of this court is determined by the individual signatories; it does not, as would have been expected, have compulsory jurisdiction over appeals from the highest national courts, although such appeals are regularly referred to it. Nor can it act as an

8. See: S. Ross, "The Common Market Tribunal—The Solution to the Conflict between Municipal and International Law in East Africa", in 1972 (21) *International and Comparative Law Quarterly,* 361-374.

9. *Treaty,* articles 43-45.

10. [1970] *East Africa Law Reports,* 457.

11. *Ibid.,* at 460; cf. Delupis, *op. cit.,* 75-76.

instrument of integration (as does the European Court of Justice) since the Treaty for East African Co-operation does not allow it to hear appeals either from the Common Market Tribunal or from the East African Industrial Court, the other regional judicial body established by the Kampala Treaty.[12]

Many other criticisms of the original structure and early functioning of the East African Community could be added to the comments made above,[13] but the principal purpose of this paper is rather to draw attention to the development of its external relationships, and, in particular those with the European Economic Community. From the outset, the three member states of the East African Community began to consider ways of extending their own machinery for co-operation to other countries in the Eastern African sub-region of the United Nations Economic Commission for Africa (ECA).[14] In the short term, however, they were principally concerned over the weakening of their external trading position because of the preferences accorded to the states associated with the EEC under the provisions of the First and Second Yaoundé Conventions and to Nigeria under the (abortive) Association Agreement signed at Lagos in 1966. They enjoyed Commonwealth trade preferences but did not grant reciprocal advantages or treatment to the United Kingdom (or their other Commonwealth trading partners) nor did they accord most-favoured-nation treatment. They sought, therefore, an association agreement with the EEC primarily for defensive purposes. In 1967, when negotiations with the EEC began, some 15 per cent of the total exports of the three countries went to the EEC member states, 11 per cent to the United States of America, and 27 per cent to the United Kingdom. Of their total imports, 24 per cent came from the EEC Member States and 32 per cent from the United Kingdom. An association with the EEC could, therefore, lead to a substantial diversification of trade and be of benefit to a major future change in trading patterns. As with the Lagos Agreement, negotiations with the EEC were conducted (by agreement with the states associated under the Yaoundé Convention)

12. *Treaty,* article 85.

13. See: *Delupis, op. cit.,* 159-161, and A. F. Ewing, "African Economic Co-operation Revisited" in 4 (1970) *Journal of World Trade Law,* 362-376.

14. See: UN ECA, A Venture in Self-reliance. Ten Years of ECA (E/CN. 14/424; 1968), 30-31.

so as to leave Commonwealth preferences untouched. Under the Treaty for East African Co-operation the signatories are not allowed to accord most-favoured-nation status in any agreement with third states.[15] Negotiations with the EEC were, therefore, concluded by the East African Community on behalf of the partner states; the Treaty eventually signed with the EEC in July, 1968, was concluded in mixed form, with the three East African Community states, the six EEC member states and the EEC Council of Ministers as signatories. The Arusha Agreement, named after the East African Community headquarters in Tanzania, had provisions which closely resembled those of the Lagos Agreement, but was valid only until May 31, 1969,[16] the date of expiry of the First Yaoundé Convention, so that it really provided only the formalisation of a negotiating position, vis-a-vis the EEC, for the East African Community countries prior to the negotiation of the Second Yaoundé Convention.

As events transpired, however, the conclusion of the Second Yaoundé Convention was delayed because of disputes within the EEC over the level of aid to be included within it and over objections to the requirement of "reverse preferences" (a characteristic of the First Yaoundé Convention) to be accorded by the associated states to the EEC. Fears were expressed that a renewal of the Yaoundé formula of association, coming so soon after the recommendation of the United Nations Conference on Trade and Development (UNCTAD) Conference in New Delhi in 1968 for the adoption of a system of global preferences in favour of developing countries, would encourage non-EEC industrialised countries to refuse new global preferences to the associated states. Transitional measures were agreed to between the signatories to the First Yaoundé Convention so as to extend commercial preferences (but not financial aid) to the associated states until a new negotiating dead-line of June 30, 1970. This development necessarily meant that a new Arusha Agreement had to be negotiated and this was in fact signed on September 24, 1969, and came into effect on January 1, 1971.[17] The Second Yaoundé Conven-

15. *Treaty,* article 7.
16. Signed on July 20, 1963; J.O. 1964, 1430.
17. J.O. 1970, L 282/54.

tion was eventually signed on July 29, 1969, and ran until January 31, 1975.[18]

The revised 1969 Arusha Agreement followed closely the lines of the Second Yaoundé Convention in its trade provisions; establishing a free trade area between the signatories with some protection for developing industries within the East African Community. There were, however, unlike the Second Yaoundé Convention, no provisions for financial or technical co-operation. The association institutions, a Parliamentary Conference and an Association Council, were functional and not over-ambitious. The Agreement specifically stated that it would not prejudice the subsequent establishment of customs unions or free trade areas between the East African Community states and third states nor would it prejudice special local arrangements on border trade; it also provided that goods originating in the member states of the EEC must not be less favourably treated than those of the most favoured third state in any such arrangement. The revised Arusha Agreement established, in short, a simple interim protectionist relationship with the EEC, which was designed as an adjunct to the central purposes of the East African Community from one side and as a balancing exercise to the privileged position of the Yaoundé states from the other. It resulted, until the enlargement of the European Communities in 1973, in a position that produced discrimination against British nationals and British goods, whilst the three East African Community states remained within the Commonwealth, and inevitably provoked further objections from within the General Agreement on Tariffs and Trade (GATT) that, as with the Yaoundé Convention formula, it was incompatible with the obligation which requires duties to be progressively eliminated between all signatories.[19]

When the negotiations between the nine member states of the enlarged EEC and the "associated and associable" developing countries opened in 1973, it was soon readily apparent that association agreements on the model of the Second Yaoundé Convention or of the Arusha Agreement were no longer acceptable; indeed, the Commission of the European Communities had itself, in its Memorandum

18. J.O. 1970, L 282/2.
19. See article 24 (8) (b) and (c) of GATT.

of April 1973, recognised that an agreement which would meet the major concerns and problems of the developing countries involved in the negotiations would have to include machinery for the stabilisation of export earnings, recognise and encourage regional co-operation, agree upon a special effort for the least favoured countries, and provide for a strengthening of the participation of the partner states (the East African Community expression) in the management of projects of financial and technical co-operation. For their part the representatives of the "associated and associable" states, including the three East African Community countries, displayed throughout a remarkable level of cohesion and unity of purpose in their negotiating positions.[20] This was especially apparent in their ministerial meeting at Addis Ababa in February 1974, which set their guide-lines for the final round of negotiations and was itself in many ways one of the most remarkable exercises in practical African economic co-operation that have yet materialised.

Relationships between the three East African Economic Community countries and the European Economic Community will be transformed when the Lomé Convention, signed on February 28, 1975, comes into effect.[21] This new agreement replaces both the Second Yaoundé Convention and the Arusha Convention; it was concluded, after some eighteen months of negotiations, between the nine member states of the enlarged EEC and forty-six developing states in Africa, the Caribbean and the Pacific (the ACP States). The ACP group of states includes (i) those countries formerly associated with the EEC under the Second Yaoundé Convention – Burundi, Cameroon, the Central African Republic, Chad, Congo, Dahomey, Gabon, Ivory Coast, Mali, Mauritania, Mauritius, Niger, Senegal, Somalia, Rwanda, Togo, Upper Volta, Zaire and the Malagasy Republic (the AASM States); (ii) a group of countries belonging to the Commonwealth, who entered into the Convention as a result of

20. See in general, *Communication from the Commission to the Council on the Progress of the Negotiations with the African, Caribbean and Pacific States* (Phases 1 and 2, November 21, 1973 to February 6, 1974), Doc. VIII/230/74 E of February 25, 1974.

21. *Lomé Convention,* article 87(1); the Convention will expire on March 1, 1980 (article 91). See: K. R. Simmonds, "The Lomé Convention and the New International Economic Order", in 13 *C.M.L.Rev.* 1976 (in the press).

the offer made in Protocol 22 [22] of the Act of Accession signed by the United Kingdom, Denmark and Ireland with the original six member states of the EEC in 1972 – these countries are (in Africa) Kenya, Uganda, Tanzania, Botswana, Gambia, Ghana, Lesotho, Malawi, Nigeria, Sierra Leone, Swaziland and Zambia (in the Caribbean) the Bahamas, Barbados, Guyana, Grenada, Jamaica, Trinidad and Tobago, (in the Pacific) Fiji, Western Samoa and Tonga; and (iii) a group of formerly non-associated and non-Commonwealth African countries – Ethiopia, Guinea, Guinea-Bissau, Liberia and the Sudan. The new Lomé Convention will come into force only when ratified by all nine EEC member states and by two-thirds of the ACP signatories. The Convention anticipates the possibility of accession on the part of any other developing country that has an economic and productive structure comparable to that of the ACP States, with the reservation that such accession has the consent both of the member states of the EEC and the ACP States.[23] In this connection, the EEC has already indicated that it will be open to approaches from the Portuguese-speaking African developing states.

The forty-six ACP States include almost all of independent black Africa and comprehend a total population of some 268 million persons. Amongst the ACP States are eighteen countries who are amongst the poorest in the world, according to the most recent average GNP figures produced by the United Nations. For the ACP States as a group, the EEC is undoubtedly already their most important commercial partner, since (in 1970 figures) the EEC takes 54 per cent of all their exports and provides 44 per cent of their imports.

It is impossible to do more in this paper than to indicate some of the innovatory characteristics of the Lomé Convention. The agreement is based upon a "co-operation rather than confrontation" approach, on both sides, and emphatically breaks with the "association" tradition. As M. Claude Cheysson, the EEC Commissioner with especial responsibility for development, explained:

"C'est aussi dans un moment ou trop de pays et d'hommes dans le tiers

22. See: *Encyclopedia of European Community Law* (ed. Simmonds), Volume B I, B9-392-395 (annotation at B9-395)

23. *Lomé Convention,* article 90; and cf. article 89.

monde, dans le monde industrialisé, parlent en termes de confrontation que, resoluement nous engageons dans une dynamique de co-operation".[24]

The preambular provisions stress the wish of all the parties to establish close and continuous co-operation in "the spirit of international solidarity" and based upon "the complete equality" of the signatories. The agreement is designed to provide a structure within which the economic progress and social development of the ACP States can be accelerated. There is also a significant reference to the wish of the parties to establish "a new model for relations between developing and developed states, which should be compatible with the desire of the international community for a more equitable and more balanced economic order";[25] this looks back to the controversial United Nations General Assembly Resolutions 3201 and 3202 on the "Establishment of a New International Economic Order" (adopted on May 1, 1974, at the Sixth Special Session of the General Assembly) and Resolution 3281 (XXIX) on a "Charter of Economic Rights and Duties of States" (adopted on December 12, 1974).[26]

The provisions on *trade and commercial co-operation* lay stress on free access to the EEC for almost all products from the ACP States and on the non-reciprocity of trade obligations. Almost all ACP products will be admitted to the EEC member states free of customs duties or charges having similar effect and without being subject to quantitative restrictions. The EEC has, in addition, considerably relaxed the "rules of origin" vis-à-vis imports from the ACP States; in a separate Protocol attached to the Lomé Convention there is provision for the treatment of the ACP group as a single customs territory and for the treatment of imports as originating from ACP States (and as thus qualifying for duty free entry) if the value added (for example, by processing) in the ACP States amounts to more than the low percentage of 50 per cent. The absence of any requirement of reverse preferences, in favour of the EEC, is one of the most important features of the entire Convention. Reverse preferences, such as those

24. In *Le Courrier Communauté Européenne-Afrique-Caribes-Pacifique*, March, 1975, at 13.

25. *Lomé Convention*, Preamble, para. 2.

26. See: R. C. A. White, "A New International Economic Order", in 24 (1975) *International and Comparative Law Quarterly*, 542-552.

provided for in the First and Second Yaoundé Conventions, have consistently been criticised as unfairly discriminatory within GATT and UNCTAD, and, most recently, were the subject of adverse provisions in the United States Trade Reform Act of 1974. The only obligation imposed upon the ACP signatories in the Lomé Convention is to accord the EEC member states most-favoured-nation treatment; their relations with other developing countries are excepted from this. In order to weaken the discrimination vis-à-vis other developing countries (for example, in Asia and Latin America) which are not comprehended within the Lomé Convention, the EEC has undertaken to extend its system of General Tariff Preferences, applicable to imports from *all* developing countries, which was established in 1971, at such date as the trade and commercial provisions of the Lomé Convention come into effect.[27]

A very important system of *stabilisation of export earnings* has been introduced by the Convention in order to protect the exporters of twelve primary products from the ACP States to the EEC.[28] This system was in fact originally proposed by the EEC in 1973 by way of fulfilling the undertaking contained in Protocol 22 of the Act of Accession referred to above, "to safeguard the interests of all countries concerned whose economies depend to a considerable extent on the exports of primary produce, and particularly of sugar". For the first time, therefore, in the Lomé Convention, industrialised and developing countries which export raw materials, have jointly established a system which guarantees to the latter a certain level of income by protecting them from price fluctuations due to market forces or the uncertainties of production. The list of products which fall within the "Stabex" scheme has been drawn up in the light of (i) the importance of the product for the level of employment in the exporting country, the deterioration in the terms of trade between the EEC and the ACP State in question, and the level of development of the ACP States in general, and (ii) the traditionally unstatic character of income from the product concerned due to fluctuation in prices or in quantities produced. Twelve principal products are covered by the scheme (groundnuts, cocoa, coffee, cotton, coconuts, palm and palm kernel

27. See: Regs. 2794-2800/71; J.O. 1971 L 287 289.
28. *Lomé Convention*, Title VI, articles 69-83.

products, hides and skins, wood products, bananas, tea, raw sisal, iron ore), together with a number of sub-products. "Stabex" is a system of commodity-tied compensatory finance which does not directly interfere with the market in the product concerned. A total amount of 375 million u.a.[28a] has been provided for the stabilisation system for the duration of the Convention. This is divided into five annual instalments of 75 million u.a., with balances at the end of each year being carried over to the following year. Financial transfers from the "Stabex" fund to ACP States will be made when their actual export earnings from the product concerned drop by an agreed percentage in a given year as compared with the moving average of earnings from exports of the same product during the four preceding years. This "activation threshold" is lower in the case of the least developed, landlocked or island ACP States, as is the "dependence threshold" – the minimum percentage earnings of total export of a product in the year preceding the year of application of the scheme.

The Lomé Convention contains special arrangements for *sugar* (in a Protocol [29]) that are almost as novel as the provisions which establish the price stabilisation scheme for primary exports. The sugar arrangements, which are in principle valid for an indefinite period, and will last for at least seven years, involve the EEC member-states in an undertaking to purchase and import at guaranteed prices cane sugar from certain ACP States. The producing countries, which include each of the three member states of the East African Economic Community, are allocated quotas (to a maximum of 1.4 million tons annually). A guaranteed minimum price is negotiated annually and is linked to the EEC sugar price; the EEC will accordingly consult with the ACP States before making its own proposals on Community prices.

The chapters of the Convention concerned with *industrial, technical and financial co-operation* [30] show that the signatories have agreed upon a greater financial effort and greater responsibility for the partner states in the management of aid. The provisions on

28a. See: *Encyclopedia of European Community Law* (ed. Simmonds), Volume B II, B 10-461.

29. *Lomé Convention*, Protocol 3.

30. *Lomé Convention*, Titles III and IV, articles 26-61.

industrial co-operation cover the whole industrial field, including industrial infrastructures, the creation of new manufacturing enterprises, research and industrial studies, the transfer and adaptation of technology, special action programmes for small and medium sized enterprises and programmes for the exchange of information on industrial promotion. A Committee of Industrial Co-operation and a Centre for Industrial Development have been established. The provisions in financial co-operation operate on the dual premises that (i) the AASM States must be assumed of keeping advantages already acquired, and (ii) equal treatment is assumed for all new signatories. For the period 1975-1980 the EEC will provide 3,390 u.a. for the ACP States (i.e. 3.7 times the amount involved in the operation of the Second Yaoundé Convention), which will be distributed (through the European Development Fund) as grants, soft loans, risk capital and through the "Stabex" scheme, and also (through the European Investment Bank) as ordinary loans. The funds distributed by the European Development Fund will be financed, according to a proportionate scale, from a non-budgetary appropriation by contributions from the member states of the EEC. As with the aid provided under the Yaoundé Conventions, the development aims of the Lomé Convention are concerned with strengthening economic and social infrastructures in the ACP States, with rural development and training programmes, and with industrial development, market and sales promotion schemes. Particular emphasis is placed upon EEC support for ACP regional and inter-regional co-operation schemes,[31] for specific aid to small and medium-sized firms, for small-scale development schemes (especially in the rural sector), and for special aid to the least developed countries. In this last respect, the Convention adopts a non-definitive list of the twenty-four least developed states; these include Uganda and Tanzania. The ACP States are given a much larger share in the management of this financial co-operation than was the case under the Yaoundé Conventions. They are free to define their own development programmes and are fully responsible for formulating their requests for financing. What the Convention does is to institute a framework within which a running dialogue between EEC and ACP representatives can take place throughout the various

31. *Lomé Convention,* articles 47 and 49.

stages of planning the aid, drawing up and appraising projects, preparing financing decisions, implementing the agreed projects and making a final evaluation of their results.

In many ways, therefore, the Lomé Convention, utilising on a basis of equality all the instruments of development aid, demonstrates convincing evidence of a radically new EEC approach to the developing ACP States. In its institutional structure [32] the need for flexible arrangements to ensure a permanent dialogue between the EEC and ACP signatories is realised. There is to be a Council of Ministers, composed of members of the Council of Ministers of the European Communities, members of the Commission of the European Communities, and members of the Government of each ACP State. This Council will be assisted by a Committee of Ambassadors; there will also be a Consultative Assembly, composed, on a basis of parity of representation, of members of the European Parliament and representatives designated by the ACP States.

The Lomé Convention represents an ambitious attempt to organise, systematically and on a basis of equal co-operation and partnership, economic inter-dependence between the EEC and a most important group of developing countries. In style and in content it is very far removed from the piecemeal and interim measures that have so often characterised relationships between Europe and the developing world in the recent past. To quote M. Cheysson again:

> "It is the first time that such a comprehensive approach to the problems of development has been agreed by industrialised countries with regard to such a large number of countries. It is unprecedented also because the whole of Black Africa has stood together, and this is politically extremely important at a time when developing countries have learned the lesson of the oil crisis that unity makes strength. Until now, this unity was expressed mostly in aggressive and sometimes negative approaches to the problems in our relationship. This time, the whole continent stands together, but in a co-operative effort with the European Community." [33]

The Lomé Convention must, of course, be viewed in the context of the current EEC negotiations, on a state by state basis, with a widely disparate group of Mediterranean countries – Israel, the Mahgreb

32. *Lomé Convention*, Title VI, articles 69-83.

33. Claude Cheysson, "Europe and the Third World after Lomé", in 31 (1975) *The World Today*, 232-239, at 235.

States, Jordan, Egypt, Syria and Lebanon, and with the special trade and co-operation agreements between the EEC and the Commonwealth countries in Asia – India, Pakistan, Bangladesh and (very shortly) Sri Lanka. We must now await the wider reactions to the Convention that will progressively become apparent during the present round of GATT negotiations. However, it is too much to hope that, in the light of the successful common negotiating position recently adopted by the African developing states, notably including the three East African Community countries, a new impetus to regional economic integration in the continent will be forthcoming? The East African Community is only one of a growing number of economic co-operation groupings in the continent; recent significant developments, of course, include the coming into operation of a multinational African Development Fund [34] and the establishment of a West African Economic Community [35] which at last may go some way toward forging lasting economic links between anglophone and francophone developing countries in this region. There is a growing recognition on the part of African governments that the various sub-regions are not and cannot be self-contained entities. It may be that the signature of the Lomé Convention will not only mark a new point of departure in their relationships with the European Economic Community but will also encourage them to re-examine the premises on which their existing regional organisations and institutions are based.[36] If this fundamental re-appraisal does take place – and there are many signs that it has already begun – then the real weaknesses of the present *ad hoc* and interim forms of regional and intra-regional co-operation, of which the East African Community is a very typical example, will be more clearly appreciated.

34. The sixteen non-African capital exporting countries which are participating in this Fund include Belgium, Brazil, Canada, Denmark, Finland, the Federal Republic of Germany, Italy, Japan, The Netherlands, Norway, Sweden, Switzerland, United Kingdom, the United States of America, Spain and Yugoslavia.

35. See: *West Africa,* May 12, 1975, at 552.

36. See: *African Declaration on Co-operation, Development and Economic Independence,* issued by the Heads of State and Government of the OAU, May, 1973. Text in (1973) 12 I.L.M., at 996.

Part II

International Trade Law

A. Universal and Regional Organisations

6

THE RECONCILIATION OF INTERNATIONAL AND NATIONAL CODIFICATIONS OF INTERNATIONAL TRADE LAW

*John O. Honnold**

At the outset, I should like briefly to relate my comments to the general theme of Universalism and Regionalism. What premises underlie the decisions as to fields of work of the *United Nations Commission on International Trade Law* (UNCITRAL), this relatively new arm of the United Nations established for the harmonisation and unification on a world-wide scale of law for international trade? What is the relationship between this work and regional approaches in this field?

The special mission given to UNCITRAL by the General Assembly of the United Nations is unification in those fields of international trade law where a world-wide approach is needed and is feasible. For reasons of efficiency, the membership of the Commission was limited to twenty-nine states, but the General Assembly's resolution specifically guarantees representation for each of the regions of the world, and assure representation of the principal economic and legal systems.[1]

The Commission has developed its work programme step by step, and on a pragmatic basis, in selecting subjects in which its world-wide approach is needed and appropriate. The work programme includes specific topics in four fields: (1) International Sale of Goods; (2) International Payments, with special attention to a Uniform Law on International Bills of Exchange and Promissory Notes; (3) Interna-

* Professor of Law, University of Pennsylvania, sometimes Chief, International Trade Law Branch, Office of Legal Affairs, United Nations, New York, The United States of America.

1. General Assembly Resolution 2205 (XXI) of December 17, 1966. This resolution appears in Volume I of the UNCITRAL *Yearbook*, pp. 65-66.

tional Commercial Arbitration and (4) International Legislation on Shipping.

In developing this work programme representatives of regional and of other international organisations have taken an active and constructive part. The consequence has been a programme in which the Commission can work towards fulfilment of its special and unique responsibility, and without conflict or duplication with the work of other bodies.

Certainly, in the Commission's work, I have seen no indication that regional economic or legal integration has reduced the need for unification, on a world-wide scale, of the basic rules of law applicable to international trade. Even the most intensive and successful regional arrangements are not designed to limit trade to that region. Indeed, such regional arrangements are often designed to encourage the rationalisation of production, with resulting efficiency and volume which augment access to world markets. And in that trade, the sellers and buyers of the region face a wide variety of national laws with which they are unfamiliar and which are unsuited to the special needs and modern practices of international trade.

In formulating proposed rules for international trade, the Commission has adopted approaches designed to accommodate regional and national needs.

The first of these scarcely needs to be mentioned: the rules apply to *international* trade, in contrast to the 1930 Geneva Convention providing a Uniform Law for Bills of Exchange and Promissory Notes and the 1931 Geneva Convention providing a Uniform Law for Cheques, both of which embrace purely internal transactions.[2]

The second approach is the development of instruments (like standard or model contracts) which become applicable on their voluntary adoption by international traders, and which consequently will be employed to the extent that the rules are found to be useful in the light of local and regional conditions and needs.

The third approach is addressed directly to regional arrangements. An example is found in the draft Convention on Prescription (Limitation) in the International Sale of Goods, which was approved by the

2. See UNCITRAL, Register of Texts of Conventions and other Instruments Concerning International Trade Law, Vol. I, pp. 154, 192.

Commission in May 1972 and has been signed on June 14, 1974 at a United Nations international conference of plenipotentiaries.[3] Article 33 (see Volume III of the UNCITRAL Yearbook, p. 139) provides, in effect, that parties to the Convention with the same or closely related legal rules may continue to apply those rules to transactions between sellers and buyers in such states.[4] The draft conventions under preparation also contain provisions for reservations preserving local rules which have special significance for certain states or regions.[5]

One could explore at greater length the measures that have been developed, in a pragmatic manner, to reconcile world-wide unification with special local or regional needs.

Let me now turn, briefly, to the use of national rules in the preparation of uniform law for international trade. Continuity in law, it has been said, may not be desirable, it is merely a necessity. For all of us who work in this field, as members of the Commission or as its Secretariat, national rules of law provide our intellectual stock-in-trade, comparable to one's mother tongue.

In work on unification on a world-wide scale, one encounters a rich variety of competing legal ideas. And, of course, one sees first hand, what an over-simplification it is to refer to the civil law, or the common law or the law of Eastern Europe. You might think that as a result of this multiplicity of legal ideas we are in a modern Tower of Babel, where communication and agreement become impossible. The difficulties are great but, I have found, the wider frame of reference offers off-setting gains.

In the first place, meeting different formulations of solutions to common problems tends to waken an exponent of a single national rule from his dogmatic slumber. It also encourages an empirical approach to lawmaking, as in our intensive examination of commercial practices, in collaboration with representatives of international

3. See UN General Assembly A/Conf.63/15, dated June 13, 1974.

4. A similar provision appears in Article II of the 1964 Hague Convention relating to a Uniform Law on the International Sale of Goods, and in Article 1(5) of the annexed Uniform Law (ULIS). See UNCITRAL, *Register of Texts,* Vol. I, pp. 34, 43.

5. See, e.g., Articles 34-36 of the draft Convention on Prescription. UNCITRAL *Yearbook,* Vol. III, pp. 139-140.

banking and trade institutions, which preceded the preparation of our initial draft Uniform Law for International Bills of Exchange and Promissory Notes.[6]

Happily, the members of the Commission, primarily commercial lawyers, accept the view that the problem is not one of bargaining for their own national rules of law (like a tariff negotiation trading a concession on chickens and watches); it is generally recognized that such an approach interferes with the solution of legal problems on their merits, and impairs the coherence and clarity of the product. The problem is one of exquisite delicacy: the need to draft rules of law, without the use of idioms that are mysterious to some (like tort or trust or dol) or which are clearly understood by all, but in a very different sense.

Perfect solutions often can not be found; but experience has shown that an acceptable and useful product is possible.

Finally, let me briefly introduce, in the context of specific provisions of UNCITRAL drafts, certain aspects of the following general question: What is the sphere of application that is given to uniform rules for international trade?

Under this heading, I want to make reference to UNCITRAL draft provisions addressed to two specific issues. They are:

(1) *The applicability of international rules and the choice of the parties.*

(a) The Uniform Law for the International Sale of Goods (ULIS) annexed to the 1964 Hague Convention – (i) Article 3 (contracting *out*); (ii) Review of ULIS by the UNCITRAL Working Group – should an Article V reservation be included?

(b) The draft Convention on Prescription (Limitation) in the International Sale of Goods, as approved by UNCITRAL at its Fifth Session (1972), Article 3(3) (A/8717); See UNCITRAL *Yearbook*, Vol. III: 1972 (E.73.V.6) (Draft and Commentary) at pp. 115 *et seq.*, esp. p. 120.

(c) Draft Uniform Law on International Bills of Exchange and Promissory Notes (A/CN,9/WG.IV/WP.2), Article 1(2) (a). See UNCITRAL *Yearbook*, Vol. III: 1972 (1972 Secretariat Draft and Commentary), p. 147. (Applicability based on use of bill of exchange stating: "Drawn subject to Convention of ......".)

---

6. The background investigation of commercial practices is briefly summarized in the UNCITRAL *Yearbook*, Vol. III, pp. 145-146. The more detailed background is set forth in A/CN.9/38, and A/CN.9/48.

(d) Revision of the 1924 Brussels Convention on Bills of Lading. See Art. 3(8) nullifying contracts withdrawing protection of Convention. UNCITRAL, Register of Texts, Vol. II (E.73.V.3), p. 133.

(2) *Required contact between the international transaction and a Contracting State.* Contrast:

(a) ULIS Art. 2 (no contact required).
(b) Uniform Laws as revised by UNCITRAL Working Group, Art. 1. UNCITRAL Yearbook, Vol. III, p. 79.
(c) Draft Convention on Prescription, *supra,* Arts. 2 and 3 (places of business in different Contracting States), UNCITRAL Yearbook, Vol. III, pp. 119-120.
(d) Draft Uniform Law on International Bills of Exchange, *supra,* Arts. 1 and 3 (no contact with Contracting State required), UNCITRAL Yearbook, Vol. III, pp. 147-148.

I must confess that these two issues were selected because they illustrate points on which different UNCITRAL drafts follow divergent approaches. This, I realize, is a reckless thing to do since it lays the foundation for this pointed question: How can you propose to unify law for the world's trade if you can't even unify your own approaches to uniform law?

Let us turn to the first issue on the outline: The effect of choice by the parties on the applicability of the uniform rule. More specifically, does the uniform rule apply to an international transaction when the contract is silent on that issue?

One approach is that the Uniform Law applies. This approach was followed in the ULIS of 1964.[7] However, it should be noted, that the Convention permits states, by reservation, to adopt the opposite approach and apply the Law only if the parties have chosen it, a reservation made by the United Kingdom in ratifying the 1964 Convention. The approach of the basic rule of ULIS, i.e. that the Law applies unless the parties contract *out,* is followed in the draft Convention on Prescription and without any provision for a reservation to reverse the rule.[8]

7. Art. 3. See UNCITRAL *Register of Texts,* Vol. I, p. 43. As to the reservation, compare article V of the Convention to article 4 of the Uniform Law, *id.,* pp. 40 and 44.

8. Art. 3(3), *Yearbook,* Vol. III, p. 120. For reasons explained in the commentary, this draft leaves to applicable law the question as to whether a choise to contract out is valid.

What approach is employed in the Secretariat Draft Uniform Law on International Bills of Exchange and Promissory Notes? (This draft is now being reviewed by an UNCITRAL working group, which held its first session in January 1973 and met again in January 1974.) [9] As can be seen from this draft, set forth in the Yearbook at p. 147, in article 1(2) (a), the Uniform Law applies only if the parties employ e.g. an international bill of exchange which states: "Drawn subject to the Convention of 1975".

Why did we retreat from the approach of ULIS and the Prescription Convention? In considering this question it may be helpful to explore issues such as these: (1) In routine international sales, how feasible is it for the parties to consider, and solve, the question of the applicable law? (2) On this practical issue, is the answer the same when banks prepare the form drafts for use in international payments? (In approaching the question, consider the experience that banks accumulate with respect to the fundamentally differing approaches to problems such as forged endorsements under the Geneva system and under the so-called "common law" approach.)

In brief it shall only be mentioned here that reliance on the parties to adopt uniform rules is at the heart of two other UNCITRAL projects. One of these [10] is the drafting by the Secretariat of general conditions of sale (i.e. standard or model contracts) covering a wider range of commodities than the existing formulations. The second [11] is the preparation by the Secretariat of draft rules for optional use in arbitration relating to international trade. The approaches to unification in the above projects have special and interesting features: A more detailed and complete approach to drafting is possible than in the preparation of a uniform law. In addition, an instrument offered for voluntary adoption can take effect without the laborious process of approval at a diplomatic conference, and without the delays attendant on ratification by states. And, of course, the choice of the parties whether to use such optional rules and the freedom to adapt them to their own circumstances, avoid any question of conflict with regional and national law-making agencies.

9. The report on the first session (A/CN.9/77) has been reproduced in *Yearbook*, Vol. IV, pp. 101 *et seq.*

10. See UNCITRAL projects summary, p. 80, *ante.*

11. See summary, p. 80, *ante.*

Now let us turn to the second and final issue: [12] Should the tribunals of a contracting state be directed to apply the Uniform Law only to transactions that have some prescribed contact with a contracting state? This brings us to the famous provision of article 2 of ULIS which, in effect says that even though an international sale has no contact with any contracting state, this Uniform Law is still to be applied. The UNCITRAL working group on sales rejected this approach in reviewing ULIS, as did the Commission in approving the draft Convention on Prescription.[13]

With this weight of authority from the Commission, what was the approach of the Secretariat in preparing the draft Uniform Law for Bills of Exchange and Promissory Notes? On examining article 3 of the draft (*Yearbook*, p. 148) it is surprising to see that the Law is to apply without regard to whether the country of the drawer or of the drawee or of the payee or of the place of payment is a contracting state.

An attempt to answer the barbed questions as to whether this approach is consistent with other actions taken by the Commission, and with sound policy must be left to future deliberations. However, there shall be a hint of a reply: Note, as was mentioned above, that this Uniform Law applies only when the parties use a bill of exchange which expressly invokes the Uniform Law. Does this fact justify a looser approach?

Do these varying approaches indicate that the choices have been inconsistent, or that they have been pragmatic? In international law-making is it practicable to build one inflexible wall around a domain called international trade? I hope that exposing some of these nerve-ends of our law-making process, will at least provoke a wider interest which should lead to a fruitful exchange of thoughts in the future.

12. See outline p. 81, *ante*.

13. As to Sales: Art. 1, *Yearbook*, Vol. III, p. 79; as to Prescription, Arts. 2 and 3, *idem*, pp. 119-120.

7

THE CONTRIBUTION OF UNIVERSAL AND REGIONAL ORGANISATIONS TO THE DEVELOPMENT OF INTERNATIONAL TRADE LAW

*Mario Matteucci**

It is very difficult to deal in a short exposition with the very complex problem of world-wide as well as regional unification. The International Institute for the Unification of Private Law (UNIDROIT) has recently devoted one of its periodical meetings especially to this important problem area at which we were presented with a particularly interesting report by Professor Limpens from Brussels, who dealt admirably with the interdependence of these two forms of unification. However, I will confine myself to a very brief account of results so far achieved. This general statement shall be followed by a short analysis of some of the problems as well as shortcomings which derive from both approaches to unification and the possible remedies.

The first organisation which tried to unify some areas of law on a world-wide level was the League of Nations. Despite its relatively short life, the League of Nations was instrumental in the achievement of some very important unifications in the field of commercial arbitration, i.e. the two Conventions of 1923 and 1927, as well as in the field of negotiable instruments, i.e. the two Conventions on the Bill of Exchange and Cheques, and the auxiliary Conventions on the Conflicts of Law. The United Nations succeeding the League of Nations have, after a certain period of hesitation, taken up again the tradition and are continuing partially the work of the League of Nations, as, for instance, in the area of negotiable instruments, commercial legislation and in all matters mentioned by Professor Honnold in his

* Councillor of State, President of UNIDROIT, the International Institute for the Unification of Private Law, Rome, Italy.

contribution.[1] The main success, achieved by the United Nations in the commercial law area during the last years was the New York Convention on Recognition and Enforcement of Foreign Arbitration Awards of 1958. Now, they are revising the Uniform Laws on the Sale of Goods and they are trying to complete the unification of negotiable instruments by introducing new negotiable instruments which may be chosen optionally for international payments by the parties. In addition, they are also revising the Brussels Convention on the Bill of Lading, but I will forego a further detailed account of the activities of the organisation here, taking the liberty to refer to Professor Honnold's contribution instead.[2] In addition to the activities undertaken by the United Nations directly, other organisations, as for instance UNIDROIT, also pursue as their main task the unification of private law. I must stress, however, that most of our work is related to economic law, because there are many areas of private law, e.g. family law, succession, real property and others which are far less suitable for unification.

The term "economic and trade law" in its modern concept is considerably wider than the original concept of the law of merchants. Commercial law, in its modern meaning, includes all matters predominantly economic in character and affecting international relationships. I think, therefore, that we should not limit our approach to matters concerning only the transfer or the exchange of goods, but include all those which are primarily of an economic character like transportation, arbitration and corporations. The concept of economic law must be enlarged, despite the imminent danger of diffusing the issue as seen particularly in socialist countries.

UNIDROIT has, after a long period of study, prepared so far two Uniform Laws on the Contract of the Sale of Goods and on the Formation of such Contracts, as well as some drafts on matters which are auxiliary to the contract of sales, like the draft on the validity of sales contracts and the draft on the protection of the bona fide purchaser.

A draft of a Uniform Law on agency in international relations of private law has also been elaborated and will be submitted to a

1. See Chapter 6, pp. 77-78 and 80-81, *ante*.
2. *Idem*.

diplomatic conference for adoption. Finally, two drafts concerning "travel contracts" and a form of testament have been presented to diplomatic conferences in 1970 and 1973 respectively.

Added to these achievements should be all unifications successfully affected in different areas of the law of transportation by other, particularly qualified, international agencies, such as the International Civil Aviation Organisation (ICAO); the Inter-Governmental Maritime Consultative Organisation (IMCO) and the International Maritime Committee (IMC).

On the other hand, there are many unifications which have been achieved on a regional level. Here, the most active agency is the Economic Commission for Europe (ECE), a United Nations affiliate. I think, without underestimating, of course, the work of other regional commissions of the United Nations, tribute must be paid to the work of the Economic Commission for Europe for its support for unification. Our own Institute has tried to assist the ECE particularly in the development of the law of transportation by inland waterways and roads. The most notable results of ECE determination are the Convention on Arbitration of 1961 and some model contracts for different kinds of goods. However, not only the Economic Commission for Europe, but also the Council of Europe is very active in the field of the unification of law. Among the drafts which have been produced are the European Convention on the Liability of Hotelkeepers concerning the Property of their Guests, the European Convention on Compulsory Insurance Against Civil Liability in respect of Motor Vehicles, the Uniform Law on Arbitration Procedure and some Conventions concerning Copyrights and Patents.

Furthermore, the Benelux countries have prepared a draft on the Uniform Law on the Sale of Goods, which has not been adopted so far. However, special reference must be made to the very important work of the Nordic countries. In Europe it is perhaps the most important unification, because it affects a very large area of law. Nevertheless, the unification in the Nordic countries is quite different from that of any other group of states, especially, as it is not the result of an intervention by an international organisation. Here, unification is achieved by collaboration of various governments and drafts are adopted unilaterally by each country, sometimes with some modifications. In the socialist countries the Council for Mutual Economic

Assistance (CMEA, often called COMECON in Western Europe) has promoted some conventions relating to transportation and other main areas of commercial law; in this context, special reference shall only be made to the General Conditions for the Delivery of Goods which are adopted and followed by all member countries of the Council.

The Asian-African Legal Consultative Committee has so far pursued some approaches to harmonisation in the field of public international law. In the private law area they have quite recently undertaken some work related to the sale of goods by the elaboration of model contracts. With regard to the Organisation of the American States (OAS), I would like to refer to the excellent contribution by Professor García-Amador.[3] Special attention shall only be drawn here to a Protocol on the Unification of Forms of Powers of Attorney in 1940, as well as the drafts on the sale of goods and negotiable instruments.

After this very quick glance on unification as achieved so far, I would like to venture an attempt of drawing some conclusions. First of all, it appears that unification on a world-wide level has achieved more important results than unification on a regional level, excluding the Scandinavian model which is of quite a different character. The main subjects which concern commerce like sale of goods, transportation and arbitration have been unified by way of universal approach, but unfortunately, many of the conventions in these areas of law have not yet been ratified by many countries. One of the main tasks remaining, therefore, is to try to extend application of these Conventions to a larger number of countries. The only Convention which has obtained a record ratification is the Warsaw Convention on the Transportation by Air.

The next step towards world-wide unification is to extend the geographical application of these Conventions to a larger number of countries. How can this goal be achieved? Professor Schmitthoff suggested already at a meeting concerned with the unification of law which we held in Rome with representatives of different international organisations, that UNCITRAL be the proper channel through which such uniform provisions should be presented to a larger forum

3. See Chapter 3, pp. 35-43, *ante*.

of countries.[4] I think, due to its dominant position among international organisations, UNCITRAL would be in an excellent position to advance the area of application of these provisions, if necessary by way of new formulations.

The second conclusion to be drawn from the very rapid synthesis of world-wide unification is that unification which has been achieved so far, shows very serious defects which must be eliminated in the future. Professor Jakubowski,[5] as well as other eminent contributors to the International Oxford Symposium on which this book is founded,[6] emphasized that it is hardly conceivable to deal with the problem of unification other than by pragmatic approach and I tend to agree with their point of view. For the moment, the only way to advance unification in the field of commercial law is to take account of the real necessity of commerce and to proceed by way of pragmatic approach. This method was followed by UNIDROIT which prepared the law on the sale of goods for international relations without having previously tried to unify the general principles on contract. The same method has been followed by UNCITRAL in its drafts. However, we should not be too complacent with these results. It appears to be true that time is not ripe for a systematic codification, but attempts should be made to look to the future. It seems that there are certain discrepancies among the various unifications so far achieved. Take, for instance, as an example, the problem area of transportation: for each kind of transport there exists a particular form of liability, sometimes absolute, sometimes based on negligence. Even though recognising the need that some means of transportation must by allowed exemption from liability under certain circumstances, nevertheless the basic concepts of liability should be the same, because it is not conceivable today, when all the means of transportation carry the same degree of danger, to discriminate between the provisions of air law, maritime law and road transportation law. There are also many gaps concerning the basic legal concept. For instance, in applying the Warsaw

4. See Clive M. Schmitthoff "The Unification or Harmonization of Law by Means of Standard Contracts and General Conditions", *UNIDROIT—Unification of Law,* IVth Meeting of the Organisations concerned with the Unification of Law, Year-Book 1967-1968, Vol. II, pp. 116-117.

5. See Chapter 10, pp. 105-110, *post.*

6. See Introduction.

Convention, there have been long discussions about the interpretation of the concept of *dol, faute équivalente au dol* and *force majeure*, were the terms used in English law are not exactly equivalent. These gaps cannot be filled, unless some general principles are universally accepted. The Council of Europe has felt this need, and while proceeding to attempt unification by way of pragmatic approach, a commission has been appointed at the same time to reconsider some basic legal concepts. This reconsideration will be very useful (a similar approach was adopted by UNCITRAL in preparation of its Draft on Prescription), because one of the fundamental necessities is to have a common understanding of principal legal concepts, a goal which cannot be reached, unless by codification of general principles. The latter proposition may seem less utopian if seen, for instance, in conjunction with the success of the Uniform Commercial Code (UCC) in the United States. It is true, all countries of the Union, except Louisiana, have a common basis in the common law, but there existed some considerable differences which, nevertheless, were overcome in the codification.

In addition, special reference must be made to a further, very important codification. It is interesting to see that the Czechslovak Code on International Trade of 1963, even though promulgated as a national code, applies to international legal relationships. The code consists of a general part on contract as well as rules governing some special contracts and results, in my opinion, in the most important success so far achieved in this field. If the idea of having in addition to the national laws governing internal relations, a special code for international relations within the private law sector, could be generally approved and extended to a certain number of countries, it would perhaps be the most useful and most perfect form of law unification.

Based on this consideration our organisation is now studying the possibility of achieving a type of codification which would obviously not be effected by a convention, but through a model law to be adopted optionally by different countries, governing exclusively those legal relationships which will be classified as international by the code itself. Even though continued efforts should be made to base unification on a pragmatic method, we should also be prepared for the future and envisage to accept a systematic code, which, in any case, will be useful as a form of reconsideration.

Finally, a brief analysis of the relationship between world-wide and regional unification. There are many methods, but I shall confine myself to draw conclusions from our experience. First of all, it seems to be absolutely necessary not to attempt unification of legal relationships on a regional level without having tried to reach an agreement on a universal level beforehand. In my opinion, the tendency, noticeable in some continents, to create a continental or regional law first, is highly dangerous. In the past, the main legal systems of the civil law and the common law have been adopted in different parts of the world, but there are still very close links between the individual countries of origin and the countries having adopted one of the above mentioned legal systems. It is most likely, for instance, that a lawyer in Australia will have the same conceptional approach to a legal problem as a lawyer in London or even in the United States, where at least some of the law is very similar to the common law of England. The same situation may be found in Africa or in any other of the English or French-speaking countries overseas; lawyers in different countries will think on the basis of the principles of the French civil code or the common law of England. Now, if we create Continental laws, we will mainly match the laws of France, England, Italy and Germany, creating a sort of amalgam called "European law". Such a development would perhaps bring an advantage to the European countries which will be governed by the same law, but we shall cut the links between the European countries (which are, so to speak, countries of the origin of law) and all other countries which have originally adopted one or the other legal system. I think, therefore, that it is a mistake to pursue solely the development of Continental laws like European law or African law, American or Asian law. On the other hand, the main problem which we have faced during our activities of more than forty years, consisted of the attempted reconciliation of the concept of the common law countries with the concept of the civil law countries, not only in Europe, but throughout Africa, America and Asia as well. I am convinced that unification on a regional basis should be pursued when necessary, to achieve some specific goals concerning the economic or social organisation of a regional group of countries. But, with regard to the general principles of the law of commerce, it would be advisable to pursue universal unification. Only if universal unification is not feasible, should one be satisfied with regional unification. To insist primarily on separate regional unifications without a link between the different continents, would be a great mistake.

In summing up, we should consider the following main questions: first of all, which remedies would help the completion of unification on a world-wide level as well as the extended application of uniform rules to a larger number of countries? Secondly, how would it be possible to bridge the anomalies existing now between the different uniform laws as a result of the pragmatic approach originally adopted in their elaboration? I venture to suggest, as a solution for further consideration, to form a model code for the general principles on contract and to avoid future competition between regional and world-wide unification by giving world-wide unification priority over regional unification, adopting the method of regional unification only if universal unification is not possible.

8

THE CONTRIBUTION OF THE EUROPEAN ECONOMIC COMMUNITY TO THE DEVELOPMENT OF INTERNATIONAL TRADE LAW

*Hans Claudius Ficker**

1. The term *regional organisation* is inappropriate if used in the context of the European Community. This term does not reflect the basic concept of the European Community – namely future political union. However, the concept does permit to speak of a contribution by the European Community to the development of international trade law.

On the other hand, it should be pointed out that it is primarily up to the European Community to contribute to this development, because the *region* of the enlarged European Community embraces most of the highly industrialized countries in Western Europe with old legal traditions in regard to their own legal systems and with old traditions as far as participation in international trade is concerned.

2. To show the rigidity of this political conviction and concept to move towards a political union, one should first mention the power and authority to create community law, directly binding on the member states by issuing *regulations*. This is unique compared with other organisations in this field. The areas concerned embrace for example trade law and competition law, where a very developed system has been established.

The second instrument is the issue of *directives* harmonising national legislations. Article 3 lit. h of the Treaty states that the Community should use approximation of the laws of member states as an instrument to the extent required for the proper functioning of the common market, and article 100 points out that all those provisions

* Dr. jur., M. C. J. (New York University), Hauptverwaltungsrat at the Commission of the European Communities, Brussels, Belgium.

should be included which directly affect the establishment and functioning of the common market. These directives cover nearly all domains of trade law.

The most important feature in the context of the Oxford Symposium on which this book is founded,[1] is to emphasise the fact that in the European Community provision is made for the enforceability of these *directives*. This means, there is a special procedure foreseen in the Treaty that the Community may enforce the realization of the *directives* in the different member states. It is even up to the Commission to bring the matter before the European Court of Justice. The existence of this court is one of the most important elements within the scope of the matter discussed here. This court has not only the political power to enforce what has been done in the field of approximation of law, but constitutes one of the great promotors of unification and harmonisation of law within the European Communities.

3. The objective of European member states is very clear—namely the setting up of a common market and, therefore, one has to be very clear on this point, the activities of the Community in all areas mentioned so far are inward-looking. The guidelines for these activities are the Treaty itself and the current state of evolution of the Community. The external effect is, at least as far as the intention of this activity is concerned, only of secondary importance. It is not meant by this that the "regional organisation" of the European Community would like to build a Chinese wall against the rest of the world, but it has to be underlined that the first interest is quite obviously its own interest. It follows that primarily the "contribution", in the sense of the matter discussed, arises more from a practical influence than from an active and deliberate collaboration with the intention really to "contribute".

There are two areas of practical influence. First of all, economic relations of the European Community and their partners are materialised in legal forms reaching from trade agreements to trade customs, legal convictions and traditions, way of thinking, law standards and so on, will shape these relations. And, even more than that, patterns adopted in the relationship between the European Community and its

1. See Preface, p. X.

partner countries may well be followed by the partners in their relations with third countries.

The second influence is the character of community legislation as a model. Under the condition that the legal problems are based on the same factual situations, a solution found in the European Community, by harmonising the laws of the member states, may serve as an example. This is primarily true in view of the transnational character and functional concept of community law.

The transnational character of the Community serves as a model for other regional organisations in their formative stages. In speaking of the functional concept it should be noted that the community system is the first legal system which is based on transnational economic objectives and *not* on the nation state, or in other words, based on twentieth century concepts, and not on nineteenth century concepts. To give an example: the European company. The Commission proposed a *Statute for a European Company* which is shaped first of all to serve the needs of the community, to allow transnational concentration movement, but which, on the other hand, introduces some quite new ideas on a transnational level, such as those on workers co-determination.

4. This is one aspect, the internal aspect. But obviously there is another aspect. Every time the special interest of the Community and its partners is to negotiate on economic matters having a direct impact to international trade, the Community will enter into those negotiations, and consequently, adapt its legislation. In this context should be mentioned the General Agreement on Tariffs and Trade (GATT) negotiations as far as they relate to non-tariff barriers. In this area the standardisation of technical requirements, for example, may be of very great importance for the development of international trade and set patterns for its legal forms.

5. Two topics can be taken to illustrate these statements. The first topic is company law as the law of the most important European participants in international trade. As mentioned, there are two aspects: the results of the harmonisation efforts on the basis of the respective articles in the Treaty set common standards for the regulation of this most important business organisation. For example, the First Directive of the Community in this field contains the rule that power and authority of the corporate officers to act on behalf of

the company are binding. They cannot be limited either by the corporate object or by the shareholders' decision. This might be a pattern, a model for a world-wide solution for this complex problem. The second example is the proposal of the Fourth Directive on annual accounts which lays down the principle of transparency of annual accounts. This also may serve as a universal standard throughout the world.

As a last example, the two-tier board system is proposed in the Fifth Draft Directive as one possible solution for the organisation of large companies.

On the other hand, the European company has already been mentioned. Here, the model character may be seen very clearly and under different aspects. There is the corporate structure itself. But, one may also look upon the Statute by seeing it as a formalised colloboration of capital investment and labour. A good example of investor protection is the minority shareholders' protection elaborated in the chapter dealing with the law of groups of companies, and the protection of the public interest in the control of large enterprises is for instance assured by the transparency of the annual accounts as well.

The second topic is the law of the sales of goods. Here, the Commission deals with product liability by starting to discuss the problem whether one should introduce a strict liability for defective products with the aim of protecting the consumer, but quite obviously mainly for industrial products as the products of modern life. The question arises, whether strict liability should be used as a world-wide standard and should, for example, also include agricultural products. Therefore, the question can be asked, whether one should really use the same rules "in both directions", from the European Communities to other parts of the world or vice-versa.

In conclusion, one may venture to express the opinion that any future community must be based upon the same objectives as laid down in article 2 of the current Treaty of Rome including an integrate system of progressive harmonisation of its member states with the support of such institutions as the present European Court of Justice in Luxembourg; only then can we expect to achieve universal harmonisation and unification of such rules which will guarantee a peaceful co-existence of mankind.

9

THE UNIFORM COMMERCIAL CODE AND THE GLOBAL UNIFICATION OF INTERNATIONAL TRADE LAW

*E. Allan Farnsworth**

The sponsors of the Oxford Symposium on which this book is founded,[1] have asked me to make special reference to the Uniform Commercial Code (UCC) in relation to the reconciliation of international and national codifications of international trade law. Although the Code has now been adopted by all but one (Louisiana) of the United States, it is still a purely domestic codification. Nevertheless, it is the most recent and most exhaustive domestic codification of trade law in the common law world, and I assume it therefore to be of particular interest. On that assumption, I intend to suggest some ways which may possibly advance international codification of trade law and some ways which could retard such a development, at least as far as my own country is concerned. My examples may well be drawn from the Uniform Law on the International Sale of Goods (ULIS) and the revising work undertaken by the United Nations Commission on International Trade Law (UNCITRAL).

Looking at the more positive aspects first, I will list four ways in which the Code may advance international codification:

1. By reducing the traditional common law resistance to codification

W. G. Gilbert, whose career as a barrister drove him to verse, reminds us of the traditional common law resistance to legislation in these lines from *Iolanthe:*

* McCormack Professor of Law, School of Law, Columbia University, New York, The United States of America.

1. See Preface, p. X.

And while the House of Peers withholds
its legislative hand,
And noble statesmen do not itch
To interfere with matters which
They cannot understand,
As bright will shine Great Britain's rays.
As in King George's glorious days.

The Code has tended to reduce this resistance in the United States by providing a domestic example. It is therefore significant that, in its ambit of codification, the Code goes far beyond its predecessor, the Uniform Sales Act. (Indeed, in one respect the Code goes far beyond ULIS as well, for it contains statutory formulations of many rules for the formation of contracts which are not dealt with in ULIS but left to a separate Uniform Law on the Formation of Contracts for the International Sale of Goods, to which UNCITRAL has not yet addressed itself.) The American lawyer will not be startled to find in ULIS a statutory rule on excuse based on impossibility of performance (ULIS, article 74); although there was no such provision in the old Uniform Sales Act, which was the law in most states before the Code, there are two new sections in the Code that deal with the subject (UCC, 2-614, 2-615). Nor will he be surprised to find in ULIS detailed rules on the effect of usages (ULIS, article 9); although there were no such rules in the old Uniform Sales Act, the Code has elaborate provisions on usages (UCC, 1-205). The same is true of the buyer's duty of salvage of rejected goods (compare ULIS articles 91-95 with UCC, 2-603, 2-604), the seller's power to "cure" a defective delivery (compare ULIS article 44 with UCC, 2-508), and the buyer's power, on seller's default, to "cover" by purchasing replacement goods at a price conclusive on the seller for the purpose of calculating damages (compare ULIS article 85 with UCC 2-712). The Code's introduction of statutory formulations of the law on these and other subjects covered by ULIS can be expected to lessen the American lawyer's resistance to codification of those subjects.

2. By presenting many common law principles in a statutory form

History reminds us that the common law has proved to be notably less exportable than the civil law, at least in part because common law principles are not stated in a form that can be easily understood by jurists from other legal systems. Countries, other than Britain's former colonies, have not hastened to invite the common law in as they have done with the great European codes. The Uniform Commercial Code, however, now puts at least some common law ideas in the more exportable form of a statute. It has not gone unnoticed abroad. Professor Lebedev, who represents the Soviet Union on UNCITRAL's working group on sales, is one of the co-translators of a Russian version of the Code (although he does not offer much hope for its adoption in any of the Soviet Socialist Republics in the near future). Professor Tunc, who has represented France in the same working group, has sponsored a French translation of article 2 of the Code on Sales, along with the official comments (although he supposes that it will be some time before it will replace the rival contribution of Napoleon's time in France). Other UNCITRAL representatives are familiar with the Code and at UNCITRAL sessions I have more than once looked to a colleague from another country to borrow a copy when I have neglected to bring my own. Those common law notions that are contained in the Code are therefore made available to civil law colleagues in a form more appealing than the collections of cases found in our libraries. Two examples should suffice: first, the rules on anticipatory repudiation found in UCC 2-610 and 2-611; second, the rules on specific relief (including replevin) found in UCC 2-716 and its comment. Although the civil law lawyer is unlikely to feel comfortable with either of these solutions, they are at least accessible to him in a form that he may understand.

3. By formulating novel solutions to many troublesome problems in international trade law

In other areas, the draftsmen of the Code have formulated novel solutions to troublesome problems of international trade in such a form that they can be easily adopted for international use. Here, Code solutions may be more appealing to the civil law jurist than where they merely restate common law rules. The Code has already served more than once as a helpful guide to the draftsmen engaged in the revision of ULIS. To take a simple example, at the 1972 meeting of the working group, the Code term "cure" was inserted, at the suggestion of the representative of Japan, as the simplest way of describing a variety of ways, including replacement and repair, in which the seller might remedy a defective tender.[2] To take another example, the revision of the provisions of ULIS article 9 on usages show the influence of the Code's provisions on usages in UCC 1-205.[3] Or to take a third, a proposal to exclude transactions in consumer goods from the scope of ULIS uses the Code's definition of "consumer goods" in UCC 9-109(1) as its basis.[4] The Code has proved, to some extent at least, an acceptable export on the level of international unification.

4. By serving as an example of a successful unification of the laws of many different jurisdictions

The Code is itself a successful unification within a federal system of the law of many states. In contrast to commercial codes in most other legal systems, which have been enacted by a national parliament, the Uniform Commercial Code has become the law in forty-nine states through the process of enactment by the separate legislatures of each of those states. Although all of the states have a common law tradition, the process has often required a spirit of compromise. For example, the principle that each party owes a duty of *good faith* in the performance of its obligations, established by case law in New York and California, has been extended by UCC 1-203 to forty-seven other states. For another example, the conflicts among the states as to the extent to which an action for damages survived *rescission* has been laid to rest by UCC 2-608.[5] Not all conflicts were so simply resolved, however, and that over the extent to which the seller's warranties extend to persons not in privity with him has left a legacy of three alternative texts, any one of which may be adopted by a state without violating the sponsor's pretensions to uniformity (UCC 2-318). But on the whole, the process of unification of state law involved in the

2. Rev. ULIS article 43 bis in UN Document A/CN.9/75, February 20, 1973, Annex 1, p. 5.
3. Rev. ULIS article 9 in UNCITRAL Yearbook, Vol. II, 64.
4. Rev. ULIS article 2(1)(a) in UNCITRAL Yearbook, Vol. III, 79.
5. See comment in sect. 1 of this article, p. 98, *ante*.

Code offers at least some inspiration to those who would unify national law.

The four ways just listed in which the Code may advance international codification illustrate, as I pointed out, the more positive aspects. On the negative side, I have listed four ways in which the Code may retard international codification.

1. By suggesting impracticable expenditures of effort

The Code is, to be sure, far from a perfect document, even for American conditions. Many of its provisions have been the target of valid criticism and its article 9 on secured transactions has recently been subjected to substantial amendments, already in the process of adoption by the states which enacted the original version a decade or so ago. But with all its faults, the Code appears to be the product of a vastly greater productive effort than that which has been spent on ULIS. Work on the Code was continuous over the years, while that on ULIS has been largely confined to the periods of several weeks only when meetings have been held. One state alone, New York, retained an army of consultants, held extensive public hearings, spent three years and $300,000 (in 1955 dollars), and produced five volumes of commentary and criticism of the first official draft of the Code, resulting in substantial amendments and a new official draft. No single country has yet to, or seems likely to, lavish such attention on ULIS. Given the greater challenges of unifying law on an international as compared to a national plane, the fact that relatively less effort appears to have been devoted to the drafting and consideration of ULIS than would be the case for comparable domestic legislation in the United States, is not likely to inspire the confidence of the American bar.

2. By affording American jurists an accessible set of norms

It is not always an easy matter for a common law lawyer to know what the case law of his country says on some matter of proposed unification. He lacks the convenient codes which his civil law colleagues carry about to resort to in such situations. And so it is more difficult for him to ascertain a clear answer when a proposed text "flies in the face" of his own law. Now, however, the American lawyer, armed with the Code, is in a position to compare almost any proposed text on sales with a text from his own law, that is not only comparable but modern. Why, he may ask, does ULIS dispense with any requirement of a writing (ULIS article 15), when the draftsmen of the Code so recently resolved to retain a minimal requirement (UCC 2-201)? Why does ULIS afford the buyer, who finds that he has defective goods on his hands, the opportunity of reducing the price "in the same proportion as the value of the goods at the time of the conclusion of the contract has been diminished because of their lack of conformity with the contract" (ULIS article 46), when in a falling market this will give him a greater recovery than that allowed by the Code (UCC 2-714)? In these and other areas the Code may, by calling attention to the compromise required, stiffen resistance to that compromise.

3. By affording American jurists an advanced set of solutions

Perhaps the appropriate response to the previous point is that the American jurist must be prepared to admit the superiority, or at least greater viability, of other solutions to those found in the Code. If the English, who gave us the Statute of Frauds three centuries ago, have now seen fit to abandon the original in even their domestic law, why should not the Americans be willing to do the same with their pale copy, at least in international transactions. Indeed, my government has consistently accepted this argument in connection with ULIS, although not without objection at home. In some matters, however, we are convinced that the Code solution is more modern and distinctly preferable to what is offered in ULIS, and that it would be a step backward to adopt the ULIS solution. *Property* (or *title*) and *déliverance* offer a leading illustration. The concept of *property* was used by the Uniform Sales Act, before the Code, as the key to the solution of such functionally unrelated problems as risk of loss and the seller's right to recover the price. A major contribution of the Code was the de-emphasis of this abstract notion of ownership and the substitution of rules that could be justified on functional grounds. Imagine, then, the reaction of the American jurist on discovering that ULIS employs the notion of *déliverance* in much the same discredited way as the old Uniform Sales Act used *property*. In our view, one of the major advances of UNCITRAL's working group has been to attempt a revision which would eliminate the abstract notion of *déliverance* much as that of *property* has been eliminated in the Code.[6] Other innovations of the Code which are accepted in the United States, but may be more advanced than in other countries, are prepared to accept in an international unification to include those allowing the parties to leave the price term "open", that is, to "conclude a contract for sale even though the price is not settled", and those affording a party who has "reasonable grounds for insecurity ... with respect to the performance" of the other, a procedure for requiring "adequate assurance of performance" (UCC 2-609). In these and similar respects, it seems likely that ULIS will appear to American jurists as less modern, less sophisticated, less advanced, and less desirable than the Code that it would in part replace.

4. By setting a standard of comprehensiveness and detail

One characteristic of the American as draftsman is notorious among civil law lawyers, whether preparing a contract or writing a code, he produces the world's longest and most detailed texts. Conversely, to the American lawyer, the civilian's style of drafting appears to leave much to be desired. The Code contains definitions of dozens of terms, including "contract" (UCC 1-201(11)), "agreement" (UCC 1-201(3)), "notice" (UCC 1-201(25)), "contract of sale" (UCC 2-106(1)) and "sale" (UCC 2-106(1)), which go undefined in ULIS. It devotes many sections to spelling out the meaning of contract terms, including "fob" and "fas" (UCC 2-319), "cif" and "c & f" (UCC 2-320), "net landed weights" (UCC 2-321), "ex-ship" (UCC 2-322), and "letter of credit" (UCC 2-325(3)), which are not spelled out in ULIS. Whatever the merits of ULIS' more laconic style in terms, for example, of greater flexibility in the development of the law, the American lawyer is likely to find it wanting since it fails to answer specific questions that are clearly disposed of by the Code.

6. See the study on *Delivery* in UNCITRAL Yearbook, Vol. III, 31.
7. UCC 2-305; see discussion of Rev. ULIS art. 57 in UN Document A/CN.9/75; February 20, 1973, pp. 30-32.

I have tried to show both sides of the coin with regard to the possible impact of the Code on the reconciliation of international and national codifications of international trade law. I can not provide a balance sheet indicating which of the two lists is the weightier. Many of the factors that will ultimately determine the American reaction to ULIS are for the future to decide. How will UNCITRAL resolve some of the remaining problems raised in connection with the amendment of ULIS? How many countries will follow the lead of those that have adopted the original version of ULIS? To what extent will American businessmen come to feel the need of unification on an international scale?

In closing, however, I would like to emphasize that I have tried to give a fair picture of how a typical American jurist might view these matters. This assessment ought not to be confused with my own view on the subject. I have devoted a good deal of time and effort to the cause of international unification, and seem to view it through that indispensible article for those engaged in international unification (especially "United Nation-style"), a pair of rose-colored glasses.

10

THE UNIFICATION MEASURES OF THE COUNCIL FOR MUTUAL ECONOMIC ASSISTANCE AND THE NATIONAL REGULATION OF INTERNATIONAL TRADE LAW BY ITS MEMBERS

*Jerzy Jakubowski**

The process of unification and harmonisation of the law in the domain of economic, scientific and technical co-operation between member countries of the Council for Mutual Economic Assistance (CMEA) is an important factor in the development of this co-operation. The unification and harmonisation of the law facilitates the co-operation and ensures a modern legal framework. One should stress the standardising effect of the unification and harmonisation of the law, i.e. the facilitation for enterprises to act in the framework of one set of rules or at least one set of principles. Another, rather more important objective of the unification and harmonisation of the law, is the creation of a modern set of rules adapted to the requirements of contemporary economic co-operation, well balanced, giving, thanks to their uniformity, to all enterprises active in the co-operation an equal legal framework.

The problem of the relationship between the community law of the CMEA countries and their national law can be considered from various angles.

One of them is the limitation of community law to regulations of so-called international situations. In this case, we have the limitation to relations between organisations, i.e. enterprises and other units of economic, technical and scientific activities from different member countries. Relations of purely internal character are, as a rule, not comprised in the scope of application of community law. This is a

* Professor of Law, Faculty of Law, University of Warsaw, Poland.

characteristic feature of the unification and harmonisation of the law within the CMEA. In contrast, the unification and harmonisation of the law within the European Economic Communities (EEC) is not limited to relations between persons from different member countries, it involves also internal relations. This difference in the scope of application of the unified law between the CMEA and the EEC reflects differences in the character and depth of the integration process among them. The main objective of the integration process within the CMEA is to contribute to the optimal development of the CMEA countries.

Another aspect of the problem is the field of operation of community law. Up to now, it is mostly the civil law (private law), not so closely connected with the economic policy as the administrative law (public law). The major acts of community law in the CMEA countries are: the General Conditions of Delivery of Goods of 1968, the General Conditions of Assembly of 1973, the General Conditions for the Technical Servicing of 1973 (these acts are new versions of documents which existed up to now, but were largely modified), the Convention on the Settlement by Means of Arbitration of Civil Law Disputes arising out of Relations of Economic, Technical and Scientific Co-operation of 1972, and the Warsaw Railway Transportation Agreements of 1950 (revised afterwards). In the course of elaboration are other instruments, among them General Conditions of Construction Works. There are also some documents aimed at the harmonisation of legal principles, not to unify legal rules, such as, for instance, in the field of co-operation and specialisation in production and with respect to joint enterprises.

The limitation of the unification and harmonisation of the law within the CMEA, as a rule, to civil law (private law) reflects the fact that the Council, in contrast to the EEC, leaves to each member country full autonomy to frame its economic relations with third countries. The Council does not interfere in the relations of the member countries with third countries. A firm principle of the socialist integration is, that it cannot harm world-wide co-operation. It is stated firmly in the preamble of the charter of the Council, "confirming the readiness to develop economic relations with all countries irrespective of the social and political systems, on the principles of equality, mutual advantage and non-interference in domestic affairs".

The effect of the limitation of community law of the member countries of the Council to the civil law has important implications with regard to the relationship between community law and the universal economic and trade law. Such character and scope of application of the unified and harmonised law cannot hamper the participation of the member countries in the developing world-wide unification and harmonisation of economic and trade law. The Socialist countries take an active part in the creation of universal economic and trade law. This is evidenced by the fact that the United Nations Commission on International Trade Law (UNCITRAL) was created on the initiative of one of them, i.e. Hungary.

Special attention must be given to the controversial question of autonomy of community law of CMEA countries towards the national law of its member countries. This question is closely connected with the problem of the ways in which to create acts of community law and to give them binding legal force.

Up to now, there were two ways. One of them is the traditional proved form of an international convention submitted to ratification. That was so in the case of the Convention of 1972 on the Settlement of Civil Law Disputes arising out of Relations of Economic, Technical and Scientific Co-operation by Means of Arbitration. The other way is the recommendation under article 4(1) of the charter of the Council. This provision reads as follows:

> "Recommendations shall be made on questions of economic, scientific and technical co-operation. Recommendations shall be submitted for consideration to the member countries of the Council.
>
> Recommendations adopted by the member countries of the Council shall be implemented by a decision of the governments or competent organs of these countries in conformity with their national legislation".

We see here three phases in the formation of a recommendation:

(1) adoption of a recommendation by an organ of the Council, composed of representatives of the member countries,
(2) acceptance of the recommendation by the given member country,
(3) implementation of the recommendation by the given member country.

Adoption of a recommendation by the organ of the Council is not binding on member countries, although the organ is composed of representatives of states. The existence of the second phase is evidence that there does not exist direct legislative power of the organs of the Council with the exception of organisational and procedural matters, in contrast to some ways of legislative process within the EEC as, e.g., the "règlements à l'application immédiate". The third phase, i.e. the implementation of the recommendation in matters of co-operation by the member countries in conformity with their national legislation consists, in the case of acts of a general normative character in the incorporation of such an act into the national legal system. That happened, for instance, in the case of the General Conditions of Delivery of Goods of 1968. It is worth mentioning that it was done in the member countries on different levels of legislative activities, in some countries on the level of decrees by the State Council, in some others by the Council of Ministers.

The requirement to implement a recommendation with an annexed act of uniform legal rules by the member countries could be regarded as depriving it of an international character. I am, however, convinced that this is not so and that the implementation is of a rather formal character and does not deprive the act of its international character. The particular acts of uniform law are composing together a special legal order on the community level. This body of rules can be called community law. The juridical literature of the German Democratic Republic, for instance, used the term "internationale Spezialregelung" (international special regulation) for this legal system. This body of rules has a separate field of application: the relations between organisations of different member countries of the Council. It is applied by tribunals which perform only the task of settling disputes in the sphere of international trade, i.e., the arbitration tribunals at the chambers of commerce of the member countries. The interpretation of the acts of the common legislative activities of the member countries of the Council is following principles, which aim at their uniform construction. This and other factors cause the relative autonomy of community law towards national legal systems. It should be added that the complex programme devised in anticipation of further deepening and improving the co-operation and the development of the Socialist economic integration of the member countries of the Council, (adopted at the 25th session of the Council in Bucharest in 1971), speaks expressly of the *common legal order* (in Russian: *obshchy pravovy poradok*).

Another problem which arises in respect of the mutual relationship between community law and national law of the member countries of the Council, is the subsidiary application of the latter in matters regulated by the former.

It should, first of all, be emphasised that the elaboration of acts of uniform law shows a tendency to completeness. This trend is also, as a rule, evident in their application by the arbitration tribunals at the chambers of commerce of the member countries of the CMEA. Particularly favourable to this principle is the legal literature; one can find there proposals going in a similar direction as the famous article 17 of the Hague Uniform Laws on Sales of 1964, so closely connected with the name of one of the participants of the Oxford Symposium on which this book is founded,[1] Professor André Tunc.

The subsidiary application of the national law is regarded as a *malum necessarium*, because solutions in the national laws differ from one another and their application leads, therefore, to an inequality between the enterprises, being parties to commercial contracts.

On the other hand, there exists among lawyers of the member countries of the CMEA a firm conviction that the completeness of the acts of the uniform law and the elimination of any subsidiary application of the rules of national legal systems can, in reality, be hardly achieved. For this reason, and to avoid the uncertainty with which national law will be applied subsidiarily, the acts of the uniform law of the CMEA countries contain conflict of law rules. As a general rule one follows the principle of the application of the law of the country where the party has its siège social, who does perform the non-pecuniary obligation, the so-called characteristic obligation in the terms of Professor A. F. Schnitzer. In the case of the subsidiary application of the rules of determined national law norms of the so-called general civil law, and not norms regulating relations between internal Socialist organisations, are applied.

This is expressly stated in paragraph 110 of the General Conditions of Delivery of Goods of 1968. The applicable norms are, therefore,

1. See Introduction.

the same as regards to relations between the enterprises of a given member country of the Council and the partners from Western countries, in cases, of course, where, according to the rules of the conflict of laws, the legal system of this country is governing the given contract. It should, therefore, be stressed that the principles of the parties' autonomy and commercial customs, especially international customs, play a dominant role as superior principles of international trade law. It was stated expressly in 1970 in a judgment of the Polish Supreme Court, that international conventions to which Poland is a party as well as international commercial customs and usages have priority over each national law; international commercial customs and usages are given preference over the applicable national law.

11

THE INTERNATIONAL TRADE CODE OF CZECHOSLOVAKIA

*Pavel Kalenský**

I

The Czechoslovak International Trade Code (CITC) came into force on April 1, 1964 [1] as the first and, it might be said, complex codification in the area of international trade relations enacted by a single state. The CITC differs from the United States Uniform Commercial Code (UCC) insofar as its provisions cover a much wider range of subject matters. The UCC aims primarily at the unification of the United States law of the contract of sale with the intention to prevent any American inter-state conflicts of law, and problems actually related to international trade have only been given secondary consideration. Equally, the CITC differs from the Yugoslav General Custom of Trade which, as it is well known, is not a statutory instrument, but only a very comprehensive collection of trade usages adopted by a resolution of the Yugoslav State Arbitration.

The enactment of the CITC has been one of the consequences of the very important changes which have taken place in socialist Czechoslovakia in connection with the fundamental restructure of social and legal institutions. The profound economic and social reasessments undertaken in Czechoslovakia since 1945 have also necessitated a new legal concept. The foundation for this new legal order was laid by the Czechoslovak Constitutions enacted after World War II in 1948 and in 1960 respectively, reflecting now the socialist character of the Czechoslovak economic system. As a consequence of the new struc-

* Professor of Law, Director of the Institute of Legal Sciences, Czechoslovak Academy of Sciences, University of Prague, Czechoslovakia.

1. By the Act Concerning Legal Relations in International Trade, No. 101/1963, Collection of Laws of the Czechoslovak Socialist Republic.

ture of the Czechoslovak economy, a number of laws were enacted by the end of 1963 and early in 1964 which, for all practical purposes, have resulted in a reorganisation of the whole Czechoslovak legal order. Perhaps the most prominent changes were made in the provisions governing property relations which had, until then, been governed by the Civil Code of 1950 as the principal enactment.

At present (since 1964), property relations in Czechoslovakia are governed by three separate codes: the Civil Code, the Economic Code and the Code of International Trade. All three codes and their provisions distinguish between social relationships arising strictly within the Czechoslovak economy and those arising in international trade. The latter have their specific economic and legal features, very often different from the former, but relationships arising in international trade are governed exclusively by the CITC.

The Czechoslovak Economic Code governs relationships arising in connection with the planning and the implementation of the national economic plans and as a result of the economic activities of Czechoslovak socialist economic organisations carried out within the framework of the municipal economic system, which do not affect the contractual relations between one of the Czechoslovak foreign trade enterprises and its commercial partners from abroad.

The Civil Code deals primarily with relations between socialist organisations and individuals as well as relations between individuals, which arise in the course of legal contacts. Without going into detail, it may be stated that the contract of sale provisions of the Civil Code impose much stricter obligations on socialist organisations than on individuals, if both the seller and the buyer are private persons.

Relations arising in international trade cannot, however, be governed by the Civil Code or the Economic Code, as a result of their different economic and legal objectives. For that reason the rights and duties of the parties to an international commercial contract are set forth, as far as the substantive law is concerned, in a separate enactment, i.e. the CITC, and the problems of private international law and particularly of the conflict of laws, are regulated by the Czechoslovak Private International Law and Procedure Act.

The CITC is a municipal codification which forms part of the Czechoslovak legal order, but which governs at the same time exclusively international trade relations between parties to international commercial contracts. In that respect it differs from foreign codes which were or are enacted primarily for municipal purposes and, consequently, do not meet the requirements of international trade very often. Realisation that international business relations and techniques of foreign trade require special rules differing from those of a purely domestic character resulted in the new Czechoslovak enactment. This phenomenon is, of course, not only characteristic to the Czechoslovak economic and legal development; it can be noted on an international level as well. The sole difference is that, as far as the Czechoslovak enactment is concerned, the source for the legal regulation of foreign trade is a special municipal Act. Contrary to the main characteristics of all unification drafts, particularly The Hague ones, the essential feature of the new CITC is, that it is not restricted to regulating only relations of the parties arising in connection with the contract of sale, but that its scope is much wider.

After these explanatory remarks concerning the basic legal character and scope of application of the CITC it will be possible to draw some conclusions in relation to universal and regional unifications. The CITC as well as other international unifications or drafts share a common base insofar as it is necessary for all to differentiate between legal relationships arising within the framework of a specific national economic order and its limited scope and those arising on the broad scale of international economic contracts in general. However, a further conclusion drawn on the basis of a fundamental comparison shows, that the scope of the legal provisions contained in the CITC goes far beyond the current objectives of all present unifications or drafts. This may be seen from the content of the CITC which shows that, apart from the introductory and general provisions, the most extensive regulations relate entirely to the law of obligations.

The Code had to define the subject matters regulated by it as well as the scope of its application. In that respect it was necessary to define the notion of *legal relationship arising in international trade.* In doing so, objective criteria were used, particularly those of locality, which do not make the application dependent on whether there are, on the Czechoslovak side, Czechoslovak foreign trade corporations participating in the individual contracts, but on a set of facts typical in international trade as, for instance, on the fact that the residence or *siège social* of the contracting parties is in more than one country, or on the fact that the contract has to be performed in the territory of a country in which neither party has its residence or *siège social*.

One of the characteristic features of the CITC is the essentially optional nature of its rules unless, of course, there is a provision to the contrary in the Code itself, declaring the rule to be of an obligatory character. The optional nature of the Code's rules guarantees sufficient liberty to the contracting parties to select the terms of their contract at their will, e.g. by referring to standard conditions, general terms of delivery, etc. A rule of interpretation provides that the provisions of the contract itself shall have precedence over the provisions of the Code. A characteristic, common to all obligatory rules, is that they are clearly identified as such in the Code itself: thus, the need for clarity in interpreting the provisions of the Code is met.

In contrast to The Hague Uniform Law on the International Sale of Goods, the CITC does not give preference to commercial usages over legal provisions; the Code admits the application of commercial usages if that is not contrary to the contract or the obligatory provisions of the Code. However, if the parties indicate in their contract that they want certain usages to be applied in the determination of their rights and duties, such usages will be given preference over the provisions of the Code, because they are seen as implied terms of the contract. Apart from such contractual provisions, lacunae in a contract or the statutory provisions can be filled by commercial usage universally observed in international trade with regard to the respective commodity. In view of the provisions adopted by the Code, the rights and duties of the parties are determined in the following order:

a) by the obligatory provisions of the Code;

b) by the contractual agreement itself;

c) by indirect contractual agreement in the form of standard contracts, commercial terms or rules of interpretation, or usages referred to by the parties in their contract;

d) by the optional provisions of the Code;

e) by usages generally observed in international trade in a particular commercial domain.

However, in the case of some contracts (e.g. voyage charter, clean and documentary collections through banks) usages have been given preferences over some provisions of the Code.

The CITC forms an integral part of the Czechoslovak legal system and its provisions are, therefore, coherent. It must be emphasized that, in the course of the drafting of the CITC, great attention was paid to making the Code correspond to the actual need of promoting international trade. Consequently, not only Czechoslovakia's own experience was taken into account, but great attention was also paid to many unification drafts, e.g. to The Hague ones (of course not in their final versions which, in 1963, were not known to the authors of the CITC). However, in view of the purpose of the CITC the provisions of the unification drafts were not mechanically copied; instead, their provisions were only taken into account after a critical evaluation, so that the final text of the Code would form a harmonious and systematic set of rules acceptable to all parties to international commercial contracts irrespective of their nationality or the social system prevailing in their particular country. In addition, the CITC deals with some problems arising in connection with, e.g., inspection contracts, prohibited re-exportation, foreign exchange and gold clauses *et al.*, which so far have not been given proper attention.

The CITC as the enactment of a single state in the area of international trade reflects the importance attributed to this area of human activities. In addition it shows that, besides participating in the elaboration of many international unification drafts, whose chances to ever become law must be regarded as highly doubtful, even one single state can succesfully regulate the complex relationships arising in this domain.

The Code had, of course, to take into consideration the existing and also the possible future regulations of the respective economic relationships on an international level. As to the regulation on an inter-state level – either bilateral or multilateral – the Code gave preference to the international regulation. Section 4 of the Code provides that the provisions of the Code shall apply unless a provision to the contrary is contained in an international treaty binding upon the Czechoslovak Socialist Republic.

As to other possible sources of the law of international trade, namely those elaborated by non-governmental bodies formulating international commercial usages, Incoterms elaborated by the International Chamber of Commerce in Paris, Uniform Customs and Practice for Documentary Credits elaborated by the latter, or the

Revised American Foreign Trade Definitions, the Warsaw-Oxford Rules elaborated by the International Law Association giving the interpretation of the *c.i.f. clause* etc., the CITC gives the parties to a commercial contract absolute freedom to refer to commercial usages or to other sources of the law of international trade. The same may be said of the various standard contracts and general conditions for specific kinds of goods elaborated under the auspices of the United Nations Commission for Europe (ECE).

The fact that the CITC does not give preference over its own provisions to what has been described as an autonomous and independent law of international trade, is due to the fact that we are here dealing with the efforts of a single state to meet the requirements of modern international trade. The Czechoslovak Code's attitude to the above mentioned sources of international trade law is clearly defined in sections 116, 117 and 118 respectively.

A contract may also be concluded by reference to commercial conditions known to both parties and relied upon by the offeror or by use of contract forms which are frequently used in commercial relations. Special provisions in the contract shall have preference over the wording of such general commercial terms or contract forms. If the parties make use in their contracts of some of the terms regulated by internationally accepted interpretation rules, they shall be presumed to intend to attain such legal effects as laid down in the said interpretation rules to which they expressly refer or which are most likely in the mind of the parties. Rights and obligations not expressly regulated in the contract shall be governed by the Code or by the commercial custom generally observed in international trade in the respective areas of business, provided they are not contrary to the contract or the Code.

II

It is, for many reasons, very difficult to give in a necessarily brief report a complete answer to the very intricate problem of the relationship of the CITC to the universal or regional unification of the law of international trade. One of the reasons which play a considerable role with respect to the universal unification is the fact that universal unification as such does evidently not yet exist and that the activities of the United Nations Commission on International Trade Law (UNCITRAL), set up with the task to promote universal unification of the law of international trade, are only just beginning to show first results. A parallel phenomenon in many respects may also be seen in the area of regional unification. This situation imposes a considerable limitation on the author's present task and consequently restricts the scope of this paper.

However, it is not too difficult to make some useful comparisons between the CITC and some other already accepted instruments of unification or unification drafts. We shall, therefore, compare the CITC with the General Terms of Delivery sponsored by the CMEA in 1968 as a unification of the international contract of delivery of goods and The Hague Uniform Laws on the Formation of the International Contract of Sale and on the International Sale of Goods. Both represent, no doubt, in their substence a unification of the international sale of goods and both went beyond the unification proposals made by various non-gouvernmental organisations. Both are the result of the activities of several countries on an international level. Nevertheless, both are restricted exclusively in their application to the international sale of goods, while the CITC does not only contain these general provisions, but also a complex set of rules embracing the entire law of contract, including all special types of contracts usually encountered within the domain of international commercial transactions. However, most of the Code's provisions which relate to the various obligations are devoted to the contract of sale (sections 276 to 404). In addition to the regulation of the obligation of the seller, the buyer and their mutual duties, special arrangements, frequently found in international commercial transactions are regulated as well (such as the right to re-purchase, the right to re-sell, sale on approval, sale and/or purchase on better conditions, right to redemption, clauses prohibiting re-exportation, agreements in restraint of trade as well as special clauses relating to prices). The CITC regulates so-called linked transactions (interdependent synallagmatic contracts and miltulateral barter transactions), the contract of barter, loan, hire, bailment, warehousing, work and labour, agency, the commission agents' contract, inspection contract, forwarding agent's contract, carriage of goods, charterparty by demise and other forms of charterparty, insurance, brokerage, commercial representation and partnership contracts. In contrast to other civil and commercial codes, the CITC includes, in a general way, the regulation of some banking transactions such as documentary credits, clean and documentary collections through banks, bank guarantees, traveller's cheques, deposits of negotiable instruments and other valuables. It is obvious from the wide scope of subject matters dealt with in the Code, that the basic features of the Code reflect the efforts of its draftsmen to cover the whole spectrum of business law.

The CITC and the General Terms of Delivery are practically limited to commercial transactions. The General Terms of Delivery represent a special legal regulation and their application is restricted to all deliveries of goods between the corporations of foreign trade in the member countries of the CMEA. This, no doubt, is due to the state monopoly of foreign trade in all socialist member states of the CMEA. The economic system of socialist states and its management are characterised as far as foreign trade is concerned, by the existence of special organisations or corporations which have the right to conclude international commercial transactions and whose activities are concentrating, therefore, on international commerce. These enterprises are different from those which do not conclude commercial transactions and are solely active in matters connected with the production of goods or municipal commerce. The socialist state has, within the frame of the state monopoly of foreign trade, the exclusive right to create foreign trade corporations and is entitled to limit the validity of the General Terms of Delivery to relations arising exclusively out of commercial transactions concluded between organisations specialising in this field. It may be said, therefore, that the application of the General Terms of Delivery is limited and that this limitation is based upon the legal status attributed to the parties to international commercial contracts.

In spite of the fact that the CITC has usually to be applied to cases in which at least one of the parties is a Czechoslovak foreign trade corporation, it did not choose to rely upon the personal quality of the parties as criterion for its application. The Code was designed to serve the needs of international trade on a universal level – in contrast to the General Terms of Delivery, which are only applicable to mutual relations of enterprises of the same kind, i.e. to foreign trade corporations from socialist states. For that reason the CITC chose the objective and not the subjective test for its application. In principle, the CITC adopted the objective approach which was also pursued by The Hague Uniform Law on the International Sale of Goods. However, as the CITC does not, as does the Uniform Law, regulate sales contracts only, but governs all legal relationships arising within the area of international trade, the scope of all provisions governing these relations had to be determined. One of the basic criteria in this respect is the territorial relationship between the parties, namely the fact that these parties have their *siège social* in the territories of different states. Thus, the CITC is not limited only to relations between Czechoslovak foreign trade corporations and their foreign partners and does not make any allowances as to which side the Czechoslovak subject finds himself on in the particular relationship. The provisions of the Code are also applicable to cases where – under the rules of private international law – Czechoslovak law is applicable to the settlement of the disputes specified in section 2, in which no Czechoslovak party is involved, e.g. two foreign parties conclude a contract on Czechoslovak territory. The CITC may also apply to the legal relationship of two Czechoslovak parties in those cases in which the Code does not require that the *siège social* of the parties should be in different countries.

In view of the wide scope of the CITC – as compared to The Hague Uniform Law – it was not possible to use the definition of the Uniform Law in article 1, paragraph 1 a – c, leaving aside the fact that its wording may result in various interpretations.

The CITC determines the scope of the commercial character of the relations it regulates by excluding relations if the relationship does not pertain to international trade on Czechoslovak territory. In order to ensure legal certainty, it is necessary for the parties to know already at the time when the legal relationship is established, whether their relation is subject to the Civil Code or the CITC. For example, the legal relationships of foreign tourists in Czechoslovakia, arising when they buy various goods, stay in hotels, eat in restaurants etc., are not governed by the CITC but by the provisions of the Czechoslovak Civil Code.

The CITC, even though rejecting personal criteria for defining its scope, is similar to The Hague Uniform Law on the International Sales of Goods which, according to its article 7, shall apply to the sales regardless of the commercial or civil character of the parties or of the contract.

Different from The Hague Uniform Laws, the CITC does not share the basic attitude of the former, expressed in its article 2, towards the conflict of laws, i.e. that the rules of private international law shall be excluded for the purpose of the application of the CITC, subject to any provision to the contrary. It must be emphasized, that the CITC came into force at the same time as the Czechoslovak Act on Private International Law. The CITC presupposes the application of the conflict of law rules, which determine the possibility of the application of Czechoslovak laws of which the Code is an integral part.

It must be said that the CITC also represents the Czechoslovak law which, according to section 110 of the General Terms of Delivery, is to be applied subsidiarily to the relations of parties to contracts of delivery of goods between the foreign trade corporations of the member states of the CMEA in cases of possible gaps in the General Terms of Delivery provided that the Czechoslovak enterprise is the seller. In contrast to the General Terms of Delivery, valid since 1968, an explanation has been given as to what is to be understood by the subsidiarily applicable law of the seller's country. This law has been defined as provisions of a general character and not as provisions of a special character adopted only with regard to relations arising between municipal economic organisations of the seller's country (as part of the economic law provisions of the country).

In contrast to the General Terms of Delivery which are applicable solely to legal relations arising in connection with the delivery of goods between the corporations of foreign trade from the member states of the CMEA, the CITC does not in any way restrict the freedom of natural or legal persons to acquire rights and duties or to undertake legal acts which would prevent some of these persons to become parties to international business transactions. Section 6 of the Code specifies unequivocally that natural as well as legal persons may be parties to legal relationships arising out of international trade.

Quite naturally, the basic criterion for determining the aforesaid freedom of a legal or natural person is determined by the rules of private international law. Section 3 of the Czechoslovak Act on Private International Law refers in this context to the *lex nationalis*. The CITC provides in section 9, paragraph 1 that "the legal status of legal persons shall be governed by the provisions of the law under which they have been incorporated". This means that, in the case of foreign legal persons, their capacity is determined by their own civil or commercial codes, their statutes or other forms of legislation. In view of the fact that the persons engaged in international trade are extremely varied as to their legal form and capacity, it was necessary for the CITC to settle quite unequivocally the theoretical dispute about the criteria used in this area. The Code has done so with reference to the law under which the specific legal person was incorporated, stating that "enterprises and other organisations shall be considered as legal persons, if the law under which they have been incorporated confers upon them the capacity to acquire rights and have obligation" (section 8, paragraph 1). The socialist nature of the Czechoslovak economy means, in no way, that it is possible to assume (and to prove successfully) the identity of Czechoslovak legal persons and the Czechoslovak State. However, in order to avoid unnecessary misunderstandings, section 11 of the Code underlines the independent liability of Czechoslovak legal persons, independent both as regards the Czechoslovak State and each other. This independent liability arises from the independent legal persona of Czechoslovak legal persons, which is quite separate from the legal personality of the Czechoslovak State. On the other hand, it means that Czechoslovak legal persons cannot raise the defence of immunity of State and its property.

In order to render a contract valid, the Code requires, in addition to the essential prerequisite that the parties must have capacity, that they should agree on at least the essential terms of the contract. These fundamental elements are either listed in the Code in the basic provisions concerning every special type of contract, or in the contract itself. These terms appear especially in the offer; acceptance of only part of the offer does not constitute a valid acceptance of the offer.

The Code proceeds from the binding nature of the offer of a contract. This principle has primarily the following two important legal effects:

a) an offer to conclude a contract may not be revoked once it has been communicated to the other party. If, therefore, the offeror wants to prevent the effect of the offer to take place, he must arrange for the revocation to reach the addressee at least together with the offer (e.g. revocation of an offer sent in a letter, by telegraph or telex). The decisive factor is the time of delivery, not the time of dispatch of the offer or the time when the addressee becomes aware of the offer.

b) A contract is concluded, if the party to whom the offer is addressed accepts it in time. Thus, after the offeror has submitted a binding offer, he cannot prevent the conclusion of the respective contract, if the offeree notifies the offeror in time of his acceptance of the offer.

The CITC is based upon the principle of liability for non-fulfillment of an obligation, irrespective of fault. Here, the Code adopts a principle which is nowadays generally accepted in modern codifications. This principle manifests itself in the fact that no difference is made between culpable and non-culpable failure to discharge an obligation. As regards the default of the debtor, no difference is made between non-fulfillment or a faulty discharge of his obligation. The fact is taken into account, that the economic consequences of a complete failure to discharge an obligation or of a discharge which is contrary to the contract, are basically the same and the determining factor is rather the manner in which the debtor has failed to discharge his obligations, i.e. how long he has been in default or to what extent the discharge is objective and, therefore, not corresponding to the intended object of the contract.

The abandonment by the Code of the principle of culpability in cases involving damages due to a breach of contractual obligations is in keeping with modern trends regarding compensation for damages. However, this provision is, as a rule, accompanied by a limitation placed upon the amount of compensation for damages. Without going into details, it is possible to say, that this is common to the Uniform Law and the CITC.

The CITC links the obligation to compensate for damages with the breach of any obligation arising under the contract and does not differentiate in this respect between a breach by the debtor or the creditor. The Code provides for similar effects to those involved in cases of damages due to a breach of contract, in the case of damages caused by

a) extinction of an obligation due to impossibility of performance;
b) extinction of an obligation due to frustration of the purpose of the contract;
c) breach of another obligation outside the contract, if an obligation set forth by the CITC is involved (e.g. in case of invalidity of a legal act, excess of authority by an agent, etc.).

However, the provisions of the CITC do not indicate the existence of an absolute liability for failure to achieve the aim of the contract. Like The Hague Uniform Act, the CITC enables the liable person to free himself of the obligation to compensate for damages caused by him, if he shows that such failure was due to circumstances excluding his liability, namely to *vis major.*

Liability is excluded in the event of the occurrence of extraordinary circumstances preventing a party for a certain time or continuously to perform his duties, provided these circumstances occur after the formation of the contract and are beyond the control of the party in question. However, circumstances connected with the personal position of the party, more particularly with his financial standing, are not considered as valid reasons to exclude liability; the same is true of obstacles preventing or hindering proper performance of the contractual obligations which the party is bound to overcome or to remove, such as the duty to obtain a licence or circumstances which arise after the party is in delay with the performance of his obligations. It is obvious from the fact that the CITC expressly exempts the failure to obtain a licence from circumstances excluding the liability for non-performance of an obligation, that the Code takes into account the day-to-day problems of international commerce arising out of the practice of granting licences for importation, exportation or for payment. The Code imposes a duty upon the seller to procure the export (or transit) licence, if such licence is required at the time of performance for implementing the deliveries, irrespective of whether such duty was already in existence at the time of the conclusion of the contract. On the other hand, the buyer is bound to procure the licence for the importation of the goods or for their payment; if the buyer fails to fulfil this duty, the seller may repudiate the contract, albeit after expiration of a period of grace.

The general comparison of the CITC with The Hague Uniform

Laws and with the General Terms of Delivery of the CMEA shows, that the CITC as a municipal enactment contains most of the principles advanced by other modern instruments of unification and drafts elaborated on the basis of an anticipated universal acceptance.

B. *International Sales*

12

THE NEED FOR UNIVERSAL UNIFICATION OF THE LAW OF INTERNATIONAL SALES

*André Tunc**

The subject has already been considered in a number of studies. At the outset, special reference should be made to two articles written by two eminent jurists, i.e. Professor Limpens [1] and Professor René David. [2] The thesis of these distinguished authors is that, for psychological, political and even to a certain extent technical reasons, regional unification in law is a necessary intermediate stage to world-wide unification.

I do not wish to engage, for the time being, in a discussion of all the problems arising out of the relationship between regional and global unification. Instead, I would like to discuss and, with respect, challenge the view of the above mentioned authors who seem to argue that regional unification is an absolute prerequisite to global unification.

It may appear obvious that regional unification is easier to achieve than global unification, as the need for unification is more strongly felt between countries which are bound by some political, economic or cultural link (Benelux, Scandinavia, European Socialist countries or even the States of the United States of America), and such ties make unification easier. However, according to Dr Matteucci,[3] the record of regional unification is not terribly impressive; I seem to remember his statement that experience of regional unification has been disappointing and that its record is even more meager than the record of

* Professor of Law, University of Paris I, France.

1. See "Relations entre l'unification au niveau régional et l'unification au niveau national, *Revue Internationale du Droit comparé* (1964) p. 13 *et seq.*
2. See *International Encyclopedia of Comparative Law* (1971), Vol. 11, cap. 5, in particular, sect. 125-137.
3. See Chapter 7, pp. 85-92, *ante.*

universal unification. In any case, this is not exactly the point I would like to discuss.

In my opinion, as regards the law of sales, the tremendous increase in international trade requires a world-wide unification of the law of international sales and we may hope for such a unification without prior regional unification, because the need for global unification is more widely and more strongly felt every year. I tried to emphasise, and this point has been made particularly clear by Professor Honnold,[4] why it would be of extreme value to many firms to be able to deal in only two laws, i.e. the national law for the national sales and a uniform law for the international sales. Of course, the biggest firms find little difficulty in the present situation. They are currently able to impose their terms. If necessary, they have the legal staff and the legal correspondents which enable them to enter into a contract embodying foreign legal concepts, or to make a contract subject to a foreign law and, in case of dispute, subject to a foreign tribunal. However, many British or French companies have much more limited legal resources, even though they may contribute to the general welfare of nations. These firms are often apprehensive to deal with someone via foreign countries, as they know that they could be involved in great legal costs if there is any dispute between the contracting parties. The elaboration of a uniform law of international sales is probably one of the main contributions that we lawyers can make towards a more positive development of international trade. Unquestionably, world-wide unification is greatly needed. But is it possible? My answer is "Yes", even though made with some reservations, of course.

The main hope for global unification, as far as I can see, is or perhaps was, the Uniform Laws on International Sales (ULIS), adopted in The Hague in 1964. It is true that the ratification of this law has been slow, but it has now also been ratified by the Federal Republic of Germany. I very much hope that France will ratify ULIS in the not too distant future, but there exist special obstacles which shall be mentioned later on. The fact that the law has now come into operation in August 1972 should draw attention to it and might multiply the number of ratifications. Professor Clive Schmitthoff has

4. See Chapter 6, pp. 77-83, *ante*.

underlined a number of times the importance of ULIS and its value as a means to global unification.[5] But is ULIS capable of a wider acceptance? I am confident enough to answer this question in the affirmative and would like to try and explain my reasons for so doing by going back briefly to the historical development.

Here, history started in 1931, when the International Institute for the Unification of Private Law (UNIDROIT) set up a special commission to draft a uniform law. Members of the commission included well known jurists such as Sir Cecil Hurst, Gutteridge, Rabel, Capitant and Bagge. The commission prepared a draft, submitted it to various governments through the League of Nations, received observations, reconsidered its draft yet, was unfortunately prevented from taking any further deliberations, because of the outbreak of war. However, the commission convened again after the war, but felt that there was need to discuss a new draft and requested, therefore, a diplomatic conference on the subject. The conference was held in The Hague in 1951. A new commission was set up which drafted new proposals. These proposals were again submitted to various governments and through the latter, to various business organisations. On the basis of observations thus gathered, the commission revised its draft and, as a result convened the 1964 conference. Finally, after three weeks of very hard work, a Uniform Law was adopted. However, one great weakness of ULIS is the fact that the commission was, in fact, a West-European commission. It consisted of experts from the United Kingdom, Germany, Sweden, Denmark, the Netherlands, Belgium, France, Switzerland, Italy, and Spain. Even the diplomatic conference was of limited geographical representation. There were some few socialist countries, yet without the Soviet Union, some few Latin American countries, no African countries, no Asian countries, not even Japan.

However, the United States, who had joined UNIDROIT only a few months earlier sent a small, but excellent delegation, including Professor John Honnold. The attitude of this delegation was very positive, even though still rather remote, as it was clear that the United States would not adhere to the Convention. The United States

5. See "The Uniform Laws of International Sales," Editorial, (1972) *Journ. Business Law* 177 and "The Law of Inter-Community Sales," Editorial, (1973) *Journ. Business Law* 4.

delegation tried to be helpful in assigning John Honnold to the drafting committee and in submitting a number of proposals to the conference. But the United States did not take part in the preparation of the draft and its delegation never pressed for one solution in preference to another.

Such a development is, of course, highly regrettable. However, we must try to look at the result. After thirty-three years of effort (i.e. a third of a century), plus three weeks hard work, the text of a Uniform Law was found acceptable by representatives of twenty-six nations.

Nevertheless, how valuable is ULIS? This main question should be divided into two sub-questions. Namely, is ULIS satisfactory for the nations which were represented in The Hague? And is it satisfactory for all other nations?

As for the nations which participated in the diplomatic conference, I would say, the provisions of ULIS are fairly satisfactory. Certainly, they are far from perfect. Nobody can be entirely satified, because of the many compromises and compromises give full satisfaction to no one. However, the work was done under reasonably good conditions and I do not see how, under the circumstances, a better result could have been achieved. Of course, discussions could have continued. But the general feeling after The Hague conference was that time for discussions had elapsed. It was time to put ULIS to a practical test. My personal hope was that ULIS would be largely accepted and that, after perhaps five to ten years of practical experience, its provisions would be reconsidered and perhaps harmonised with the Uniform Commercial Code (UCC). The UCC is certainly the result of a more advanced standard of legal thinking; the code has undoubtably practical values which cannot be found in ULIS and I had hoped that after some years of operation, it would be easier to assess the values and defects of ULIS as well as of the UCC better. Furthermore, the UCC would be more widely known (that is the reason why I took the initiative of having it translated into French, so that we could get accustomed to it). It was my hope that, perhaps by 1980, we would really have a world-wide uniform law, a final realisation of Cicero's dream.[6] I was impressed when, at the first meeting of the Oxford

6. "Non erit alia lex Romae, alia Athenis, alia nunc, alia posthac, sed et apud omnes gentes, et omni tempore, una eademque lex obtinebit".

Symposium on Universalism and Regionalism in International Economic and Trade Law on October 1, 1973,[7] Professor Barry Nicholas expressed exactly the same anticipation, hoping that the revised ULIS would be harmonised with the UCC. Thus, ULIS is probably satisfactory for the twenty-six nations which were represented at The Hague. But, what about the other nations? Frankly, I do not see any reason, especially any technical reason, why the Uniform Law could not be adopted by them. ULIS was acceptable to common and civil lawyers alike, even though we have to agree that there is no such specific person as a civil lawyer. In France, for instance, we have traditions which are somewhat different from the German or Italian ones, but the Uniform Law was acceptable to the Germans, English, French, Italian and all other nations represented at The Hague. The socialist countries did not take part in the preparation of the draft, but some of them were at The Hague and a number of delegates told me that they were impressed by the complete openness of the discussions. There was a political or geographical coalition, despite the fact that delegates from the Common Market were expected to meet separately from time to time. In fact, there was not one meeting, not one minute of common discussion between the members of the Common Market.

We solely tried to do our best and to maximise our achievements within the short period of just over three weeks. We tried to devise the best law we were capable of. Therefore, I understand the somewhat emotional reaction of nations which were not members of the commission and did not participate in The Hague conference. To ask: "Why should we accept a draft, if we did not take part in its preparation?" seems to me quite human. It may seem paternalistic to insist that it could, nevertheless, be of interest to all nations to ratify ULIS. But, to be frank, I am expressing here only a personal opinion. ULIS could be very useful to the many countries which were not present at The Hague. The Uniform Law was not in the least set up against any of them nor particularly for the members participating in The Hague conference. It was done with a view to help everyone. To me, ULIS seemed the cristalisation of a great work for world-wide unification. I regret to be less optimistic now.

There is, of course, hope for a second chance, if the revision of

7. See Preface, P. X.

ULIS, made under the auspices of the United Nations Commission on International Trade Law (UNCITRAL), does succeed. You will have heard about UNCITRAL. You may also have read about UNCITRAL, particularly in two recent articles by Professor Allan Farnsworth.[8] You know, therefore, UNCITRAL and its most important task. One point however, has not been made clear. If I am not mistaken, credit to UNCITRAL should, to a great extent, be given to Professor Clive Schmitthoff. It was he who was asked by the United Nations for the report, on the basis of which UNCITRAL was created. We should be most thankful to him for that, because I am certain that UNICTRAL is and will be very useful.

However, as regards the revision of ULIS, I have some misgivings, which are well known to my friend John Honnold. Nevertheless, I anticipate three main advantages for such a revision.

First, of course, wider geographical representation from a psychological and political point of view may be of great help.
Secondly, experts of great value will be involved (but, I would like to point out that the situation was already the same at the conference and in the commission; I presume, because in the commission, I was but a "beginner", witnessing the great debate between giants).
Thirdly, the main assets of UNCITRAL will be the leadership of John Honnold and I hope to be forgiven for such a frank statement, but I feel that I have to be sincere.

The beginning of the revision has been extremely slow and again, I would like to refer to Allan Farnsworth.[9] A new procedure has been adopted to accelerate the process of revision and within a year, a new draft is to be agreed upon. Will it be better? Perhaps, but as I pointed out already earlier on, ULIS, in its present form is in my opinion quite satisfactory.

When will this draft be accepted? It has to be prepared by a working group and ratified by UNCITRAL. I will pass details of the

8. See "UNCITRAL – Why? What? When?" *American Journal of Comparative Law,* Vol. 20, p. 314 *et seq.*, as well as "UNCITRAL and the Progressive Development of International Trade" in the excellent *Festschrift für Professor Clive Schmitthoff, Law and International Trade* (1973), p. 145 *et seq.*

9. See Chapter 9, pp. 97-104, *ante.*

procedure which is to follow afterwards. If the procedure is the same as the one used before The Hague conference, it will be a long one. The draft submitted in 1964 was a revision of the draft agreed upon by the members of the commission in 1958. It takes a very long time to submit a draft to various governments, who, in turn, want to submit it to business organisations, who take their time to study the proposals and report back to their governments, who, in turn, submit amendments. Will UNCITRAL and the working group meet again to achieve a final draft and submit it to a diplomatic conference? Such a process takes years. I hope, other ways and means will be found to speed up the development. However, I remain impressed by Professor Farnsworth's question: "When will the revised ULIS be more widely acceptable?" Probably soon, but, I am afraid that, on the other hand, the work presently done by UNCITRAL certainly prevents many nations from acceding to the existing ULIS. Why should a nation, at the present time, adhere to ULIS, when the law is in the process of being revised? Therefore, my hope that ULIS would advance global unification is now slightly dimmed. Furthermore, what will China's attitude be? Will China take the same view as taken by a number of countries and say that it will not adhere to a draft in the preparation of which it did not participate? At the moment, China tries to appear modest and reasonable. It may be the same in ten years from now, but the situation may also be completely different and the revision may have to be revised with the participation of China.

Finally, when a new draft is accepted as a revised version of ULIS, I hope that many nations will accept the Uniform Law. However, whill it be accepted by those countries who, by then, will have accepted the 1964 version? I hope so and Dr. Matteucci has explained why and for what psychological reasons they could be made to adhere to the new version.[10] But nobody knows whether they will. If ULIS is in operation between the members of the Common Market or, at least most of them, will they accept to adhere to a new version? Again, I hope so, but we cannot be sure. Will the United States accept ULIS under any circumstances, as the Uniform Law is bound to be less elaborate than the Uniform Commercial Code?

The situation, therefore, which we may have to face in ten or fifteen

10. See Chapter 7, pp. 89-90, *ante*.

years from now, might well confront us not only with national laws, but also with a so-called Uniform Law in the form of ULIS and another Uniform Law which will be contained in the revised version of ULIS, as well as the UCC or, perhaps, other regional unifications and many nations will see no purpose to adhere to the original version of ULIS rather than the revised form. For me, the achievements generate a great amount of confusion and I am afraid that we may have a great diversity of uniform laws. To be frank, in The Hague I felt that if ULIS was not widely accepted, there was no hope for unification of the law of international sales before the advent of the XXIst century. I hope to be proved too pessimistic, I am not sure. However, everything is accelerating, so perhaps the present efforts will be fruitful earlier than expected.

There is a third possible avenue to unification, if not of the law of all international sales, at least, of the law of certain international sales. Here, I refer to the draft of the General Conditions for the sale of some basic commodities, initiated by the Economic Commission for Europe (ECE) in Geneva under the initiative of Dr. L. Kopelmanas.[11] Here, in my opinion, we find documents comparable to ULIS.

Keeping in mind that they are drafted by a limited number of persons, but representing, nevertheless, examples of regional unification capable of a world-wide expansion. How is the work done?

The ECE organised a meeting with the participation of experts from socialist countries and from so called free market economy countries, from countries which are mainly buyers of a certain commodity and countries which are mainly sellers, with the participation of common and civil lawyers from various countries with different legal traditions and the Secretariat tried to bring all the experts to agree on a certain draft. However, no agreement has been reached, nothing is done. If, on the other hand, a draft seems generally acceptable, it is published as a General Condition for the sale of the given commodity. But it will only be a model. It has no statutory value of any kind, it is a model which is offered to merchants. Again, I do

11. For further reading on the importance of these General Conditions see, in particular, Peter Benjamin, "The ECE General Conditions of Sale and Standard Forms of Contract", (1961) *Journ. of Business Law* 113 *et seq.* and an article by the author himself, in *Revue International du Droit comparé* (1960), p. 108 *et seq.*

not see, why those General Conditions should not be acceptable to people of two nations outside of the ECE. They have been considered by the various Economic Commissions of the United Nations. I was pleased to see that they are now considered by UNCITRAL.

Certainly, such work can be very useful as it would complement ULIS and, with regard to the committee to which it applies, the provisions may even be more satisfactory, since ULIS deals at the same time with commodities as different as, lets say, coal and citrus fruit. In my opinion, such work is one of the important achievements gained through ULIS.

In conclusion I would like to quote René David: [12]

> "The Uniform Laws agreed upon at The Hague are far from perfect. They are a compromise and nobody is completely satisfied. – However, we have some doubts whether it would in fact be possible to improve the Hague Laws very much." He explains why and continues: "It would be very discouraging to see the effects of so many years reduced to nothing. – The Hague Uniform Laws seem to us to be most favourable, especially to developing countries. The contrary has been said. – We think otherwise. – The Hague Uniform Laws seek to establish a just compromise between the interests of the seller and those of the buyer, without there being any reason for seeking to favour one or the other. They are perfectly acceptable to developing countries and those countries, if they accept them, will have the grat advantage that their courts will only have to apply one or two systems of law: The domestic legislation for internal sales and the Uniform Law (accepted by their government) for international sales."

Well, I regret to seem to represent the old guard. That is not my habit, and, I hope, it will not become my habit. Perhaps, I am still avant-garde on certain legal problems. I very sincerely hope that I have not been too pessimistic without serious justification, but it would not have been honest on my part not to express doubts.

12. See "Conclusion", *International Encyclopedia of Comparative Law* (1971), Vol. II, cap. 5, sect. 371.

13

THE HAGUE UNIFORM LAWS OF INTERNATIONAL SALES

*Freiherr Wolfgang Marschall von Bieberstein**

When we contemplate respective aims and changes of universal and regional unification in the field of international sales law, it must be kept in mind that we have already restricted the object of our examination. We confine ourselves to sales of an international character, because we realize that a universal unification of law covering all sales – domestic as well as international – is out of the question. The restriction is the price we pay, in order to achieve the desired unification.

As Professor Tunc has already pointed out,[1] such universal unification has good chances under present conditions. Commercial needs have always provided the strongest impulse for unification of legal rules on every level, national, regional and universal. The exchange of goods is not restricted to limited regions.

In the field of international sales, the needed unification is facilitated by a growing awareness that differences between various legal systems are basically not as great as they might appear at first. The comparative analysis undertaken by lawyers of many nations in the process of preparing The Hague Uniform Laws has shown that the views with regard to the basic obligations of the seller and the buyer, as well as to a fair balance in the distribution of risks between the two parties, are in greater harmony than one might at first expect.

Even the frequently cited examples of a marked difference between certain legal systems lose some of their importance on closer scrutiny. Thus, the sphere of application of article 16 of The Hague

* Dr. jur., Professor of Law, Director of the Institute of Comparative Private Law and the Law of Civil Procedure of the Johann-Wolfgang-Goethe University of Frankfurt, The Federal Republic of Germany.

1. See Chapter 12, pp. 127-135, *ante*.

Law on International Sales, intended to preserve the existing common law rule on specific performance, should not be overestimated. Even, where a judgment for specific performance can be obtained in another legal system, enforcement of such a judgment presents difficulties and becomes almost impossible, if the items to be delivered, cannot be found in the possession of the judgment debtor, To my knowledge, however, cases of enforcement of such a judgment are rare in the field of international sales.

In the case of goods which fail to conform to the specifications given in the contract itself, the buyer's right to claim damages is limited in some countries to certain specified situations, while general provisions are made in other countries as well as in The Hague Law on International Sales. In practice, however, the difference does not seem as great as evident from a recent study of German case law.

The real problem of universal unification in the law of international sales seems not to be one of substance, but rather of procedure and drafting techniques. As already pointed out, in particular by Professor Schmitthoff at the Hamburg meeting of the German Association of Comparative Law in September 1973,[2] it is regrettable, especially for psychological and political reasons, that representatives of the nations of Asia and Africa as well as most Latin American and Socialist countries were not participating in the preparation of The Hague Uniform Laws and that representatives of the United States took only part in the final stage of the discussion. However, an opportunity to participate should be given to all countries; it is a chance which should be recognised as a justification for the re-examination of The Hague Laws even by those, who cannot see that the shortcomings of the existing texts are of such a nature as to warrant a fundamental revision even before the law has undergone any practical test.

It is another problem to harmonise the different approaches individual legal systems apply to the task of legislation, a problem, which can be observed in the use of different drafting techniques. Thus, Professor Tunc in his commentary to The Hague Sales Laws

2. Clive M. Schmitthoff, "Methodik der Vereinheitlichungsbestrebungen des Handelsrechts durch die UNO", *Arbeiten zur Rechtsvergleichung, 69. Methoden der Rechtsvergleichung,* 1974, p. 19 *et seq.; idem* Diskussionsbericht, p. 53.

observed[3] that the law attempts to provide detailed provisions for different situations in which the parties may find themselves. He pointed out that many lawyers would have preferred a much shorter text with rules of a more general character. On the other hand, Professor Farnsworth has mentioned earlier,[4] how especially lawyers of common law countries have criticised The Hague Laws precisely for being too vague and for their lack of precise definitions of many terms. Some of the proposals of the working party on sales of the United Nations Commission on International Trade Law (UNCITRAL) have also been concerned with the improvement of the draft of The Hague Uniform Sales Laws.

In looking at the chances of any unification of sales law, the function of the intended law must be kept in mind. Traditionally, sales law has been regarded as a "gap-filling law". The sequence of sources of law to be applied to the relations of two parties are:

1) The individual agreement of the parties relating at least to the description of the goods to be sold, the price, the place of delivery, etc.

2) supplementary rules contained in general agreements of the parties, whether they are embodied in a form contract of adhesion or, whether the parties have entered into a general framework contract.

3) statutory or case law to be applied only in filling gaps in those contractual provisions which exist, because the parties have deliberately left such points open or, because they have overlooked the problem during their negotiations.

The situation is different, when the law has the function of providing certain mandatory rules which have to be obeyed and from which parties may not deviate. This may be called the "yardstick-function" of a legal rule against which every contractual agreement has to be measured in order to decide whether it is compatible with the statutory or judicial yardstick-rule.

If we keep this in mind we can understand, why attempts to achieve a uniform unification in the field of sales law, have so far been restricted to international sales. In this area, no great need has been

3. André Tunc, Commentary of the Hague Conventions of July 1, 1964 on the International Sale of Goods and on the Formation of Contracts of Sale, pp. 2 *et seq.*

4. See Chapter 9, pp. 97, 98 et seq., *ante.*

felt to develop international rules of a yardstick-type. Thus, difficulties of reaching agreement among nations with a different background, different political institutions and different economic needs can be overcome more easily as long as unification can be achieved by developing only rules of a gap-filling type.

The problem is different, when we look at attempts of regional unification. So far, such attempts have not been restricted to sales of an international character. Restriction is not necessary as long as it seems possible to achieve complete unification of all sales laws within one region, because the participating jurisdictions are in harmony in respect of the goals and legal policies pursued, when they are willing to use the same yardstick.

That is the case, when jurisdictions which are involved belong to the same legal family or, if they are at least closely connected for historical or other reasons. The task of unifying the law in such an area does differ only in degrees – but not in substance – from the task of unifying the law among member states of a federation. The German Commercial Code of 1861 and the American Uniform Commercial Code can be cited as examples of such successful unifications. Here, as well as in a number of countries with a common background, the pressures of commercial interests have proved strong enough to achieve a unification not restricted to sales of an international nature, but covering the law of *all* sales, including those of a domestic nature. Especially the Scandinavian Sales Law is an early example of such a regional unification.

This situation has changed though with the growing tendency to introduce statutory provisions for the purpose of protecting the general public or, at least, certain groups of persons against certain dangers inherent to the principle of freedom of contract. In the law of sales, the first rules of such a character were special regulations for the protection of instalment buyers.

Now, a great number of proposals are designed to regulate and restrict contracts of adhesion (i.e. General Sales Conditions – Allgemeine Geschäftsbedingungen (AGB) and Formularverträge) in general or at least with regard to consumer sales; other proposals provide for special consumer protection, some of which have been enacted. Such provisions of the law serve the function of providing a yard-stick against which the fairness of contractual provisions has to be measured. They are the tools with which to carry out special legal policies.

Differences between members of a regional unification project as to aims and to the extent to which such policies should be pursued go to the substance and not only to procedure or techniques of unification. As long as such policies exist, the desired unification cannot be achieved and an existing unification can be endangered. The new development in Scandinavia offers a good example. As I learned recently from Professor Hellner, it is Finlands declared intention to adopt the Scandinavian Sales Law, but only in a modernized form. But so far, a re-examination and modernization could not be achieved by the member states which is partly due to the differences in certain protective policies. Sweden has now, apart from the general sales law, enacted a special consumer sales law. Thereby, the desired new rules can be created without endangering the existing unity which remains unchanged with respect to all sales and is only being supplemented in the case of consumer sales.

Unification of sales law in the European Community

The Scandinavian example shows that the chances for regional unification of law will be reduced whenever questions of public policy are regarded as being of great important in a special area. This may be one of the reasons, why the European Communities have, so far, not attempted to achieve a complete unification of their sales laws. It is well known that six original members have only agreed to enact the Hague Uniform Laws, and the United Kingdom ratified the Convention even before entering the common market, although only with the reservation provided for in article V of the Convention.

It is to be welcomed that the members of the European Community have taken The Hague Sales Laws as a ready made set of provisions for the desired unification instead of starting to work out a new set of rules. This helped to further the aim of a more universal unification to which a new project of a regional character could be an obstacle.

But, it must be asked, whether the restriction to apply The Hague Sales Laws only to sales of an international character, should be upheld even within the European Community. The resulting fraction of the sales law into an international and a home market sales law could lead to certain difficulties within the framework of the Community which are not necessarily felt to the same degree in a purely international setting.

One example are the so-called "back-to-back contracts" *contrats de suite*. Whenever an exporter into another common market country has to obtain export goods from a seller in his home market, the exporter is interested in entering into a contract under which the liability of his supplier will be in accordance with the exporter's own liability towards the buyer in the other country with whom he has contracted. Not only liability for delay, for nonconforming goods and for other breaches should be in harmony, but also the requirements, especially the time limits for exercising contractual rights, must coincide. This can be achieved by the use of the same standard conditions for both transactions or by a provision providing for application of the same law to both contracts. The latter is of special importance whenever an agreement as to standard provisions cannot be reached as in some of the well known cases of the "battle of the forms". The advocates of The Hague Law on International Sales hope, of course, that in such situations the parties to an internal transaction will choose The Hague Law as applicable in accordance with article 4 of that law. But, it should not be overlooked that The Hague Law is a "new" law, not yet well known in commercial circles. In commercial circles, at least in Germany, the view is expressed that in such situations the exporter will rather try to reach an agreement that his national law (or even another national law) shall be applied to both transactions. The tendency to exclude application of The Hague Law (in accordance with article 3) could be a serious handicap for the desired unification, especially, in view of the provision that such exclusion may be implied (article 3, second sentence). The use of a contract form using certain legal terms of a particular national system might be sufficient to exclude application of The Hague Law on International Sales under such circumstances.

It should be asked, whether the line should be drawn between international and national sales. As long as no national policies for protecting consumers in the common market or other special groups are involved, it seems that the member countries have a broad common background to make the restriction of The Hague Laws to international sales – necessary for the sake of its universal acceptance – unnecessary.

A comparison of the commercial sales contracts actually in use is needed in order to show to what extent basic differences as to the substance, and not only to procedure and technique of the applicable provisions, still exist. If such a comparison shows that the actual differences are not as great as to prevent unification, it would be possible to adopt The Hague Law as the only sales law within the common market with respect to commercial sales. It would then be left to the member nations to enact special provisions for consumer sales which could supplement or replace the general sales law in this special field. In view of recent experiences, it seems better to create such special provisions for all consumer sales and not to restrict the possibility of exceptions to the narrower field of the different forms of selling goods by instalments. The difficulty of drawing a line between general sales is not unsurmountable. The Hague Law has, for many reasons, not restricted its application to commercial sales.

Recent national legislation for the protection of consumers offers certain guidelines as to how such sales can be defined in order to achieve a clear delimitation.

Summing up

1) A universal unification of the law of international sales seems possible, since no basic differences as to public policies with regard to the field of international sales can be found.
2) In order to avoid conflicts with the desired universal unification, new regional projects should not be restricted to international sales. But a regional unification is useful and can even further universalism, as long as it is designed to cover all sales contracts of a commercial nature within such a region.
3) Unification cannot be successful insofar as different views as to public policies to be pursued exist between the nations involved. But such attitudes do not prevent all unification. It is only necessary to design a unified sales law in such a way as to permit respective nations to supplement it by additional provisions for the purposes of fulfilling such policies, especially in the field of consumer protection.
4) No unification of statutory provisions can be successful as long as

sellers and buyers are not aware of the advantages of the new law and develop a tendency to exclude its application by contractual provisions. It will be a great task for all those desiring unification to "sell" their idea and to develop new contract forms and general conditions which are based on the new unified law.

C. International Carriage by Sea

14

UNIVERSALISM AND REGIONALISM IN THE LAW OF CARRIAGE BY SEA

*Kurt Grönfors**

To a large extent, transportation is international by nature. This is true, as far as maritime and air transportation are concerned; these areas of law might be characterised as global or universal. Carriage by rail, road and inland waterways are geographically less extensive activities, often regional only, but, as parts of combined transports, they still bear the hall-mark of universality. Universal activities require universal legal rules. Obviously, maritime law of today is universal in this sense of the term, founded as it is, on a series of conventions, adopted and adhered to by a great number of nations and based on more or less common traditions of two thousand years. One reason, why uniformity has been such a success in this field of law, is to be found in the traditional machinery of procedure, designed especially to create universal rules, corresponding to the commercial needs of shipping.

In 1897, an international group of maritime law experts founded the International Maritime Committee (*Comité Maritime International—CMI*). National CMI associations were formed in all member countries.

The "transmission belt" for creating new conventions was arranged in the following way. The *Bureau Permanent* of the CMI would choose a suitable subject for a new convention and entrust it to some leading member who would start an initial investigation, usually by sending some sort of questionnaire to other national associations in order to detect the main lines of thought prevailing among experts in various countries. Based upon the information

* Professor of Law, Göteborg Institute of Legal Sciences, University of Göteborg, Sweden.

obtained from the answers would be a provisional draft, which was critically discussed and improved *ad hoc* by an international sub-committee, consisting of representatives from a restricted number of countries. Often, after presentation of an amended second, sometimes even a third or more versions, a draft was presented to an international CMI conference, to which all member countries were invited. At the conference, further amendments were introduced and, finally, a new CMI draft convention was adopted. Up to now, the whole work had been kept within the framework of this private organisation of maritime experts.

Then the project was transferred to government level. At the time, the CMI passed the draft convention to the Belgian Government, which sent it out to other governments with an invitation to a diplomatic conference in Brussels. At this conference, government officials met who would frequently be the same persons as those who had worked within the CMI on the project, thus creating a link between the two stages of development. Further amendments were introduced and, finally, a new convention was adopted and later ratified by countries participating at the conference or adhered to by other countries.

The technique just described, is based on the supposition that it is wise to start a project on a small scale and to widen the circle of individual participants and countries gradually. The effect is the same, as if a person throws a stone into a pool of water; the rings on the surface of the water are small at first, but grow subsequently bigger and bigger. In addition, another important basic idea was to keep maritime law problems as long as possible on an expert level, thus avoiding political difficulties and national prestige.

Surprisingly, this traditional pattern for international maritime legislation has proved itself extremely successful. An impressive number of conventions have been adopted and some of them are of a widely accepted international uniformity. Few branches of law show an equal success.

Obviously, everyone should be most content. Unfortunately, however, this pattern has few chances, if any at all, to operate also successfully in years to come.

A changing world demands changing methods of international legislation.

One reason, for changing the present situation, is a growing difficulty to keep legislative work of this kind on an expert level. Transportation policy is an increasingly important part of trade policy as well as politics as a whole. Thus, governments cannot afford to be passive for long, meeting only at international diplomatic conferences, where so many problems have already been settled at an earlier stage by unofficial experts, with the result that government influence is more or less restricted to details. Governments want to have a steering influence in the preparatory work from the very beginning. As a consequence, international legislative work in maritime law has been entrusted to inter-governmental organisations, like the Inter-Governmental Maritime Consultative Organisation (IMCO) (e.g. the 1969 Liability Convention on Oil Pollution Damage, the Passenger Liability Convention and the Revision of the Global Liability Convention of 1957) and the United Nations Commission on International Trade Law (UNCITRAL) (e.g. revision of the 1924 Convention on Bills of Lading). Both these organisations have an important function in the field of international legislative work today.

Furthermore, the traditional pattern, as referred to, has been an arrangement that is special to maritime law. In other branches of transportation law one has found other means of handling legislation problems. Only the development of air law before the Second World War seemed to follow maritime law procedure closely. The Warsaw Convention was drawn up by a private group of experts in the field of air law, the so-called International Technical Committee of Legal Experts on Air Questions (*Comité International Technique d'Experts Juridiques Aériens*—CITEJA), and adopted by a diplomatic conference held at Warsaw in 1929. But, as a result of the Second World War, this procedure was changed into a governmentally run pattern, and the International Civil Aviation Organisation (ICAO), being the air agency of the United Nations, now presents itself as a natural centre.

Since the end of the nineteenth century, European railways, mostly state owned and operated, have their own organisation in Berne, where governments meet regularly to amend the railway conventions. The road hauliers of Europe got their liability convention through governmental work carried out by the Economic Commission for Europe (ECE) within the framework of the United Nations. The first fundamental preparatory work was done by the International Institute for the Unification of Private Law (UNIDROIT) in Rome, an expert organisation attached to the United Nations and thus being a governmental organisation. It would appear, therefore, that a natural framework for collaboration in the field of transportation law must be seen today in the big conglomerate of regional and world-wide organisations of the United Nations. This must also be true, as far as maritime law is concerned, as this branch, in fact, integrates with other branches of transportation law through the development of combined transports and container traffic and cannot exist in isolation any longer.

Another factor of fundamental importance is that the structure of the world community has changed considerably during the last years. The decolonization has forced us to reconsider the position of developing countries in relation to developed countries. The creation of the United Nations Conference on Trade and Development (UNCTAD), as a special forum for the developing countries within the United Nations, is only one example of the radically changing situation. Governments of developing countries do not look upon maritime legislation as a speciality without any political impact, but as one of many policy questions, influencing the position of developing countries in the world economy.

Thus, they do not want to entrust the main part of the preparatory work to small groups of experts originating only from developed countries. From the very beginning, work must be carried out by sufficiently representative bodies, which means that they expand necessarily into large groups. And here, we reach the natural limit of efficient co-operation when pioneering new drafts. At the same time, possible conflicting interests between developed and developing countries polarise at such an early stage of work, that problems are not yet sufficiently elaborated and analysed to allow meaningful arguments on the subject. This is a very effective method of destroying any project from the very beginning.

All these changes of working conditions have created serious difficulties in applying a traditional pattern to create universal rules on maritime law as well as other transportation laws. It is my belief that the golden days of the traditional conventions, aiming directly at global acceptance, have now come to an end. It is extremely difficult to achieve unanimity, or, at least, a substantial majority for the detailed legal rules on carriage of goods at one single conference or, at least, at a few international conferences. The legislative history of the Draft Convention on Combined Transport of Goods (TCM) offers one good example, because it has now been tossed around for years between various United Nations organisations like IMCO, ECE and ICAO. The United Nations Commission on International Trade Law (UNCITRAL) revision of The Hague rules seems to be very successfull, however, after having been completed, it has to pass its test: the approval by a substantial majority of nations. The amount of work required today, in order to reach this goal, is undoubtedly much greater and much more complicated than before. Thus, the risk of failure has increased.

Under these circumstances, the vital question of today must be this: "Are there any other procedural means to achieve uniformity of maritime law, except by way of drafting and adopting international conventions aiming at universality?"

Fortunately enough, this question can be answered in the affirmative and I will endeavour to elaborate my points of view on this subject a little further.

One way out could be to concentrate on adopting regional conventions, in the hope that they will be able to prove their suitability and thus, eventually, be adopted by such a wide circle of nations that they deserve to be called universal. Such a hope is not necessarily in vain. If I may refer to my earlier illustration, this is one way of regaining some of the efficiency of the lost effect of the rings on a water surface growing successively bigger.

Once again, the Warsaw Convention offers a useful example. It originated *de facto* as a European convention, influenced mainly by French and German legislative traditions. England did participate in the preparatory work, but obviously looked upon the efforts as of more or less Continental concern, English vital interests not being severely affected, and the United States had sent only two observers.

The unusual concise and generally framed articles can only be explained by the small number of nations participating in the preparatory work as well as their legal background. Transocean flights became a reality during the thirties and forties; the South Atlantic route was mainly developed by the French, the Asian route by the

Dutch and the North Atlantic route primarily by two United States carriers. The practical thing to do for establishing routes was to adhere to the Warsaw Convention, which thus expanded into a world-wide legal arrangement.

The development of railway laws in Europe gives another example, how a regional pattern can be expanded. The Berne Convention inspired a Railway Convention for Eastern Europe, the Agreement Concerning the International Rail Transport of Goods (Russian initials: *SMGS*) which, as far as liability is concerned, comes very close to the Berne Convention. In addition, special rules on co-operation between the two Conventions, in principle with the effect that westbound traffic over the border line follows the Berne Convention and eastbound traffic the SMGS, have harmonized the West European-East European law of railway transportation in an admirable way.

In the future, a third possibility might be offered by the Convention on the Contract for the International Carriage of Goods by Road (CMR). In reality, this Convention is a common market project, adopted also by some other states geographically surrounding the common market. A growing roll on-roll off traffic with the help of trucks between the European and the North American market would make it desirable and worth while to adopt the CMR in the United States and Canada. Though, no official moves have been made in this direction, the idea of taking this step from regionalism to universalism has been informally touched upon many times.

Regionalism does not necessarily imply that countries, co-operating and forming a region, must also be neighbours in the geographical sense of the word. A number of geographically divided countries could have a "regionally" common interest to accept one convention. This method might be applicable as one way of solving the difficulties connected with the Draft TCM Convention on Combined Transports. Developing countries have opposed to follow a particular legal system, and the real interest of having a new convention in this matter is represented by the big maritime nations, highly industrialized and with sophisticated transportation systems between the European, North American, Japanese and Australian markets, i.e. more or less between the industrialized or "Western" countries. As a general rule, I think, we should try to avoid polarizing the interests of developed and developing countries. But, in so far as the interests of the latter group are not effected, as seems to be the case if the convention is made optional, and leave old trade patterns unharmed as long as merchants want to follow them, the interests of those, really wanting to have the convention for the traffic of their own without imposing it on other countries, could be preserved by such a regional project.

Regionalism becomes even more valuable if it is no longer combined with the old dogmatic concept of international conventions, as the only effective way of creating uniform legal rules and thus harmonizing law. In fact, there are many other methods at hand.

One method is the creation of a model law, like the Uniform Commercial Code (UCC) in the United States which will be followed in the future by many nations when they form their national statutes. The "radiation effect" of the UCC on North American state legislations has been most impressive. The same effect could develop on the international level too. The draft TCM Convention has already inspired important documents launched by international organisations, e.g. the FIATA Bill of Lading by the International Federation of Forwarding Agents Associations (*Fédération Internationale des Associations de Transitaires et Assimilés*—FIATA), the Combiconbill by the Baltic and International Maritime Conference (BIMCO) and the document form on combined transports in preparation by the International Chamber of Commerce (ICC).

Another method is, to leave it to the organisations of commercial life, to create standard rules that can be incorporated in contracts by reference. One option offers the INCOTERMS. Close to this method comes, for instance, the adoption of rules on minimum requirements, which could also offer a solution to the problem of combined transports.

No doubt, any solution which is not based on the traditional concept of conventions will have its drawbacks, since there will be no guarantee for real uniformity. In fact, experiences of various standard documents for combined transport is evidence enough. On the other hand, speed and flexibility will be gained, while the drawing up and conclusion of international conventions is a time-consuming affair, not to speak of the time it will take for a convention to enter into force. Much less time is needed by commercially interested parties to agree upon the terms of standard documents which, in any case, can be easily amended to meet particular needs.

Commercial law has, for many centuries, proved its tremendous power of introducing uniform rules for international trade. None has shown the development of the new law merchant as a legal system of its own in a more persuasive way than Professor C. M. Schmitthoff. However, one condition for future success is to look in an unconventional way at the tools available for the harmonization of law. International legislation has to find additional new roads. If it works open-mindedly, it will also succeed in the future, irrespectively of any difficulties some lawyers and politicians might create.

15

UNIVERSALISM AND REGIONALISM IN THE LAW OF CARRIAGE BY SEA: THE IMCO EXPERIENCE

*Thomas A. Mensah**

The Convention which established the Inter-Governmental Maritime Consultative Organisation (IMCO) envisaged that IMCO would provide for consideration of any matters concerning shipping and, more specifically, for the consideration of matters concerning "unfair restrictive practices by shipping concerns". In spite of this expectation IMCO did not, for reasons which fall outside the scope of this paper, concern itself directly with the law relating to carriage of goods by sea, until very recently. Since 1969, however, IMCO has acted as the forum for a number of activities in relation to the liability of shipowners.

Following the "Torrey Canyon" disaster of 1967, the Council of IMCO set in motion a programme of work in the legal field which has resulted in two diplomatic conferences and four conventions namely:

1. The 1969 Convention Relating to Intervention on the High Seas in Cases of Oil Pollution Casualties
2. The 1969 Convention on Civil Liability for Oil Pollution Damage
3. The 1971 Convention on the Establishment of an International Fund for Compensation for Oil Pollution Damage, and
4. The 1971 Convention Relating to Civil Liability in the Field of the Maritime Carriage of Nuclear Material.

* Head of the Legal Division of IMCO, the Inter-Governmental Maritime Consultative Organisation, London, England.

The views expressed in this paper are solely those of the author. They are not in any way to be attributed to the Organisation or to its Secretariat.

In addition, IMCO is currently engaged in preparing draft instruments on:

(a) The conditions of carriage of passengers and their luggage on board ships
(b) The limitation of liability of the owners of sea-going ships.

As is well known, IMCO co-sponsored with the Economic Commission for Europe (ECE) the programme for developing a Convention on Combined Transport of Goods (TCM). This attempt proved abortive in the event; but the work so far done can be expected to have a significant influence on the eventual international instrument which, it is hoped, will emerge on the subject in the near future.

In addition to work which it has sponsored on its own or together with others IMCO has, of course, keenly followed and actively participated in the work of the United Nations Conference on Trade and Development (UNCTAD) on international legislation on shipping.

However, with the exception of a very limited number of projects, the main thrust of IMCO's work in this field has been more oriented to the liability of the shipowner, vis-à-vis third parties as a result of the operation of the law, rather than with the liability of the shipowner towards the shipper, consignee or other persons entitled to goods carried on board ships. In other words (and perhaps oversimplifying the matter somewhat), IMCO's work has been principally concerned with the *tort law* in the field of shipping rather than with the *law of contract*. This is, of course, not entirely true of all IMCO's work. The work which was done in connexion with the TCM Convention was aimed at producing a Convention on a Combined Transport Contract, and to provide for the contractual rights and obligations of the carrier (CTO) and the shipper. And the work being currently done on a Convention on the Carriage of Passengers and their Luggage will, in a real sense, regulate the rights and obligations of passenger-ship operators which arise from contracts of carriage entered into with passengers. Similarly, the projected work on the revision of the 1957 Convention on the Limitation of the Liability of the Owners of Sea-Going Ships will involve consideration of the obligations of shipowners both to persons with whom they contract as well as to "third parties".

In spite, however, of these exceptions, it has to be admitted that the bulk of IMCO's work in relation to shipping law has been and will probably continue to be directed more towards the regulating of the rights and obligations of shipowners to "the world at large" rather than towards the development of uniform contractual norms to regulate the relationship between shippers and shipowners.

But, although the direct impact of IMCO's work in the law of carriage by sea is limited, the lessons to be drawn from this work may not be so irrelevant to the work in other organisations. After all, IMCO was the first body of global participation and orientation to be engaged in the work of developing international shipping law. Previous to, and for a long time after, the establishment of IMCO, this work had been done in organisations which were not, and could not even pretend to be, global in participation or in outlook. The International Maritime Committee (Comité Maritime International – CMI), which has perhaps played a greater and more influential role in this field, has, throughout its successful career, drawn contributions and support mainly from the developed maritime countries of Europe and North America and has never really been able to attract much attention, support or sympathy from the countries of the third world; and the participation of socialist countries in the CMI is a very recent phenomenon. It is not necessary here to give an explanation as to why this was so, and why, to a large extent, little has changed in the meantime. The reasons are many, not all, or perhaps even most of them, may justifiably be laid at the door of the CMI. Be that as it may, the fact remains that, even now, many countries of the developing world do not participate in the CMI and do not consider that participation therein would be of any benefit to them. On the other hand, IMCO was conceived as an organisation in which all countries, developing as well as developed, could and were expected to operate on an equal footing. And although the attitude of these countries to IMCO has, in the past, been rather lukewarm, there has always been some developing country representation in IMCO, a representation which has increased considerably in recent times. Indeed, it can now be said that the factors which operate in the United Nations organisations, such as UNCTAD and the United Nations Commission on International Trade Law (UNCITRAL), have been and are at work in IMCO, if not to the same degree and with the same results, at least in the same general way. Therefore, the IMCO experience can, with some justification, be said to be typical of the experience of the truly and effectively global organisations which have concerned themselves in this area.

As with most United Nations organisations IMCO, although an inter-governmental organisation with a global mandate and global memberships, has, in almost all it does, to take account of the circumstances, interests and wishes of governments of states and countries which belong to given regions, particular political orientations or groupings determined by some other criteria. Indeed, it may well be said that the need to give special attention to these sectional needs and desires, is a necessary consequence of the global nature of the Organisation's objectives; but this is a matter of opinion and, in any event, its discussion need not concern us here. The fact, however, remains that in the work of the United Nations and its organisations, special emphasis has always been placed on the special needs and problems of groups of states. One of the groups whose interests and needs have been consistently emphasized throughout the United Nations system has, of course, been the group of developing countries.

Similarly, the United Nations system has pratically institutionalised certain groupings of states for a whole host of purposes. The most interesting and relevant one for our purpose is the grouping of the governments in UNCTAD into the group of developed market economy states, the group of socialist states of Eastern Europe and the Group of seventy-seven being the group of the developing countries of Africa, Asia and Latin America. While this grouping of states operates as a formal arrangement only in UNCTAD, it operates, in effect, in almost all United Nations organisations, including IMCO. And in matters relating to economic development and trade, the positions of the states in these groups are almost predictably uniform. This has been particularly so in the work on the development of the law of international shipping and the law of carriage by sea. While IMCO work has been spared (or denied) the full effects of this phenomenon, it has had to take it into account in a real sense; and the trends which have emerged in IMCO appear to be more or less the same as those observable in other United Nations organisations. For this reason it appears to me, that it would be more accurate and more helpful if we looked, not at the IMCO experience, but at the United Nations experience. And it is with the lessons and trends to be drawn from the United Nations experience as a whole that I intend to deal hereafter. These may be summarized as follows:

The developed maritime states (including the developed maritime states of the East European socialist block), with their long-established maritime tradition and an acknowledged rôle in the development of the existing international rules of law relating to carriage of goods by sea, have been willing, and in some cases anxious, to use the machinery provided by IMCO and other United Nations organisations to extend the scope of existing maritime law régimes and to modify these régimes only where this is necessary in order to take account of the changes which have occurred in the pattern and character of world trade since these régimes were developed. The developed states have proceeded on the assumption that the régimes themselves are basically sound, requiring adjustments and modifications in parts, but not, in any way, in need of a complete change or even a drastic overhaul.

On the other hand the developing countries are mainly "shipper" countries without long-established maritime traditions, and they did not participate in the development of the existing legal régimes. For this reason they have generally taken the view that the régimes, which were developed in the past to regulate the relations between different developed countries, are no longer suitable to regulate the relations between developed countries and developing countries, or even between different developing countries. They have, therefore, tended to demand entirely new régimes which should be elaborated in United Nations fora (in which the developing countries feel they have a truly effective say) and which can, therefore, be expected to take more account of the facts of to-day, including the needs and special circumstances of developing countries.

This basic difference in attitude is illustrated by the respective positions taken by developed states and developing countries in connexion with the revision of the Hague-Visby Rules on Bills of Lading. When UNCITRAL considered this subject at its fifth session in April/May 1972, representatives of the developing states expressed the view that the existing rules on Bills of Lading were "outmoded and the UNCITRAL working group should, therefore, draft a new

Convention rather than merely revise the 1924 Brussels Convention and the Hague Protocol of 1968". In particular, it was suggested that "the new Convention should be based on the carriers' contractual responsibility for the safe delivery of the cargo" and further that "the new rules should be patterned after other international conventions concerned with the transport of goods." In direct opposition to this, the representatives of developed countries felt that, while the 1924 Brussels Convention should be revised, this Convention's provisions "were based on substantial experience which should not be cast aside. Consequently, proposals for changes should be carefully considered and implemented only with a view to the practical advantages that might be derived from such changes". Some of the delegations observed, in particular, that it should be borne in mind that conditions of ocean transport were still very different from those of other modes of transport.[1]

The same disagreement manifested itself in the discussions concerning the liability régime of the TCM Convention, with the developing countries (this time supported by the United States of America and Canada) demanding that a new and stricter system of liability, analogous to that operating in air transport, be adopted while the maritime states of Europe and Japan contended that nothing should be done, at least in the TCM Convention, to subsume the régime of liability under maritime law to other régimes whose circumstances, according to these states, were different from those of maritime transport.

There has also been disagreement between the developing countries and the developed countries as to the means of achieving the required modifications in the legal régimes. While the developing countries believe that the development of what they consider to be an equitable and effective régime can only be achieved by means of state action at national level and inter-governmental agreement at the international level, the developed countries do not appear to have so much belief in the appropriateness or efficacy of state intervention in this field. They tend generally to favour self-regulation by the parties involved and

1. See Report of UNCITRAL on the work of its fifth session – Official Records of the General Assembly, 27th session: Supplement No. 17 (A/8717), pages 26 and 27, paragraphs 47 and 48.

such self-regulation is, no doubt, promoted and aided by the operation of market forces. This basic disagreement is exemplified by the attitude of the developing and developed countries as to the appropriate and useful rôle which UNCTAD or UNCITRAL may play in the development of international shipping legislation. The developing countries have generally been in favour of a decidedly activist rôle for these bodies. Both, in relation to the revision of the Hague-Visby Rules, the development of a Code of Conduct for Liner Conferences and in the discussions of the TCM Convention, developing countries delegates insisted that UNCTAD and UNCITRAL should have the task, not merely of encouraging and co-ordinating work carried out elsewhere, but also that they should themselves undertake work on their own "in order to reduce and remove obstacles to the flow of international trade". The position of the developing countries is exemplified by the following statement from the Chamber of Shipping of the United Kingdom: "The increasing trend towards governmental intervention is evident in some countries and in UNCTAD. British shipowners stand for free enterprise and free competition ... what they say is, let the forces of the market place work. ... UNCTAD in this has an important part to play which, wisely used, can assist shipping and world trade. If, however, it allows itself to develop into a machine for the furtherance of discrimination and of nationalistic tendencies on the part of one group of countries against another or of erecting the paraphernalia of bureaucracy on an international plane to control, what are essentially commercial matters, then world trade (quite apart from shipping) will suffer. This is not to argue for a policy of laissez-faire. Control of some sort is necessary; but in the view of British shipowners, this should be through self-regulation and the commercial settlement of disputes". The statement went on to describe the achievements of the consultative machinery established through liner conferences and shippers' councils. It concluded: "The benefits are clear, not only in practical terms, but also as a demonstration of the irrelevance of governmental intervention where no constructive results ensue or where it merely amounts to interference, for the sake of interference, in commercial matters".[2]

2. See Annual Report of the Chamber of Shipping of the United Kingdom, 1968, pp. 29 to 30.

The disagreement reflected by the above quotations has been, and remains, basic to all the discussions in IMCO and elsewhere in the United Nations system, on the future of development of international law relating to shipping in general and the carriage of goods by sea in particular. And this disagreement is not based on regional attitudes or regional conditions as such. It is based primarily, if not solely, on the stage of economic development and hence on the commercial power of individual countries. The position of states have been less influenced by their regional location and more by their state of economic and industrial development. Thus Japan, geographically an Asian country, consistently and, in some cases, more emphatically shares the views of the developed countries. Similarly, Australia and New Zealand adopt generally a position much closer to the Western Europeans and North Americans than the position of, say, Indonesia which is their geographical neighbour.

In this, the position of the socialist countries of Eastern Europe is particularly revealing. While, in most other political issues, these countries readily make common cause with the developing countries as against the "developed market economy" countries, this alliance does not function in the discussions relating to the law of international shipping. Here, the position of the socialist states is, in general, barely distinguishable from that of the developed market-economy states. Thus, the socialist states join the developed market economy states in defending the present system of shipping law and advocating only minor adjustments thereto. Similarly, the insistence on the application of market forces and self-regulation has not been confined to the traditionally capitalist states. This insistence has been equally championed by the developed countries of the socialist block. In the discussions on the Terms of Shipment at the third session of the UNCTAD Committee on Shipping, representatives of a socialist country of Eastern Europe states that a central organisation had been established in that country to deal with freight rate questions, but it had been found, on the basis of experience, that no one principle could be applied in arranging the terms of shipment and, besides, that the terms of shipment must be fixed mutually by the sellers and buyers themselves.[3] It is interesting to compare this with the position of the

3. See Report of UNCTAD Committee on Shipping on its Third Session, 9 to 25 April 1969 – TD/B/240, TD/B/C.4/55, p. 4, paragraph 6.

representatives of the developed market economy countries who stated that in their opinion, "the selection of the most appropriate terms of shipment should be decided by the parties freely exercising their choice. They stated that it could have harmful effects on trade to state general principles on the line of policy to be followed in respect of terms of shipment." [4]

In the discussions on the TCM Convention the position of the socialist countries was the same as the position taken by most of the developed market economy countries, not only with regard to the need for a convention, but also with regard to the necessity or advisability of a revision of the present régime of liability in respect of the maritime leg of combined transport operations.

There has been occasional disunity in the ranks, even of the developing countries, where the economic interests of various countries have not been exactly the same. Thus, while UNCTAD was discussing the subject of terms of payment at the third session of the Shipping Committee, the representative of a Latin American country indicated that "his country's experience and practice with regard to terms of shipment was somewhat different from other Latin American countries, and more advantageous than theirs". He described how, by the use of the liner conference arrangement, his country had been able to obtain more favourable terms.[5]

It is true that the countries of certain regions such as Western Europe (and especially the Nordic and Scandinavian countries), generally take common stands on questions of shipping law but this is due, not so much to their regional location as to the fact that these states happen to have the same economic and commercial interests. Mexico, for example, does not take the same position as the United States, and in certain cases, as in the case of liability of shipowners (whether to shippers in respect of loss or damage to cargo or to third parties in respect of pollution damage), the position adopted by the United States and Canada approximates that adopted by the developing countries, since both countries regard themselves, in this particular regard, more as shipper and "coastal" states than as "maritime" or shipping states.

4. See Report, p. 4, paragraph 5.
5. See Third Report, p. 3, paragraph 4.

At the 1969 IMCO Conference on Marine Pollution Damage and, to a lesser extent, at the 1971 Conference to adopt a Compensation for Oil Pollution Damage, it was noticeable that the more developed countries among the developing states, especially India and Brazil (which also happen to be relatively important shipping nations), took a slightly different position from that adopted by the developing countries. Brazil and India were openly against imposing strict liability on the shipowner in respect of pollution damage, and joined major shipping countries from Europe (West and East) and Japan in insisting on liability based on fault. When they failed to get this accepted, they made their acceptance of the 1969 Convention conditional on the establishment of a fund to which contributions were to be made by the oil industry and which would provide, *inter alia,* some relief to shipowners in respect of the financial burdens imposed on them by the 1969 Convention. It is significant that in this the United States, Canada and Australia shared a common cause with the rest of the developing countries, while the Soviet Union and Japan joined the Western Europeans, Brazil and India. Very little evidence of regional groupings or solidarity was to be seen in this line up. The same alignment of countries emerged in the discussions of the draft TCM Convention with the Western European and the Socialist countries, plus Japan, in favour of the net-work system (which left the maritime law liability régime intact where the damage or loss was known to have been caused during the maritime leg), while the United States, Canada, Australia and New Zealand joined the developing countries in supporting a uniform system of liability based on strict liability. Here were a few defections from the Western European camp, notably by France and, at a later stage, by the Nordic countries, which attempted to promote a compromise designed to persuade the developing countries to drop their total opposition to the TCM Convention. On the whole, therefore, it can be said that the position adopted by states does not depend on a regional association but on economic, industrial or commercial considerations.

Another significant fact, which emerges from the experience of IMCO and of other United Nations organisations is, that even though the countries of the same "economic grouping" generally take a common stand on most issues, none of these groups suggests, or would accept, that the solutions they advocate, should be applied only within their groups. On the contrary, it is always the main purpose of the groups to persuade the others to accept their preferred solutions for application on a universal basis. Thus, when the developing countries advocate the adoption of a new law on the bills of lading and on liner conferences and when they firmly demand that these new laws should be adjusted to the needs and requirements of developing countries (sometimes even to the extent of affording preferential treatment to such countries) they, at the same time, demand that the new law should be applicable globally. And this is only reasonable and natural. For it would be of no use to the developing countries if any such new laws were to be applicable at regional level, since the very purpose of the developing countries is to have new (and more favourable) laws to regulate the trade relations between them and the developed countries. It is with the developed countries that the countries of the developing world have their most significant trade relations and it is in respect of this trade that the need for more favourable trade laws is most felt. Hence, the solutions which are devised at regional level and with regional needs most in mind are meant, and acknowledged to be, for global application. Similarly, when the developed countries, for instance, promoted the adoption of the TCM Convention and, when they defended the continued application of existing laws and practice (in some cases by opposing the making of any general law at all), they did not limit their concern to the relationships between themselves. On the contrary, they insisted that there was need for a common system and régime which should apply to the trade relationship of all nations. They advocate acceptance of this principle and acceptance of a common law and practice where appropriate only, because they are concerned that discriminating policies and governmental intervention at national or regional level would not be in the interest of shipping and world trade. Both in IMCO and in UNCTAD, the developed countries had stated over and over again that they were in favour of "international uniformity in the legal regulation of multimodal transport" and stated that "the application of a uniform legal régime to international combined transport of goods would bring considerable benefit to international trade".[6]

6. See Report, p. 6, paragraphs 36 and 39.

It is true that some developing countries advocate the right of state intervention, but this is usually to enable them to deal with particular problems in their countries and in any case, they always insist on this right being accepted and acknowledged universally. As far as they are concerned, what is advocated is a universal recognition of the necessity and appropriateness of governments intervening in this field, where the conditions and circumstances permit or require such intervention. This right of intervention is claimed for countries whose conditions require them to do so, irrespective of their regional location.

It is very rare to find a group of governments suggesting that a solution, which appears to them to be just and acceptable, should be applied only in some regions. The nature and pattern of world trade relations do not make such "regional rules" either realistic or useful. Those, who formulate rules and systems on the basis of regional solidarity (or, more accurately, solidarity based on common economic, industrial or commercial circumstances), are almost always interested in getting these rules and systems applied universally. Hardly ever do they suggest or agree that, what they propose, should be applied among themselves while others apply their own rules and practices. When at the UNCTAD Committee on Shipping (Second Special Session) the representatives of the developing countries suggested that, "if a group of countries was willing to take the risks involved (in a TCM Convention), those countries could experiment with the application of an interim convention among themselves," it was more in reply to the threat from some developing countries that failure to adopt a TCM Convention in the United Nations might result in a regional or less global convention with which some of the developing countries would be obliged to live in their trade with states which became parties to the new instrument. The suggestion, that action could be taken by a group of states was therefore more of a taunt than a serious proposition. The underlying argument was not whether a uniform régime was desirable, but whether such a régime was feasible and opportune at the time.

It appears clear, therefore, that whether countries group together by virtue of a common economic interest or regional solidarity or by virtue of some other criterion, they do so, to agree on common solutions, to be urged on other groups of states for adoption and application on a global basis. The motives for particular solutions may be, and usually are, sectional. But, they are put forward as appropriate for universal application.

Conclusion

There is very little evidence that, in the development of the law of carriage by sea in IMCO and other United Nations organisations, regionalism as such has played a major rôle either with regard to positions adopted by states as to the laws to be adopted or in regard to the law and practice of individual states. There have, no doubt, been groupings of states which have adopted common positions, both in respect of the laws which should apply and also in regard to the changes which should be made in such laws. But, those groupings have been based more on economic and commercial factors rather than a regional consideration. Where countries of the same region have taken a common stance, as has generally been the case with the developing countries of Africa, Latin America and Asia or the developed countries of Europe, the reason has been that they have common or more or less common, economic and industrial interests. Where there are no such common interests, different countries in the same region take different positions, and the alignment of states transcends regional location. There is no evidence that this tendency will be reversed; all the evidence would appear to indicate that this will remain a feature of the United Nations process in this field.

It is also significant to note that, whilst the various groupings of states – not necessarily or even often regional in outlook – will continue to adopt common positions and co-ordinate their policies and practices, they will continue to advocate the universal or wide acceptance of these policies and will work for the application of their suggested régimes, not on a regional or other sectional basis but rather on a global international plane. The impact of regionalism (or more strictly the effect of state groupings based on a function of economic development and industrial and commercial power) will, I believe, continue to be in the formulation of the objectives which motivate the various policies proposed, in the devising of the methods by which they are urged on the international level and in the results which such urging will eventually have in the final solutions adopted and applied at world level. And the objectives and strategy adopted by states will depend less on regional thinking than on straightforward national economic and commercial interests. The more it becomes true to say that the economic and commercial stake of the various countries in a uniform world order is the same (and the more the majority of states are enabled to recognize that this is so), the less likely it is that regional or sectional approaches will loom large in the development of the law of carriage by sea and the general law of international trade. But, unless the states of different regions come to recognize that global uniform rules are relevant to, compatible with and adequate to satisfy their particular needs, they will either seek to change these rules in order to give themselves the advantages they want, or failing that, they will seek to construct sectional arrangements of their own. It is such sectional arrangements, erected in frustration and pique, which would have a disruptive effect on a much-needed world order. So far, the regional or sectional movements have, at least in the field of maritime carriage of goods, been aimed at infusing sectional objectives into world-wide régimes, with a view to making these régimes universally acceptable. If this trend continues, as I hope it will, then there will be no reason for pessimism about the attainment, in time, of that uniformity which alone is desirable because it is obtainable.

D. International Commercial Arbitration

16

UNIVERSALISM AND REGIONALISM IN INTERNATIONAL COMMERCIAL ARBITRATION

*Clive M. Schmitthoff**

The reasons given for the popularity of arbitration in international commercial transactions are normally that arbitration is held in private and avoids publicity, that it is less formal than the procedures of many national courts, and that it is cheaper and more speedy than court proceedings, although those experienced in commercial arbitration know that the last mentioned two reasons are not always correct. Avoidance of publicity and informality are certainly reasons for the preference, by merchants, of arbitration to litigation but the main reason for the popularity of arbitration in international business transactions is that that it is the only means of settling disputes appropriate to the international character of the transaction. We have no international commercial court. The only alternative to international arbitration is to commence proceedings in a national court. That, however, imports a degree of uncertainty. First, it has to be ascertained whether a particular national court has jurisdiction to entertain the action. If several national courts are competent, the claimant can engage in the practice of forum shopping, i.e. he can choose the forum which he considers most favourable to him. Some lawyers regard the possibility of forum shopping as regrettable, but the present author does not accept that view; he thinks that, as the claimant has the choice of deciding whether to pursue his claim at all or to desist, it is not unfair that he should be allowed to choose the

* Dr. jur. (Berlin); LL.M., LL.D. (London), F.I.Ex., Barrister, Visiting Professor of International Business Law at the City University and the University of Kent at Canterbury, England; Hon. Professor of Law at the Ruhr University, Bochum, The Federal Republic of Germany; Editor of the Journal of Business Law.

battleground. More serious objections to national litigation arise from the danger of multiplicity of actions in several national courts. This can happen in various ways. A plaintiff starts proceedings in country A; he encounters difficulties, e.g. a demand for security for costs, and he then commences proceedings founded on the same cause of action in country B. Or one of two co-plaintiffs starts proceedings in country A and the other in country B. Or the plaintiff brings his action in country A and the defendant who thinks that he has a claim arising from the same transaction against the plaintiff sues in country B. In all these cases a procedural mechanism must be devised to avoid multiplicity of proceedings in several national courts. Further, in some countries the national courts are not suitable to deal with international commercial transactions. That applies, in particular, to the countries of state-planned economy. The disputes which arise in their national courts are basically different from those in which their foreign trade corporations, which enjoy a monopoly in export and import trade, may become involved. That is the reason why all these countries have established foreign trade arbitration commissions. These tribunals are essentially arbitration tribunals but in some respects they can be compared with the commercial courts which are constituted in many countries of the free market economy.

Since international arbitration is the only type of procedure appropriate for the settlement of disputes arising from or connected with international business transactions, one should expect that international commercial arbitration is one of the topics which are uniformly regulated throughout the world. That, however, is not the case. The reasons for the absence of a truly world-wide uniform regulation of international commercial arbitration are not far to seek. They are partly historical; thus, the great commodity associations with world-wide ramifications have devised their own arbitration procedures. Partly they are economic; thus, the preponderant position of the United States in international trade has led to the expansion of the influence of American arbitration rules. Partly, they are of economic-political character; thus, the division of the world into countries of free market economy which all accept the co-existence of a private and public sector of business and are, therefore, sometimes referred to as countries of mixed economy, and those of state-planned economy is a divisive factor in international arbitration. While thus the regional element is still strong in international arbitration and a characteristic feature of the pattern, as it presents itself today, there exists in recent years a growing tendency to universalism in this field – a hopeful sign which finds its clearest expression in the publication of the United Nations Commission on International Trade Law (UNCITRAL) Arbitration Rules adopted on April 28, 1976.[1]

The four areas of international commercial arbitration

In view of the inherently international character of the arbitration rules to be considered here it is not appropriate to arrange this subject according to regions, because a region has a local connotation. It is better to refer to the four great areas of international commercial arbitration.

These four areas are:

(1) the countries of free market economy, in which the Rules of Conciliation and Arbitration of the International Chamber of Commerce (ICC) [2] have special significance;

(2) the area in which the Commercial Arbitration Rules of the American Arbitration Association (AAA), amended and in effect as from November 1, 1973, apply; [3]

The AAA Rules are widely used in the international trade of the United States with Latin America, Japan, Australia, Asia and Africa;

(3) The area covered by the arbitration rules of the Council for Mutual Economic Assistance (CMEA).[4] These are the Arbitration Rules under the General Conditions of Delivery of Goods between

1. UNCITRAL Report on Ninth Session (UN Doc. A/31/17).

2. The latest version of the ICC Rules on Conciliation and Arbitration is that of 1975.

3. The Rules are reproduced in *International Commercial Arbitration* (ed. Clive M. Schmitthoff, Oceana, 1974), p. 329.

4. The CMEA includes the following countries: the Soviet Union, Poland, Czechoslovakia, Hungary, Romania, Bulgaria, the German Democratic Republic and Albania.

Organisations of the member countries of the Council for Mutual Economic Assistance 1968.[5]

(4) The fourth area of international commercial arbitration is covered by the arbitration rules of the great commodity associations, as they exist, e.g. in the United Kingdom, and the Federal German Republic. As illustration, reference may be made to the Arbitration Rules of the Grain and Feed Trade Association (GAFTA, London), effective as from October 1, 1973, those of the Federation of Oils, Seeds and Fats Associations (FOSFA, London) and those of the *Waren-Verein der Hamburger Börse e.V.*

This arrangement is not exhaustive. There exist arbitration arrangements which cannot be classified into any of these areas, although they are derived from rules falling thereunder. Thus, the Arbitration Rules of the Economic Commission for Asia and the Far East (ECAFE) of 1966 [6] are influenced by the American practice, and the Rules of Foreign Trade Arbitration of the Federal Economic Chamber of Yugoslavia of October 9, 1967 [7] have a similarity with the CMEA Rules, but are, in practice, administered more leniently.

Before leaving this subject, a few observations may be made on the arbitration rules just referred to. The ICC Rules have three peculiarities which are adopted by some of the other institutional arbitrations. First, the Arbitration Court of the ICC provides a procedure and a permanent Secretariat and examines the awards with a view of rendering them technically enforceable. The Court itself does not decide, but appoints an arbitrator – and this is the second characteristic feature – of a nationality different from that of the parties. Thirdly, arbitration is preceded by conciliation and the matter proceeds to arbitration only if conciliation fails. The arbitrator is always a person different from the conciliator.

Further, commodity arbitrations are often two-instance arbitrations, viz. an appeal is lodged from the arbitration tribunal to an appeals committee. It is one of the great advantages of institutionalised commodity arbitration to admit an appeal procedure within

5. These Rules are reproduced in *International Commercial Arbitration, op. cit.* in note (3), *supra,* p. 169.

6. *International Commercial Arbitration, op. cit.* in note (3), p. 161.

7. *Ibid.,* p. 239.

the framework of arbitration. In some countries, such as France, an appeal lies from the award, unless given by *amiable compositeurs,* to the ordinary courts.

International arbitration arrangements

Turning now to arrangements on commercial arbitration on the international level, the following are the principal sets of rules which should be mentioned here:

1. First, two international agreements have been concluded in Geneva, the Protocol on Arbitration Clauses of 1923 and the Convention on the Execution of Foreign Arbitral Awards of 1927.[8] They are annexed to the United Kingdom Arbitration Act 1950 as schedules 1 and 2. They are given effect in the United Kingdom and some forty other countries. They deal principally with the mutual recognition and enforcement of foreign arbitral awards.
2. Then, there is the important United Nations Convention on the Recognition and Enforcement of Foreign Arbitral Awards of June 10, 1958.[9] This Convention is designed to supersede the Geneva Protocol and Convention and to introduce a considerable simplification of the procedure for mutual recognition and enforcement of foreign arbitral awards. The New York Convention has been adopted by some forty countries, including the United States of America, the Soviet Union, France and the Federal Republic of Germany. The United Kingdom has enacted the Arbitration Act 1975 which provides the legal basis for giving effect to the New York Convention in the United Kingdom.
3. A European Convention on International Commercial Arbitration was signed at Geneva on April 21, 1961 and came into force on January 7, 1964.[10] A number of important trading nations adhere

8. *International Commercial Arbitration, op. cit.* in note (3), pp. 1 and 5.
9. *International Commercial Arbitration, op. cit.* in note (3), p. 9.
10. *International Commercial Arbitration, op. cit.* in note (3), p. 107. This Convention was amended by the Agreement of Paris relating to the Application of the European Convention on International Commercial Arbitration, December 17, 1962.

to it, including the Soviet Union, France and the Federal Republic of Germany but it has not been accepted by the United States and the United Kingdom. A feature of the European Convention is the constitution of a special committee which consists of a representative of the chambers of commerce of the states in which national committees of the ICC exist (the Western chambers of commerce) and a representative of the Eastern chambers of commerce, under a chairman who holds office for two years and is elected in alternating rotation by the Western and Eastern chambers of commerce. This Convention is of particular importance for East-West trade.
4. Of importance is further the Washington Convention on the Settlement of Investment Disputes between States and Nationals of Other States of October 14, 1965 which was sponsored by the World Bank.[11] On June 30, 1975 not less than sixty-five states had become parties to the Convention, including the United Kingdom which gave effect to the Washington Convention by the Arbitration (International Investment Disputes) Act 1966. On June 30, 1974 five arbitrations were pending under the Washington Convention.
5. On April 28, 1976, UNCITRAL adopted the final draft of the UNCITRAL Arbitration Rules.[12] These Rules are not effective yet, but there is no doubt that they will be eventually effective and, perhaps widely used. They are intended for "optional use in *ad hoc* arbitrations relating to international trade". They are not in the form of a convention, but rather in the form of a uniform law which can be adopted by the parties if they so desire. Although, according to their stated object, they are intended to apply to *ad hoc* arbitrations, they provide that they may be used if the parties have agreed on an "appointing authority".[13] If the parties agree that the arbitration shall be administered by a designated appointing authority, that institutution can perform the following functions: appoint the arbitrators if the parties fail to do so, decide whether a challenge of an arbitrator is justified, collect the deposit for arbitration costs from the parties, and perform other administrative duties. If the parties do not agree on arbitration by a designated

11. *International Commercial Arbitration, op. cit.* in note (3), p. 35.
12. *Op. cit.* in note (1), p. 173.
13. Article 6.

arbitral institution, the UNCITRAL Rules provide procedures for dealing with these matters but in some cases these procedures are necessarily more complex than under an administered arbitration. The Rules also provide that arbitrators must decide according to the law, "taking into account the terms of any contract between the parties and the usages of the trade,"[14] but the arbitrators may decide *ex aequo et bono* (as amiable compositeurs) if the parties have authorised the arbitrators to do so and the arbitration law of the country where the award is rendered permits such arbitration.

Bridging attempts

It is evident from the preceding observations that, apart from commodity arbitrations which, in any event, are in a special category, the areas covered by ICC, AAA and CMEA arbitration are generally speaking, self-contained. That limitation contravenes the fundamental idea explained in the introduction of this essay that international commercial arbitration should be truly international. Particular attention has therefore to be paid to the attempts to bridge the gulf which divides those three areas of arbitration.

1. We have seen [15] that under the European Convention on International Commercial Arbitration of 1961 a special committee is constituted with the object of resolving technical difficulties that may arise in East-West arbitration. This is the most advanced institutional attempt at breaching the dividing line between the areas of international commercial arbitration.
2. Further—and this is a remarkable development—the CMEA countries have constituted a committee of presidents of the national foreign trade arbitration tribunals of the member states of the CMEA and that committee is in regular contact with the Arbitration Court of the ICC. Although this link is informal and tenuous, it is of considerable practical importance. This arrange-

14. Article 33.
15. See p. 176, *ante*.

ment augurs well for the future co-operation in the development of international trade law.

3. Thirdly, the AAA has arrangements with a considerable number of organisations in other countries. These bilateral arrangements aim at the determination of the venue of arbitration and of the application of arbitration rules if the parties have failed to regulate these matters in the arbitration clause. The AAA has such arrangements with the ICC, the Japan Commercial Arbitration Association, the London Court of Arbitration, the Manchester (England) Chamber of Commerce, organisations in Spain, India, Pakistan, Australia, Italy, Poland, Korea and other countries. Typical is the following clause which is taken from the AAA-Japan agreement:

> "Two joint arbitration committees shall be established, one in Tokyo and the other in New York. These committees shall be composed of one US citizen, one Japanese citizen, and a chairman from a third country. Disputes and determinations as to the place of arbitration shall be submitted to the joint committees."

It will be noted that these bridging committees are constituted differently from the special committee constituted under the European Convention of 1961 and their functions are more restricted than those of the special committee.

The bilateral arrangements of the AAA have not been a success. Mr. D. B. Straus, President of the Research Institute of the AAA, writes: [16]

> "I am forced to conclude that bilateral arrangements of the kind described above do not seem to have won much enthusiasm either from the organisations that promoted them or by international lawyers or businessmen. One reason, I suspect, is that, after these agreements are negotiated, they are soon forgotten by those who participated in the negotiations and by their successors. None of them were widely publicised except at the time of their signing. Few members of the AAA staff even know of their existence today, and, of course, even fewer attorneys would be aware of them. Nevertheless, every now and then a case does occur under these joint clauses, and is handled in accordance with their provisions".

4. Lastly, a few years ago an International Committee on Commercial Arbitration was formed. It has its origin in international

16. *International Commercial Arbitration, op. cit.* in note (3), p. 173.

conferences on arbitration held in Moscow, Delhi, and other places. It is informal and its activities are still at the beginning, but it is clear that they are designed to narrow the gulf between the various areas of arbitration.

The future

It has become increasingly obvious that disputes arising from or in connection with international commercial transactions are inherently unsuitable for cognizance by the national courts. The international business community has recognized this, and, hence, the growing trend to international arbitration.

The logical conclusion which one might be tempted to draw from this experience is, that the ultimate goal should be to establish a world-wide network of arbitration tribunals, culminating in a supreme arbitration appeal tribunal to which appeals from all commercial arbitration tribunals would lie in an obligatory and automatic fashion – a hierarchy of commercial arbitration on a world-wide basis, comparable to the hierarchy of national courts which one finds in the administration of justice on the national level. Pure logic would appear to demand such a blue print of a brave new world of international commercial arbitration.

Logic is always a dangerous method in law, because law deals with social and human affairs which are much too multiform to be purely logical. The logical conclusion sketched here is not only utopian and impracticable but, even as a final goal, probably quite undesirable. It overlooks the varying degree of sophistication already achieved in arbitral proceedings and the far from uniform requirements of different types of international transactions.

The most sophisticated organisation of arbitral proceedings known today are the commodity arbitration procedures. Many of them admit already an appeal to an appeal committee. In many countries exists a link between the arbitral tribunals and the courts although outside England and Wales, and now Scotland, the link is not constituted by the special case procedure [17] which has been

17. Scotland introduced the special case procedure by the Administration of Justice (Scotland) Act of 1972 but, unlike in England and Wales it can be contracted out. See Professor W. A. Wilson in (1974) J.B.L. 231.

evolved as the result of the English doctrine that there must be no ouster of the jurisdiction of the courts in questions of law. Moreover, commodity arbitrations are suitably adapted to the requirements of a particular trade. This should not be understood as implying that commodity arbitrations can be regarded as perfect. They are capable of considerable inprovement and modernisation, but this is not the place to discuss that topic. Suffice it to state that, taking an overall view, the area covered by commodity arbitration appears to be the most advanced one.

The preceding observations admit, it is believed, four conclusions. *First,* no attempt should be made to unify arbitration procedures on a world-wide basis. The strength of international commercial arbitration lies in its multitudinous form. There is room in the world of business for institutional and *ad hoc* arbitration and for simple as well as sophisticated arbitration proceedings.

Secondly, it would be useful to devise a world-wide, universally applicable code of arbitral conduct in the first place for *ad hoc* arbitrations, but also for institutional arbitrations. The UNCITRAL Arbitration Rules may, in due course, become such a code. This is the beginning of a development which, it is to be hoped, will be successful.

Thirdly, those who have experience in the conduct of arbitration will generally agree that institutional arbitration is superior to *ad hoc* arbitration. Arbitration clauses are often defective,[18] and gaps in arbitration clauses can be filled more speedily and efficiently if there is an institutional framework for the arbitration. But institutional arbitration can be divisive. It should not have the effect of perpetuating the division into regional areas of arbitration. For that reason bridging attempts should be encouraged and expanded. The goal should be a rapprochement and friendly co-operation between the many different arbitral institutions.

Fourthly, as a result of the progressive complication of disputes which are dealt with by arbitrators, it is desirable that all arbitrations involving difficult questions of law or questions of general interest should, on principle, be two-instance proceedings. There should exist the possibility of invoking an appeal tribunal unless the institutional

18. Clive M. Schmitthoff, Defective Arbitration Clauses (1975) J.B.L. 9.

rules of procedure admit already an appeal to an institutional appeal tribunal, as is the case in many commodity arbitrations. It will, in the end, be necessary to establish an international arbitral appeal tribunal. The jurisdiction of such a tribunal should not, however, be obligatory and automatic for all commercial arbitrations in the world. The greatest degree of flexibility is appropriate. The tribunal should be competent only if the parties desire the review of the award by a higher tribunal and have given it jurisdiction in their arbitration agreement. The autonomy of the parties' will must remain the ultimate source of arbitral jurisdiction. In time, of course, it may become a normal term to provide such review in arbitration clauses, both in *ad hoc* and institutional arbitrations, if the institutional rules do not provide for an appellate review. If the international arbitration appeal tribunal is thus used as a stand-in, available to the parties when no other review possibility exists, it could make a valuable contribution to the internationalisation of commercial arbitration and the development of a modern international law merchant.

17

PERMANENT AND *AD HOC* ARBITRATION TRIBUNALS

*Aleksandar Goldštajn**

It is universally accepted today that one of the reasons for the universal similarity of the law of international trade is the fact that this branch of law is based on three fundamental assumptions, one of which being arbitration.

This universalism rests on the fact that differences in the social structures and legal systems are by no means an unsurmountable obstacle to the evolvement of uniform rules. Thanks to the existence of a world market, rules governing commercial transactions in this branch of law are showing an increasing tendency towards equalisation and uniformity. This fact is, in our opinion, a precondition for the development of arbitration.

Since the great differences prevailing among various municipal legislations have an adverse influence on the existence of an international market, the provision of an arbitration clause in international commercial contracts is an essential requirement for the existence of an autonomous law of international trade. It could be said that there exists an interdependence between the law of international trade and international commercial arbitration in that they exercise an influence upon each other.

For, the more economic relations between socialist and other countries continue to develop, the greater will be the need for the availability of a reliable, impartial settlement of disputes. This is an important factor affecting also the expansion of commercial relations between the East and the rest of the World.

As regards the Socialist countries there are two politico-economic

* Doctor of Law, Professor at the Faculty of Law, University of Zagreb, Yugoslavia.

areas in which arbitration is regulated. There are, first of all, Socialist countries in general, i.e. all Socialist countries regardless of where they are located, to which region they belong, and how they are politically and economically interlinked. The second area includes Socialist countries – members of the Council for Mutual Economic Assistance (CMEA).

According to the present situation, it can be said that, regardless of the above-mentioned division, arbitration is generally accepted in all Socialist countries whenever international commercial transactions are involved. It can be further asserted that despite differences, the legal systems of the Socialist countries are generally in favour of arbitration in the settlement of disputes of this kind.

As regards the CMEA countries three characteristic features of their law of arbitration could be mentioned:

(a) In all CMEA countries economic disputes between domestic state enterprises are heard by state arbitration. This is actually neither arbitration nor a court; state arbitration differs from conventional arbitration and regular courts;

(b) Disputes between enterprises from CMEA countries arising from contracts are settled by arbitral proceedings before an arbitration body set up in the country of the defendant, or, by mutual agreement of the disputing parties, in a third CMEA country, as provided in paragraph 90 of the CMEA General Conditions of 1968. According to paragraph 91 (3) arbitration awards are to be final;

(c) As regards disputes between enterprises from CMEA countries and other countries, the contracting parties are allowed to stipulate permanent or *ad hoc* arbitration by mutual agreement, so that in practice, we find arbitration agreements providing for the jurisdiction of permanent or *ad hoc* arbitration.

As regards arbitrability, in all Socialist countries arbitration can, as a rule, be stipulated for commercial disputes between a domestic and foreign enterprise.

The selection of arbitrators for institutional arbitration follows in all Socialist countries, with the exception of Hungary and Yugoslavia, the rule whereby foreign parties may not propose foreigners as arbitrators, but only members of the panel of arbitrators, who are not foreigners.

On the other hand, there are no essential differences between arbitration in the Socialist and many other countries regarding the agreement to arbitrate, the selection of foreign arbitrators for *ad hoc* arbitration, the qualification of arbitrators, the choice of law, and enforcement of foreign trade arbitration awards.

The East-European Socialist countries, members of CMEA and Yugoslavia are signatories to international arbitration agreements and they cooperate in the United Nations Economic Commission for Europe (ECE) whose Standard Contracts and General Conditions provide, as a rule, for the settlement of international commercial disputes by arbitration. (Cuba acceded also to the European Convention on International Commercial Arbitration in 1961).

Numerous and varied proposals and efforts have been made to date with a view to achieve universalism in international arbitration. Among the views from the Socialist countries we should, in particular, mention the Report on International Commercial Arbitration by the distinguished Special Rapporteur Mr. Ion Nestor from Romania [1] and the proposal by Professor Jakubowski from Poland, made at the Third International Arbitration Congress in Venice, in which they suggested that a non-governmental, international organisation of commercial arbitration should be established, because international arbitration will become increasingly important for all arbitration institutions.[2]

As regards numerous differences in municipal legislation and the practice of various kinds of arbitration, we think, that we should first try to find out whether or not the present economic and political climate is such as to warrant determined efforts to establish universalism in international commercial arbitration. It seems that in both respects, there is a wish for co-operation. Economic relations between the socialist countries and the rest of the world are being increasingly expanded. Commercial transactions with non-socialist countries are

1. United Nations General Assembly, Doc. A/CN 9/64, 1 March 1972.

2. Jakubowski, J., Promotion of Co-operation in the Domain of International Commercial Arbitration Practice, in Carnacini/Minoli (ed.) "Cooperation among Arbitration Organisations, IIIrd International Arbitration Congress, Milano 1970, p. 344.

assuming growing proportions, a fact which, by itself, calls for devising a better system of settlement of international commercial disputes by arbitration.

In view of the aim of this Symposium, we consider that the purpose of the present paper will be fulfilled if, in the present-day practice, it succeeds in presenting some of the most important issues that deserve our special attention, either because of their significance in practice or because they reflect a legal philosophy from which it would not be easy to deviate.

Among these issues I would like to mention the following:

1. Ad hoc arbitration and institutional (permanent) arbitration

It appears that permanent arbitration should become an element of contemporary international trade. Many authors concur in the view that the future of international commercial arbitration lies in its institutionalization, and that *ad hoc* arbitration is in the decline. Mr. Ion Nestor is right in saying that institutional arbitration involves a permanent body, which does not take part itself in the settlement of disputes, but plays a part at the administrative level.[3] *Ad hoc* arbitration is not just arbitration agreed upon in each particular case by the parties, but also arbitration in which the parties follow the rules of a given institution or association which participates in the conduct of the proceedings.[4] Professor Martin Domke states that institutional arbitration also serves to standardise business transactions and trade practice and to control the business ethics of the participants, and that the trend to institutional arbitration is obviously based on the recognition of the value of pre-established rules and control of the procedure through such administrative measures of the agency. But Professor Domke gives also examples of using *ad hoc* arbitration clauses throughout the construction industry, in maritime arbitration between owners and the charterers, and between merchants and carriers, as, e.g., in an agreement with the members of the India,

3. Nestor, J. in Report n. 1 *ante,* p. 104.

4. Lalive, P. A., Problèmes relatifs a l'arbitrage international commercial, in Recueil des Cours, Académie de droit international, The Hague 1967, p. 665.

Pakistan, Ceylon and Burma Outward Freight Conference.[5] The Special Rapporteur of the United Nations Commission on International Trade Law (UNCITRAL), Mr. Nestor, states rightly that there is no substantial difference between *ad hoc* and institutional arbitration.[6] One of the features of institutional arbitration is its technical facilities, whereas an arbitration tribunal is always constituted for each particular case.

The advantages of institutional arbitration bodies of considerable repute are quite evident, especially in view of their influence on extra-legal sanctions. Nor should we overlook the fact that in trade relations between East and West and the centres of international trade and the new states mutual confidence in institutional arbitration bodies can be gradually gained through experience. The divergence between institutionalized and *ad hoc* arbitration is not so wide as was generally believed.[7] Some writers hold that the role and importance of institutional arbitration have often been exaggerated.[8]

With regard to the organisation of arbitration, the Geneva European Convention on International Commercial Arbitration of 1961, placed permanent arbitral institutions and *ad hoc* arbitral procedure on the same level, by stating explicitly that "the term 'arbitration' shall mean not only settlement by arbitrators appointed for each case (*ad hoc* arbitration), but also by permanent arbitral institutions" (article I, paragraph 2 (b)), and that, therefore, "the parties shall be free to submit their disputes to a permanent arbitral institution or to an *ad hoc* arbitral procedure" (article IV, paragraph 1 (a) & (b)). The ECE General Conditions of Sale and Standard Forms of Contract No. 574, designed for use in East-West trade, provide that the arbitration procedure "shall be such as may be agreed between the parties" referring only to the settlement of disputes "by arbitration", whereby the General Conditions No. 188 refer to the Rules of Conciliation and Arbitration of the International Chamber of Commerce. Finally, the United Nations New York Convention on the

5. Domke, M., The Law and Practice of Commercial Arbitration, Mundelein 1968, pp. 10, 11 and 36.

6. Nestor, J., n. 1 *ante*, p. 105, para. 158.

7. Straus, D.B., in "Cooperation among Arbitration Organizations", *ante* n. 2, p. 135.

8. Kopelmanas, L., n. 2 *ante*, p. 90.

Recognition and Enforcement of Foreign Arbitral Awards of 1958 provides in article 1, paragraph 2, that "the term 'arbitral awards' shall include not only awards made by arbitrators appointed for each case, but also those made by permanent arbitral bodies."

The reasons, why we wish to emphasize the equivalence of the settlement of disputes in international trade by permanent and *ad hoc* arbitration lie in the fact that some Western circles are reluctant to accept institutional arbitration in the Socialist countries, and *vice versa*. All this is, in the last resort, a matter of confidence gained through the practice of individual institutional arbitral bodies but, at the same time, considerable changes in the structure of some permanent arbitration bodies are expected.

In a recently published study entitled "Commercial arbitration in the Socialist Federal Republic of Yugoslavia" an English author said that "the foresight and tolerance as regards arbitration as seen in Yugoslav national law and practice can only enhance and encourage international trade", and speaking of the Foreign Trade Arbitration Court in Belgrade, the same study says: "There are few other arbitration courts which can claim to have so consistently reached impartial and acceptable awards." [9]

Since international commercial arbitration is the only acceptable means for the settlement of commercial disputes, the variety of forms at the disposal of the parties will facilitate acceptance of foreign and/or international arbitration bodies. Experience to date has shown that enterprises in the Socialist countries recognize arbitration bodies in third countries which have made a name for themselves, because of their expertise, speed and objectivity. Whether institutional or *ad hoc* arbitration is selected, "what is important," to quote Professor Domke, "is the knowledge that resort to arbitration is available".[10] The law of Socialist countries allows agreements to stipulate the competence of *ad hoc* arbitration at home or abroad for commercial disputes between domestic enterprises and foreign natural or legal persons. In this respect, there are no restrictions with regard to the place of arbitration, the qualities of arbitrators, their

9. Lew, J. D. M. in Arbitration Journal, Vol. 28 (1973), p. 49.

10. Domke, M., Promotion of Diffusion of International Commercial Arbitration, note 2 *ante*, p. 353.

nationality, etc. Exceptions have been made in the CMEA General Conditions for disputes between enterprises of the CMEA member countries. In the practice of CMEA member countries, institutional arbitration is strongly favoured.[11] Therefore, Professor Schmitthoff's conclusions should be quoted: "It should not be inferred from these observations that *ad hoc* arbitrations have become obsolete. This procedure is of particular importance where 'neutral' arbitration is desired, particularly in East-West commercial relations. The European Convention on International Commercial Arbitration, undoubtedly the most progressive measure of international legislation on arbitration, rightly accords equal status to *ad hoc* arbitration and arbitration by permanent arbitral institutions; it provides that the parties shall be free to submit their disputes to either form of arbitration." [12]

2. Choice of forum

Following the 1968 CMEA General Conditions of Delivery of Goods between Organisations of the member countries (which do not differ essentially from those of 1958), parties frequently stipulate arbitration to take place in the country of the defendant, with arbitrators to be chosen in accordance with the rules of the arbitration agency in that country. This was the practice of all Socialist countries with the exception of Yugoslavia. This approach did not safeguard the intention of the parties in all cases and could lead to manoeuvring by the parties to ensure designation as a defendant.[13] However, as confidence in international arbitration centres has considerably strengthened, there has been an increasing tendency to have disputes arbitrated by them. A number of commercial contracts provide for

11. General Conditions for Delivery of Goods of CMEA countries, para. 90.

12. Schmitthoff, C. M., The Law of International Trade, its Growth, Formulation and Operation, in Schmitthoff's "The Sources of the Law of International Trade", London 1964, p. 25.

13. Goldštajn, A., Investicije (Investments), Zagreb 1969, p. 61; Starr, R., A new Legal Framework for Trade between the United States and the Soviet Union, the American Journal of International Law, Vol. 67, No. 1 (1973), p. 76.

arbitration in a third country, for example Switzerland or Sweden, either by the ICC Court of Arbitration or by an *ad hoc* arbitration. An arbitration clause, stipulating the competence of the ICC Court of Arbitration, is no longer a rare exception in contracts entered into between enterprises from socialist and non-socialist countries frequently with a seat in Switzerland. *Ad hoc* arbitration tribunals, stipulated by enterprises from socialist and Western countries, have their seat in third countries, frequently in Switzerland or Sweden.

Yugoslav enterprises most frequently stipulate the competence of the Court of Arbitration of the International Chamber of Commerce with the proviso that the seat of the arbitration tribunal be in Zürich (*ad hoc* arbitration in Zürich, as well as the Arbitral Tribunal of the Zürich Chamber of Commerce).

A number of Chinese commercial contracts provide for arbitration in a third country, for example Sweden or Switzerland. In some agreements, concluded between Chinese and Yugoslav enterprises, the arbitration clause provides for the jurisdiction of the Foreign Trade Arbitration Commission of the China Council for the Promotion of International Trade in Peking. However, there are also contracts providing for the competence of the ICC Court of Arbitration. A certain number of "sales confirmations", stating that the parties have agreed to close the transaction, do not contain any arbitration clause, so that the most likely, "the defendant's country clause", will be applied.

It can be noted that enterprises from Socialist countries tend to give preference to arbitration in those European countries which are known for their fairness, such as Switzerland.[14] In Yugoslavia, there is no difficulty in obtaining the consent of the foreign trade corporation, which enjoy considerable independence from the state, to arbitration outside the country.[15]

14. McCobb, Jr. J. B., Foreign Trade Arbitration in the Peoples Republic of China, New York University Journal of International Law and Politics, Vol. 5, No. 2 (1972), p. 213: Schmitt, A. H., Standard Form Contracts in the International Commercial Transactions of the Peoples Republic of China, in the International and Comparative Law Quarterly, Vol. 21, Januar 1972, p. 139; Schmitthoff, C. M., The Export Trade, London 1975, p. 377; Starr, op. cit. n. 13 *ante*, p. 76; Lagergren, G., The Limits of Party Autonomy, in Schmitthoff's "Sources ...", n. 12 *ante* p. 222.

15. Schmitthoff, C. M., The Export Trade, n. 14 *ante*, p. 377; Goldštajn,

3. The law applicable by permanent arbitration institutions of socialist countries

As Professor Schmitthoff has pointed out the sources of the law of international trade are: international conventions and international custom. This viewpoint was also accepted in the United Nations Secretary-General's Report on Progressive Development of the Law of International Trade.

The rules of permanent arbitration institutions contain, *inter alia*, the following provisions on the application of trade usages:

Bulgaria: The Court of Arbitration bases its decisions upon the law and commercial usage which should find application in the particular case in accordance with the norms of international private law (paragraph 47).

German Democratic Republic: The Court of Arbitration shall take into consideration the trade customs covered by the matter in dispute, in particular, as far as the recognition of these customs has been agreed upon by the parties, or when the governing law provides for their legality (section 27, paragraph II).

Poland: The tribunal shall take into consideration the principles of equity, of good faith and of custom in so far as they are permitted by the proper law (paragraph 31 section 1).

U.S.S.R.: The tribunal may request the opinion of experts to elucidate questions requiring special knowledge which arise during the examination of the case, including questions as to existence of particular commercial usages (paragraph 23).

Yugoslavia: The arbitrators judge the facts by free judgment and render their award on the basis of the applicable legal prescriptions and trade customs (article 29, paragraph 2).

The application of trade customs shows an international approach on the part of institutional arbitrations, and respect for the autonomous law of international trade. In practice, further progress has been

---

A., Ugovor o stranim privatnim investicijama u Jugoslaviji I, Zagreb 1972 (Contracts on Foreign Private Investments in Yugoslavia), pp. 121-123 in Vol. I.

achieved towards the application of commercial usages.[16] Many decisions of the Yugoslav Foreign Trade Arbitration Court have been rendered with the explanation that they conform to the "general principles of commercial law", or "existing customs in international trade", or "to generally accepted rules in international trade" and similar formulations.

4. Hearings

It is a rule of arbitral proceedings that hearings are normaly held in private. One of the chief factors moving in favour of arbitration is the desire for privacy. On the other hand, according to the rules of permanent arbitral bodies in Socialist countries, hearings are in principle public, unless the parties request that they be held in private. The issue is decided by the arbitration body. An exception in this

16. Lunz, L. A., Conflict of Laws in International Sale: Theory and Practice of Socialist Countries, Recueil de Cours, Academie de droit international (1965) I; Bystricky, R., Pravo mezinarodniho obchodu, Praha 1967, p. 16; Szaszy, I., Legal Regulations of Foreign Trade Transactions in Eastern-European Socialist Countries, "Questions of International Law", Budapest 1968, pp. 232-233; Ramzaicev, D. F., Primenenie mejdunarodnih obitchaev v commerchescom arbitrage, Sovetskii ežegodnik mojdunarodnoga prava 1961, Moscow 1962; Ramzaicev, D. F., Pravo primenjaemoe vnešnetorgovymi arbitrajnymi sudami socialističeskih stran, Sovetskoe Gosudarstvo i Pravo (1965) 12, pp. 54-60; Enderlein, F. (ed.), Der Aussenhandelskaufvertrag, Berlin 1971, p. 80; Ramzaitsev, D. F., The Law Applied by Arbitration Tribunals, in Schmitthoff's "Sources ..." n. 12 *ante*, pp. 151-153; Goldštajn, A., Međunarodno trgovačko pravo (The Law of International Trade) Zagreb 1970, pp. XVII; Karlòcai, J., In the "Self-Regulatory Character of the International Sale of Goods, in "Questions.." note 16 it is stated that merchants have always sought the simplest solutions possible, thus shaping customs and usage and it is in the interest of everyone in the trade to know these practices, in whatever legal or social system he may live, (p. 133); according to the decision of the Supreme Court of Poland in 1970, arbitrators in international commerce are to apply first of all provisions of international law arising either out of respective conventions or of respective established customs. Only in the absence of such rules is municipal law to be applied, whether Polish or foreign. See: Jakubowski, J.: The Autonomy of International Trade Law and its Influence on the Interpretation and Application of its Rules, in Fabricius, F. (ed.), Law and International Trade, Festschrift für Clive M. Schmitthoff, Frankfurt 1973, p. 211.

respect is Poland where "at a motion of one party the hearing shall be *in camera*." [17]

It can be assumed that this uniform standpoint has been adopted under the influence of legal philosophy and, consequently, under the influence of principles applicable to regular court proceedings wishing to assure public control. However, as Professor Jakubowski rightly considered, very important is the fact, that these arbitration proceedings are formally or factually not held in public.[18] This is in conformity with article 29 of the Arbitration Rules of the United Nations Economic Commission for Europe of 1966, which reads: "The proceedings shall be held *in camera* unless both parties request that they be held in public." In accordance with the Convention on Settlement of Investment Disputes between States and Nationals of Other States (article 48, 5) and the Arbitration Rules, as a matter of principle, arbitration proceedings should not be public. (rule 31).

The request that hearings in arbitration proceedings be held *in camera* has its justification. Publicity of commercial litigations is adverse to the interests of both parties. Many trade secrets may be exposed, damaging the interests of the defendant as well as the plaintiff. Furthermore, the private atmosphere creates a climate favourable to the continuance of business relations. Finally, arbitration is different from the all or nothing attitude of the law. For, all that privacy is in line with the nature of arbitration. The contrary uniform standpoint, adopted by permanent arbitration institutions of Socialist countries, can be traced to historic and political reasons. In any case, in practice to date this has not been a problem, although it does not mean that this stand does not deserve to be re-examined. A compromise could perhaps be reached in this way that the proceed-

17. Article 17 Reglement concernant l'instruction des affaires par la Commission d'Arbitrage pour le commerce exterieur d'Albanie; Article 21 of the China Provisional Rules of Procedure of the Foreign Trade Arbitration Commission; Section 23, paragraph 2 of the Rules of the Arbitration Court of the Chamber of Commerce of Czechoslovakia; Article 10, paragraph 8 of the Rules of Procedure for the Court of Arbitration at the Hungarian Chamber of Commerce; Paragraph 26 of the Rules of the Court of Arbitration at the Polish Chamber of Foreign Trade; Paragraph 160 of the Rules of Procedure of the Foreign Trade Arbitration Commission of the U.S.S.R.; Article 34 of the Rules of the Foreign Trade Arbitration Court of Yugoslavia.

18. Jakubowski, J., n. 2 *ante*, p. 339.

ings shall be held in public unless one party requests that they be held *in camera.*

5. Other questions

In addition to these basic questions, there are other issues which should be considered, in respect of which institutional arbitration bodies in the socialist countries do not, however, basically differ from one another. Differences are sometimes greater between the arbitration systems of the Western countries than between systems of the Socialist and other countries.

6. General conclusions

According to the Special Rapporteur of UNCITRAL, Mr. Nestor, "the institution of arbitration won international acceptance under the pressure of the requirements of the international trade." It seems to us that world-wide co-operation in the field of international commercial arbitration could be achieved, if international arbitration were separated from domestic commercial arbitration. This approach has already formally been accepted in the sphere of unification of the law of international trade. The Socialist countries have, in a great measure, accepted international conventions on international arbitration, and in 1972, Moscow was host to the Fourth International Arbitration Congress.

A world-wide system of international commercial arbitration could therefore be developed because there are no doctrinaire differences that would hinder it. The difficulty lies in finding fair solutions, acceptable to the largest possible number of countries. Since the East-European Socialist countries also take an active part in the work of UNCITRAL, we should look optimistically upon UNCITRAL's suggestions that uniform rules on international commercial arbitration should be prepared. It should be noted that present-day differences are more a matter of historic conditions, so that the creation of a world-wide system of arbitration can be hoped for. This highly desirable aim could be achieved by a gradual removal of discrepancies in municipal rules. Since co-operation in the equalisation of the law of international trade is already well under way, we see no obstacle to achieving the same progress with respect to international arbitration.

It seems necessary to focus our attention on the following questions:

i. Efficient organisation of arbitration courts which decide international commercial disputes;
ii. Improvement in the arbitration rules of procedure; and
iii. Unification of the substantive law to be applied.

International commercial disputes are settled by national courts of arbitration or by the Court of Arbitration of the International Chamber of Commerce. Some changes in the structure of various permanent arbitration courts have become indispensable, at least in cases when individual courts of arbitration pretend to be recognized as international arbitration courts. The Court of Arbitration of the International Chamber of Commerce deserves, in this respect, special attention. Practice has shown that it is necessary to re-examine some solutions contained in the ICC Rules of Conciliation and Arbitration. Thus, for example, under article 19 of the above rules, before beginning the hearing of the case, the arbitrator shall draw up, on documents or in the presence of the parties, a statement defining his terms of reference. This statement must be signed by the parties and arbitrators and, thereafter, approved by the Court of Arbitration. This preliminary procedure, without any significance for the settlement of the case, has, in practice, been a cause of delay of proceedings and a superfluous burden, and has been criticized within the framework of the ICC Court of Arbitration.[19]

Another example relates to the approval of awards by the Court of Arbitration. According to the ICC rules, before completing the award, the arbitrator shall submit the same to the Court of Arbitration, which may lay down modifications as to its form and, if need be, draw the arbitrator's attention even to points connected with the merits of the case, but with due regard to the arbitrator's liberty of decision. No award shall, under any circumstance, be issued until approved as to its form by the Court of Arbitration. The re-examina-

19. Eisemann, F., Welthandelsschiedsgerichtsbarkeit – Heute, Vortrag vor dem Oesterreichischen Nationalkomitee der IHK am 4. Oktober 1971 in Wien.

tion of this article would most likely lead to a more expeditious settlement of cases and to the clarification of some controversial issues.

As regards the national composition of its arbitration tribunals, the ICC Court of Arbitration has come to be considered today as being international and neutral, since each of the parties nominates an arbitrator, while sole arbitrators and third arbitrators must be nationals of countries other than those of the parties. This is not the case with many national arbitration courts, because their respective arbitration panels are exclusively composed of nationals. The attractiveness of such arbitration courts for the settlement of international commercial disputes depends on whether or not a particular arbitration court is neutral, because the arbitrators are not nationals of any country of the parties, and on whether or not this arbitration court has gained reputation for its expertise, fairness and speed. There is, however, a difference between permanent arbitration courts of the CMEA and other countries: when the defendant's clause is applied to disputes with parties who are not from the CMEA countries, the arbitration court is not from a third country. Therefore, the possibility for a foreigner to nominate an arbitrator would result in greater confidence in the arbitration courts.

It seems, that more flexibility in the structure of the institutional arbitration courts is desirable, giving greater possibilities to meet the requirements of the parties.

As regards the arbitration rules of procedure, a solution is easier to find. The Arbitration Rules of the United Nations Economic Commission for Europe of 1966, and the experience of permanent arbitration courts can help in the elaboration of arbitration rules acceptable both for *ad hoc* arbitration relating to international trade, and for permanent arbitration courts which want to decide international commercial disputes. It would, therefore, by useful if the arbitration rules for optional use in *ad hoc* arbitrations relating to international trade, which are currently being prepared by UNCITRAL, were also acceptable and applied by permanent arbitration institutions and incorporated into their rules of procedure.

In the last resort, doctrinaire, historical or political reasons may be a basis for adhering to some solutions regarding the organisation and the rules of procedure of permanent arbitration courts. However, to what extent partners in international trade will accept individual permanent arbitration courts, will depend on risks that are taken into account, on the economic strength of the partners, on interest in concluding individual transactions, on the will to make compromises, and other circumstances which motivate them to accept a particular arbitration court. But, such cases cannot be generalised. Therefore, the trend towards improving international commercial arbitration in general is justified by the need to do away with the various shortcomings that have been noted to date. As regards permanent arbitration institutions, it will be opportune to adjust them to the requirements of the greatest possible circle of participants in international trade, because, as already pointed out by Professor Clive Schmitthoff, "the insufficiency of the present position is demonstrated by the frequent resort to *ad hoc* arbitration".

Much has been done to date to promote exchanges of views and co-operation, but not enough to satisfy the international business community. Historic, economic and political reasons do not fill us with illusions of a sudden spectacular success. However, a characteristic feature of our times is the increasing autonomous development of arbitration. The needs of international trade, sooner or later, result in the removal of the barriers, and these needs have certainly never been greater than today.

By stipulating the law of a third country as the proper law of the contract, and by agreeing on an international court of arbitration for the settlement of possible disputes, the contracting parties accept the international standards of behaviour in line with the law of international trade. Consequently, the differences, which exist in this field, are the result of historic and political conditions which have been transcended by the present-day economic requirements of the contemporary world. The consistency of legal systems is not, in our opinion, an obstacle to the harmonization and unification of the law of international commercial arbitration.

Further approach to universalism seems to be closer, and will depend upon the interdependence between substance and form, so to speak, as well as the influence of the law of international trade.[20]

20. Goldštajn, A., The New Law Merchant – Reconsidered, in Fabricius, F. (ed.), Law and International Trade – Festschrift für Clive M. Schmitthoff, Frankfurt 1973.

E. International Trade Law and World Peace

18

THE UNIVERSAL AND REGIONAL HARMONISATION OF INTERNATIONAL TRADE LAW AS A MEANS OF MAINTAINING WORLD PEACE

*Fritz Fabricius**

A. Introduction

"Un jour viendra où il n'y aura d'autres champs de batailles que les marchés s'ouvrant au commerce et les esprits s'ouvrant aux idées." "Some day, there will be no other battle fields than the markets open to commerce and minds open to ideas." With these words the French author Victor Hugo inaugurated the International Peace Congress on August 22, 1849.[1] He thus stated that world trade would stabilise world peace. Today, one hundred and twenty-five years after these words were spoken, it appears that we have not come nearer to attaining this goal, and that, on the contrary, we have receded from it. The world is not only divided into capitalist, socialist and communist states, into rich and poor nations, but there are also nations having a mixed racial composition; often, serious conflicts of interest and ideology occur between many states. Nevertheless, in view of the dangers connected with the invention of the atomic bomb, the longing for peace among the greater part of the world population has increased, and is stronger than ever before. The question is therefore justified, if and to which extent the development and unification of international trade law might help to secure world peace. The work of my highly esteemed teacher and friend Clive M. Schmitthoff induced

* Dr. jur., Professor of Labour Law, Economic Law, Company Law and Mercantile Law; Director of the Institute of Social Security of the Ruhr University Bochum, The Federal Republic of Germany.

1. See Hans-Jürgen Schlochauer, *Die Idee des ewigen Friedens – Ein Überblick über Entwicklung und Gestaltung des Friedenssicherungsgedankens auf der Grundlage einer Quellenauswahl,* Bonn 1953, p. 137.

me to go into this question more deeply. Today, I will deal with it under the special aspect of the universal and regional harmonisation of international trade law.

Let us begin by outlining the problems.

B. The problems

1. The concept of peace

Contemporary scholars within the field of peace research include within its ambit the avoidance of conflicts, concerning social, psychological, political, religious, ethical, paedagogical, economic and legal matters.[2]

2. International trade law as a means of promoting peace

Seen from this point of view international or world trade must be taken into consideration as a peace stabilising factor. Thus, the Soviet scientists V. Arkhipow and A. Bykow state that: "The successful development of mutually profitable trade between countries ... is a major means of strengthening world peace and understanding".[3] This applies even more to International Trade Law. For millenia, mankind has recognised that one of the main functions of the law is to promote peace or, as the French author Raymond Aron [4] says, to maintain peace is the dominant aim of a legal system.

In principle it is the task of law to prescribe the occasions on which power can be exercised in society, and also to state the limits of such exercise. In considering all social phenomena, we may, however, observe an "interplay of contradictory forces and tendencies", as was pointed out by Karol Lapter [5] of the Polish Institute of International

2. See Paul Noack, *Friedensforschung—ein Signal der Hoffnung,* Freudenstadt (Lutzeyer) 1970, p. 31 et seq.

3. See their work, *Free Trade or Exclusive Blocs,* Moscow 1971, pp. 7, 8.

4. *Frieden und Krieg, Eine Theorie der Staatenwelt,* Frankfurt/M. (Fischer) 1963, p. 831; translation of *Paix et guerre entre les nations,* Paris 1962.

5. In his article *Äußere und innere Ursachen Internationaler Spannungen,*

Affairs in Warsaw. The increase in power of certain interest groups may lead to demands for law reform, which sometimes can only come about as the result of force, such as strikes, revolutions and wars, as Professor Röling [6] from the Polemological Institute of Groningen University quite rightly states. So it follows that the connection between peace and law is only a relative one.

In spite of the latter considerations, we must ask if the maintenance of world peace can be promoted only and exclusively by a unitary world trade law, and if regional regulation of international trade law harbours the germ of conflicts. One must remember that the regional systems of international trade may serve as a means of increasing the economic strength of a power bloc which may also increase its military power. For this reason we might say that a universal system of international trade law is to be preferred, and that regional systems, if they are to promote world peace, must pursue common aims which are not incompatible with this ideal. This statement will be qualified later on.

3. *The relationship between law, power and state authority*

The concepts of law and justice have a close connection with the power of the states, who create the law and, when necessary, enforce it by means of sanctions. The Catholic theologian Heinrich Gross [7] points out that in the societies mentioned in the Old Testament, only power guarantees peace, which is connected inseparably with the concept of law. We thus must pose the question whether an effective system of international trade law is dependent on the existence of a world state. If we are unable to create such a state, we must pose the question whether international law can be regarded as true law. In the

---

which appears in *Weil wir überleben wollen, Modelle für eine neue Welt,* herausgegeben von Robert Jungk und Hans Mundt, a translation of the English original edition "Conflict in Society", 1966, by Professor Dr. Otto Kimminich, München 1970. Note especially p. 332 et seq.

6. In "Die Rolle des Rechts bei der Konfliktlösung", an article in the volume referred to in note 5; note especially pp. 311-313.

7. See his work *Die Idee des Ewigen und Allgemeinen Weltfriedens im Alten Orient und im Alten Testament,* Trier 1956, pp. 17, 26, 28.

present connection, we think of the names of Kelsen [8] and Austin [9] on the one hand, and of Wolfgang Friedmann,[10] Georg Schwarzenberger [11] and of the sociologist Talcot Parsons [12] on the other hand. Even though, one must consider that there are different stages of integration of the various legal systems, and that evolution towards effective enforcement measures proceeds by degrees, and that legal systems make themselves effective generally through voluntary compliance rather than by compulsion; [13] is apparent, however, that some sort of generally accepted authority is necessary in order to permit the creation of law, and we must therefore deal with this question.

C. The classical liberal concept of a world economy

The possibility of creating law without state authority and state compulsion has been considered theoretically by laisser-faire economic liberalism of the nineteenth century. Certainly, nineteenth century liberal economists also saw the development of international trade as conducive to international peace. A brief examination of the concepts of laisser-faire liberalism follows:

1. The concepts of laisser-faire individualism

The idea of laisser-faire liberalism concerning trade was based on the following ideas:

8. See especially his discussion of the question as to whether international law is true law in Kelsen and Tucker, *Principles of International Law,* 2nd ed., 1966.

9. For an elucidation of this question, see Wolfgang Friedmann, *Legal Theory,* 5th ed., London 1967, at pp. 258-9, and P. S. James, *English Law,* 6th ed., London 1966 at pp. 4-5.

10. In *Legal Theory,* op. cit. note 9, p. 279.

11. See his article "Krieg und Frieden im internationalen System" in *Krieg und Frieden in der modernen Staatenwelt, Beiträge der Sozialwissenschaft II,* Gütersloh 1966, p. 37.

12. See his article "Ordnung und Gemeinschaft im internationalen System" in *Krieg und Frieden im industriellen Zeitalter, Beiträge der Sozialwissenschaft I,* Gütersloh 1966, p. 290 et seq.

13. Note the work by Heinrich Henkel, *Einführung in die Rechtsphilosophie,* 1964, p. 109 et seq.

According to Adam Smith, the idea of laisser-faire liberalism as to trade was based on the following principles:

> "Each man is best fitted to be the judge of his own actions. Individual interests are not in conflict, but are subject to a natural harmony. Therefore, the selfish actions of individuals lead to the welfare of all, and the continuous regulation of government is unnecessary. The best results can be obtained if the state follows a policy of let-alone, of laisser-faire." [14]

The free market, being directly regulated by perfect competition is the centre of all actions of the individuals:

> "The main thesis of the theory of perfect competition was, as I will be allowed to recall, that if the economic units are infinitesimally small in relation to the size of the market, and if they do not act together, then no unit can by its own actions have any influence in the market. If anybody should decide to change his behaviour – i.e. his demand or supply – it would have no perceptible effect on the total demand and supply for the product, nor, consequently, on the price. The market and the prices were, therefore, to the individual, whether he acted as a buyer or a seller, independent variables, a set of objective and given conditions for his behaviour. They were as entirely outside his control as the seasons and the weather, to which he had to adjust in order not to perish. Under the assumptions implicit in the model, the price formation in the market performed continuously and smoothly the change of the primary conditions." [15]

This theory, as it was developed by Ricardo, led to a belief in the desirability of a world state.[16] The Frenchman François Quesnay held that the merchants of all nations were to be seen as a Trade-Republic. Jean Batiste Say, having systemised the ideas of Adam Smith in France, which then were also espoused by Frederic Bastiat, thus employed the concept of the existence of a universal economic community in order to accept the idea of the general freedom of trade,

14. See in the present connection P. T. Ellsworth, *The International Economy,* 3rd ed., New York/London, 1964, pp. 46-47.

15. Note also Gunnar Myrdal, *Beyond the Welfare State,* London 1958, p. 22.

16. In the present connection see especially Fabricius, "Internationales Handelsrecht und Weltfrieden – Eine Bestandaufnahme" in *Law and International Trade,* Festschrift für Clive M. Schmitthoff, ed. by Fritz Fabricius, Frankfurt/M. 1973, p. 101 and pp. 113-115.

similar to Adam Smith's opinion that national economy were to be replaced by "World Economy". The idea of a "Cosmopolitan Economy" is closely connected with the idea of peace, especially that of world peace. In Germany it was Kant who in his famous essay "On Eternal Peace" which was published in a great number of editions, pointed out that trade had had the special function of causing nations to enter into peaceful relations with each other ... that "the spirit of trade could not co-exist with war".

In England James Mill and, to a greater extent, John Stuart Mill and Jeremy Bentham stressed the connection between world trade and world peace. John Stuart Mill may be cited:

> "It is commerce which is rapidly rendering war obsolete, by strengthening and multiplying the personal interests which are in natural opposition to it. And it may be said without exaggeration, that the great extent and rapid increase of international trade, in being the principal guarantee of the peace of the world, is the great permanent security for the uninterrupted progress of the ideas, the institutions, and the character of the human race."

The legal order too was thought to function by itself along these lines, its enforcement being looked after only by international arbitral tribunals created by contract. War as a means of enforcing the law was denied.

2. Some doubts as to the validity of laisser-faire liberalism

This concept of international free trade was held to be a Utopian one already by Fichte, who, in his essay "The Autarchic State" [17] expounded his contrasting model of an economically self-supporting, corporate state, domestic trade also being subject to state regulation. He objected to any form of foreign trade on principle. Friedrich List,[18] the pioneer of the German Zollverein (Customs Union), stated that the free trade theory lacked all sense of reality and so rejected it.

Contemporary economic historians doubt whether international

17. See Johann Gottlieb Fichte, *Der geschlossene Handelsstaat, ein philosophischer Entwurf als Anhang zur Rechtslehre und Probe einer künftig zu liefernden Politik*, Tübingen 1800.

18. See his work, *Das nationale System der politischen Ökonomie*, 1841, New Print Tübingen 1959, pp. 138, 139.

trade between the developed nations in the late nineteenth century took place in accordance with the laisser-faire model. It must not be forgotten that trade in the nineteenth century was mainly carried on between the European colonial powers and North America under the leadership of Great Britain, and that it had the special object of obtaining preferential access to their colonial markets where cheap consumer goods could be sold. Thus, international trade was very much conditioned by colonialism in the nineteenth century. One must ask further questions as to the validity of the concept of free trade before it becomes possible to use it to show how it may foster world peace.[19]

3. The present situation of the international economy [20]

For our further investigation it is important to understand that the present situation of international economy is the result of basic patterns of development which have occurred since the beginning of World War I.

a. The period until World War I

We shall assume, despite the doubts already mentioned, that the concept of international, multilateral free trade did function more or less among the developed nations of the world. It was generally thought that laisser-faire liberalism would promote the maximisation of profits and of economic growth, and that maximisation also necessitated international monetary stability, which was guaranteed by the acceptance of the gold standard under British leadership. This acceptance necessitated "certain generally accepted modes of thought and attitude in the world of banks and the existence of certain taboos which were respected by all politicans. An international capital market, working on this basis, provided the necessary

19. In this connection see also Fabricius, "Internationales Handelsrecht und Weltfrieden", op. cit. note 16, pp. 118, 119.

20. In the present connection see also Fabricius, in *Festschrift für Schmitthoff,* op. cit. note 16, pp. 119-123, and also the work of Gunnar Myrdal, *An International Economy, Problems and Prospects,* New York/ London 1964, and *Beyond the Welfare State,* London 1958.

foreign capital at very low rates of interest for the world of trade."

Labour, of course, was an important factor for keeping this system functioning, but because of the actual situation at the time, this fact could be neglected. For labour was to be obtained in the labour market at minimal wages because it was there in abundance, especially so in the colonies where poverty reigned. Unemployment was accepted as a matter of course. In those times full employment was not deemed to be a relevant factor in economic planning or in political programmes. During the period in question, the state intervened sporadically rather than in a planned and co-ordinated way.

b. Development trends since the outbreak of World War I

A sudden change of the situation was caused by the outbreak of World War I, as it interrupted foreign trade to a great extent and necessitated stringent economic measures. Hopes for a return to the former position after the end of the war were not fulfilled generally. The general post-war trend was for the more developed nations to espouse certain measures of economic planning.

As Gunnar Myrdal points out in his book *International Economy* the longterm trend in all developed countries is against the free market economy based on free competition, and towards increasing intervention of governments and organised groups. The causes of this trend in the individual national states are firstly changes in the structures of markets and enterprises by the formation of combines and cartels, and further, the growing political voice of the less wealthy part of the population of the developed Western nations, which alone can be taken into consideration here. The increasing political power of the poorer sections of the population have led to demands for greater social justice.

These tendencies were accelerated by economic crises of the inter-war period and further by World War II and the circumstances of the post-war period. Where mergers of enterprises cause a distortion of the balance of the market, such distortion has been held to require state interference, which may include interference in the organisation of the market. Since the end of World War II, demands for economic growth, for price stability, for increased wages and especially for full employment are of paramount and equal importance. Democratic governments must take all these demands into consideration, if only in order not to alienate strong interest groups and to stay in power. These demands which cannot all be complied with at the same time, require state planning which will give more decisive importance to national interests than to international interests and which will consequently lead to fragmentation of the international economy. We speak of a general trend towards the welfare state, where welfare does not only mean welfare for the poorest section of the community, but "a high level of production per head of the population and a wide distribution of economic, cultural and social advantages". This trend is to be noticed in all rich industrial nations of the West, though the welfare state "has not been attained yet anywhere".

The national trend towards the welfare state necessarily has a disintegrating effect on the principle of international free trade. The preconditions for international free trade, as pointed out above, namely freedom of trade in the international sphere, market equality, international convertibility of currencies, and a free international labour market have gone, even in the small world community of the developed nations as it existed up till 1914. Since the Second World War, there is no hope of re-establishing the "old order". This conclusion is re-enforced by the fact that the future pattern of world trade will include the socialist states as well as the under-developed and the less developed members of the world community.

At present, world trade can only be realised, within the limitations of the above constraints, by means of entering into suitable multilateral and bilateral agreements. It is no longer possible to realise world trade within the liberal economic framework.

c. *Some legal consequences of the above considerations*

It appears necessary, given the above facts, to create international economic law on a bilateral or multilateral basis, which system of law would become the basis of and have supremacy over international trade law which governs private transactions. International economic law has as important a function as international trade law in promoting world peace.

d. *Some important questions*

The results of the above investigation, namely the absence of a world trading community, and of world economic or trade law, posit the question as to, given these circumstances, how the development of international economic law and international trade law can be promoted best. International trade may be influenced by political consideration, as in cases where it is decided to restrict trade with communist countries. Patterns of international trade may reveal themselves as a simple exchange of goods, but may involve closer degrees of economic co-operation and integration. Thus the EEC embraces in principle the whole economics of the participating states. Where the harmonisation of international trade law is technically motivated, as in the areas of air transport and containerisation, such harmonisation is more likely to be successful than in cases where a basically political decision is called for, as in the creation of a common market.

D. The creation of international economic law and international trade law on a universal basis

1. The competence of the United Nations

At present there does not exist any unitary world law of economics nor a unitary world trade law. The Charter of the United Nations, however, provides an institutional frame for the development of a universal international economic and trade law. It would be a work of superogation in the present company to attempt a detailed exposition of the preamble and articles 1, 13, 55-60, 62 of the United Nations Charter. It will suffice to cite that members of the United Nations are determined "to save succeeding generations from the scourge of war ... and for these ends unite our strength to maintain international peace and security ...". They have resolved to "combine" their efforts "to accomplish these aims". The purposes of the United Nations are to develop friendly relations among nations ... and take other appropriate measures to strengthen universal peace, to achieve international co-operation in solving international problems of an economic, social, cultural, or humanitarian character ... (article 1, paragraph 2, 3). In order to accomplish these aims the General Assembly is to initiate studies and make recommendations for the purpose of ... encouraging the progressive development of international law and its codification, and for the purpose of promoting international co-operation in the economic, social, cultural, educational and health fields ... (article 13, paragraph 1).

With a view to the creation of conditions of stability and well-being which are necessary for achieving these aims the United Nations demand:

> "higher standards of living, full employment, and conditions of economic and social progress and development solutions of international economic, social, health, and related problems; and international cultural and educational co-operation ..." (article 55)

The Economic and Social Council was established in order to accomplish these tasks. The General Secretary of the United Nations called it the "pivot" of the economic and social organisations within the UN. The Council may, under article 62:

1. make or initiate studies and reports with respect to international economic, social, cultural, educational, health and related matters and may make recommendations with respect to any such matters of the General Assembly, to the members of the United Nations, and to the specialised agencies concerned;
2. make recommendations for the purpose of promoting respect for, and observance of, human rights and fundamental freedoms for all;
3. prepare draft conventions for submission to the General Assembly, with respect to matters falling within its competence;
4. call, in accordance with the rules prescribed by the United Nations, international conferences on matters falling within its competence.

The Economic and Social Council is the parent organ of the four economic commissions, i.e. the United Nations Economic Commission for Europe (ECE), the United Nations Economic Commission for Latin America (ECLA), the United Nations Economic Commission for Asia and the Far East (ECAFE) and the United Nations Economic Commission for Africa (ECA).

Of the semi-autonomous bodies the United Nations Conference on Trade and Development (UNCTAD) should be mentioned; of the special organisations, the International Monetary Fund (IMF), the International Bank for Reconstruction and Development (IBRD), also known as World Bank and the Food and Agricultural Organisation of the United Nations (FAO). The General Agreement on Tariffs and Trade (GATT) is not an organisation of the United Nations, but it co-operates with the organisation very closely indeed. In this connection we must mention especially the United Nations Commission on International Trade Law (UNCITRAL), which was created with the assistance of our honoured friend Clive M. Schmitthoff.

2. Some aspects of setting up a world state

The United Nations do not have any legislative competences, but may draft international multilateral conventions, which are submitted to the General Assembly, which then, in its turn, asks the member states to sign and ratify the convention. Those, who feel that the realisation of world peace can be attained by a world state, an idea which can be traced back to Dante, do not deem the competence of the United Nations to be sufficient. Even before World War II, H. G. Wells and Bertrand Russell developed plans for a world state holding full sovereignty. David Mitrany [21] drafted the model of a world state on a functional and federative basis which is still now worth considering: the legislative, administrative and judicial powers were to rest primarily with regionally combined groups of states of a relatively similar standard of social and political development, excluding the great powers who were to remain independent.[22] As regards economic relations, Mitrany held that these could be organised on world level only if they were to be constructive and peaceful.

The idea of a world state has been intensively discussed again since World War II. I will only mention the comprehensive book by Grenvill Clark and Louis Sohn [23] *World Peace through New World Law*. It makes extensive proposals for the amendment of the United Nations Charter, but expressly excludes any competence of the United Nations "in the regulation of international trade".[24] The

21. See his work *The Progress of World Government*, London 1933.
22. For further details see Mitrany, op. cit. note 21, p. 107.
23. See their work *World Peace by World Law*, Frankfurt/M. 1961.
24. Op. cit., p. 46.

authors are, however, of the opinion that "a proper world system must be created", "in order to diminish the great differences in the economic circumstances of the different regions of the world, differences, the continuance of which may cause "instability and conflicts".[25] So, the plan proposes "to set up a world development authority, which is to promote the economic and social development of the developing regions in the world, especially by actual assistance and loans free of interest".[26]

It is generally agreed that, at the same time, there do not exist any real possibilities for the establishment of a world state. As the English historian A. Toynbee [27] points out, "the cement of a common culture is needed, which does not exist yet". Apart from social and cultural solidarity, in order to secure its existence, a state requires a government having effective power, and that pre-condition does not exist either. Toynbee holds that only the institution of a world authority for controlling atomic energy and another one for the supervision of production and distribution of food are possible now.

3. *Some pre-conditions for a world economic law and a world trade law*

If it is true, as Mitrany suggests, that the peaceful and constructive organisation of economic relations between states can only take place on a world basis, we must pose the question as to why this has not been done.

a. *Premises*

In order to examine the question, we shall begin from three premises:

1. that the exchange of goods and services in the world is necessary or at least desirable;
2. that the ideal situation would be reached if individual persons, legal persons and states could bring about the exchange of goods and services only by negotiating and concluding contracts, which

25. Op. cit., p. 15.
26. Op. cit., p. 27.
27. In this connection see Arnold J. Toynbee, *Change and Habit – The Challenge of our Time,* London 1966, p. 138 et seq.

would imply that the world had become a common market;
3. that the attainment of this state of affairs only appears to be possible where social, economic and political conditions are roughly equal in the nations concerned.

b. Factors in opposition to the above premises

Three facts are in opposition to the above premises, namely:

1. that the world is divided into industrialised and non-industrialised states, into suppliers of raw materials and of valuable industrial products, into poor and rich nations,
2. that the trend towards the welfare state has divisive effects in the world, and
3. that the world is divided on an ideological basis.

The first-mentioned factor is, I think, the most important one. As Dag Hammerskӧld said already in 1954, the deep gulf between the poor and the rich nations is a problem, which "in the long run will be more dangerous than conflicts which demand our attention at the present time". U. Thant, in his report of 1962 wrote "that the present division of the world into rich and poor countries ... is more real and more serious ... and lastly far more explosive than the ideological divisions in the world". The effects of trade must be considered in relation to the division into rich and poor nations, into suppliers of raw materials and industrialised nations. The position of the suppliers of raw materials may worsen in the event of fluctuations in prices of industrial products, which have a considerable influence on the prices of raw materials in the world market, and in the event of economic recessions and crises. Such events may cause poorer states to lose more than they gain in aid from the developed nations.

It should be pointed out, however, that this model tends to over-generalise, and is inapplicable to the petrol producing countries at the present time. According to a recent report it is inapplicable to Kenya, the economic independence of which has become more and more apparent during the past ten years, largely on account of the fact that it is a coffee exporting country and coffee is said by experts to rank next to petrol as a valuable commodity in world trade.[28] Other

28. Professor Letiche of the University of California at Berkeley, a

examples might be pointed out. Thus the individual case may not conform to the model already mentioned.[29]

It will only be necessary to consider a few factors in relation to the trend towards the welfare state. This has been one of the contributory causes of such impediments to world trade as the absence of fixed exchange rates, differences in internal taxes, export and import restrictions, and also to differences in social and industrial laws which have their effect on prices. National legislation may contain different requirements in relation to the qualities of products, and national health and pollution regulations may be different. Quite apart from ideological differences between nations, all the factors recently mentioned can cause impediments to the free flow of trade. An attempt will now be made to consider, how regional systems of economic and trade law can mitigate the effect of such factors.

E. Regional economic law and trade law

In our analysis of the question as to how important regional economic law and trade law may be for the maintenance of peace, we shall examine the Regional Economic Commissions of the United Nations, and above all the European Economic Communities (EEC) and the Council for Mutual Economic Assistance (CMEA). The European Free Trade Association (EFTA), and the Latin American Free Trade Association (LAFTA), however, shall only be mentioned briefly here.

1. The Regional Economic Commissions of the United Nations

The Regional Economic Commissions are not independent organs, authorised to create economic or trade law for a certain region. They are subsidiary organs of the Economic and Social Council, which is itself an organ of the General Assembly of the United Nations. According to articles 55 and 62 of the United Nations Charter, the General Assembly's aims are stated to be of universal character. If it

---

participant in the Oxford International Symposium 1973 (see Preface), kindly directed my special attention to these facts.

29. See the report in *Handelsblatt* Nr. 226, 1973, p. 8.

is assumed that in order to realise the task of the unification of economic and trade law, one must first secure improvements in economic, social and political conditions throughout the world in accordance with articles 55 and 62 of the United Nations Charter, then regional efforts toward this end should be of great value. Such efforts are consistent with the aims of the United Nations, as the regional commissions being subsidiary organs of the United Nations have to work for the same aims. As we know from experience, special reference may now be made to the United Nations analysis "Five-Year Perspective 1960-1964, Document E (3347) Rev. 1", for a number of purposes, but effective work for a universal goal can only be carried out on a regional basis. The solution of many economic problems is not possible without them being considered in relation to a larger supranational background. If the non-industrialised countries are to become fully economically developed, quite a number of tasks are of a universal nature, for example, combating infant mortality and starvation, and the mechanisation of agriculture and industrialisation. The tasks can be carried out by world-wide organisations.[30] On the other hand, it is clear, that different climatic and other conditions, as well as differences of mentality and cultural development present tasks which can only be carried out effectively on a regional basis. In addition to that, we have to consider a psychological barrier insofar as it will be almost impossible in the near future to awaken a consciousness of the existence of a world economy in the inhabitants of developing countries, whose awareness is often limited. Thus, we have to recognise the possibility of integration in limited areas where relatively equal economic conditions prevail and where the parallelism of interests may make a real chance of integration possible.[31]

30. As to the changes in the structure of the World Economy see "Der Weltwirtschaftliche Strukturwandel, Rückblick auf die Sechziger Jahre und Ausblick" in *Die Weltwirtschaft, Halbjahresschrift des Instituts für Weltwirtschaft an der Universität Kiel,* herausg. von Herbert Giersch 1970, p. 19 et seq., esp. pp. 68, 84, 86; see further the basic study of Gunnar Myrdal, *The Challenge of World Poverty; A World Anti-Poverty Programme in Outline,* first published in the United States 1970, published in Pelican Books 1971.

31. See Detlef Dicke, *Die administrative Organisation der Entwicklungshilfe durch die Vereinten Nationen,* Frankfurt/M. 1972, p. 29 et seq.

As regards the achievements of the different Economic Commissions, the ECLA has been the most successful. The decisive factors which have promoted the integration of this region were the common culture and history, and the attitude taken by Latin-American States towards the hegemony of the United States. In this region this Commission initiated the creation of the free-trade-zones of CACM and LAFTA.[32]

The ECAFE met with much greater difficulties in its region due to solely adverse factors, namely:

> "The division into numerous geographical sub-regions and the existence of religious, cultural and language differences as well as deep-rooted political tensions. The economic situation of the different countries cannot always be compared. The region includes three highly developed industrial countries (Japan, Australia and New Zealand) and states which, even in comparison with other developing countries, must be called poor, for example, Afghanistan, Burma, Laos and Nepal. While the hegemony of the United States in the American region has led to a sense of community among the Latin-American countries, the hegemony of the Soviet Union and China in the Asiatic region has led to the disunity of the region. Thus the efforts of the ECAFE at integration must remain limited to single projects."[33]

The question as to whether and to what extent economic law and trade law can be harmonised on a regional basis will be discussed when the CMEA and the EEC have been considered by way of example.

2. The Council for Mutual Economic Assistance (CMEA) and the European Economic Communities (EEC)

It has already been stated that in order to create a world economic and world trade law economic, social and political conditions must be approximately similar throughout the world. The economic and political aspects have been dealt with when the Regional Economic

32. This statement is based on events occuring before 1966; see Dicke, op. cit. note 29, p. 37 with further references. Events occuring since do not lead to such conclusions, as has been reported by Professor Brewer Carias in his report to the Oxford International Symposium 1973, see Chapter 3, pp. 13-33, *ante*.

33. See Dicke, op. cit. note 29, p. 38.

Commissions were discussed, so it is not necessary to consider these matters again. But, it is very interesting to look at the CMEA and the EEC, because these institutions may be considered as representing the socialist camp and the capitalist camp respectively.

a. Common features

To begin with, it must be pointed out that the statute of the CMEA as well as the preamble to the Treaty of Rome express the determination of the states concerned to contribute towards the safeguarding of peace in the world. Further, the preamble of the Charter of the CMEA states, that the contracting parties are convinced that co-operation between their countries will help to reach the aims laid down in the United Nations Charter; in the preamble to the Treaty of Rome we find the express intention "to promote the welfare of overseas countries according to the principles of the United Nations Charter". This, I think, shows that both organisations feel themselves bound by the fundamental principles accepted by the United Nations.

b. Differences in the structures of the two organisations

1) EEC

The differences in the structure of both these organisations arise from the fact that the EEC is a supranational institution, the nucleus of which is the formation of a common market, and consequently the intention to co-ordinate the economic policies of the member states. The harmonisation of the provisions of national law so far as this is necessary for the proper functioning of the common market thus becomes necessary. Consequently, customs are being abolished, a common law of competition is being developed and the harmonisation of the law of taxation, labour and social law, and of company and trade law is in the process of development, or is at least projected. The EEC proves the above thesis to be right, namely that a common economic law is the necessary basis for a unitary trade law.

2) CMEA

In contrast to the EEC, the CMEA is not a supranational organisation, but has only the function to co-ordinate the efforts of the member states represented in the Council and to develop the national economies of their peoples according to plan. The Council makes only recommendations to the governments of the countries concerned which, subsequently, have to be accepted by the respective governmental organs in order to achieve co-ordination of the economic plans of the member states (article III, IV). The CMEA General Conditions of Delivery of Goods of 1968 provide for certain measures of unification of law in relation to contracts involving the delivery of goods made between legal persons in the member states.

c. Political aspects

One must consider the political aims of the two regional economic blocs when considering their possible function in maintaining peace. Although both, the Rome Treaty and the Charter of the CMEA refer to the safeguarding of world peace and to the promotion of the aims of the United Nations, the two blocs have opposing political aims. In the communiqué on the foundation of the CMEA, as printed in the "Pravda" of 25 January 1949, p. 2, we read:

> "The conference further stated that the governments of the United States, England and several other West-European states actually boycott the peoples' democracies and the Soviet Union, because they feel that it is impossible for them to submit to the dictation of the Marshall Plan, as this would violate their sovereign rights as well as the interests of their national economies".
> Considering these circumstances the conference negotiated the creation of an organisation ...

In the essay by V. Arkhipov and A. Bykow,[34] the EEC, as well as other organisations are called an "instrument of discrimination in World Trade",[35] "an instrument of economic hostility against third parties" [36] whose "real aim is to unite in the economic and political struggle against the world socialist forces, extend the front of the "cold war" ..." [37] and finally it is called "the economic foundation of the aggressive bloc of NATO", "and a force capable of rallying the West-European imperialist forces against the Socialist Community".[38]

34. See *Free Trade or Exclusive Blocks*, Moscow 1971.
35. Op. cit. note 34, p. 74.
36. Op. cit. p. 77.
37. Op. cit. p. 78.
38. Op. cit., pp. 80, 89.

There is no need to attempt an evaluation of these contentions for our present purposes. We may say, however, that regional economic and trade groups may contribute to world peace, quite apart from the verbal declarations of their protagonists, if the regional groups have their basis in common values and aims. We may thus ask, where to find an ideological basis for transcending differences between the two power blocs in order to develop regional blocs, which will serve the same purpose. Let me remind you here of the words of Victor Hugo, cited above, that a day will come, which will know of no other battlefields than the markets open to trade and the minds open to ideas. At the present time, the opening-up of world markets definitely depends on human minds being open to common ideas and values, on which a world economic law might be based.[39]

d. The principle of a democratic welfare state as one capable of bridging the ideological differences between the two power blocs

The two power blocs which are dominant in world politics in our present time are the Western Bloc on the one hand and the Eastern Bloc on the other hand; the Third World and China will, for the moment, not be taken into consideration. As regards these two blocs, we might think that the "principle of peaceful co-existence" was their common political basis. But it is not yet clear, whether this principle merely describes the existing state of affairs, namely co-existence as the result of the actual balance of power, but fails to describe a common ideological basis for the existence of the two blocs.[40]

The common basis for East and West, which may also be found to hold good for the relations with the developing countries and China, is the principle of a material, liberal, democratic, legal state. This idea originates from the fact that the principles of freedom and equality have their roots "not only in the ideas of Western democracy", but that they are of fundamental importance in classical economics and that Karl Marx' economic philosophy is also based upon them. It seems that the principle of human freedom and equality is the

39. Upon the need for utilising explicit value judgements, see Gunnar Myrdal, *The Challenge of World Poverty*, op. cit., note 28, p. 41 et seq. with further references.

40. See Fabricius, "Internationales Handelsrecht und Weltfrieden", op. cit. note 16, pp. 125, 126 for further information.

common root.[41] The differences between the Western and the Eastern system arise from the fact that these principles have not been carried into full effect in countries belonging to either bloc; they have not been materially realised in actual life to the extent that might have been practically possible. If these principles are more fully realised, the two blocs may be expected to move more closely together.

Arnold J. Toynbee describes the differences in his work "Change and Habit – The Challenge of our Time" [42] as follows:

> "Communism has erred, not in insisting on justice, but in sacrificing liberty for the sake of it. Individualism has concentrated on the Christian valuation of human souls as being infinitely precious in the sight of God, as God himself has signified by suffering for their redemption. Individualism has erred, not in insisting on the sacrosanctity of human personalities, but in sacrificing social justice to this."

These ideas, in essence, hit the nucleus of the problems. The constitutional developments in Germany, which were based on Kant's philosophy, led to the evolution of the liberal, democratic, legal state, a development similar to that in other West-European states, which in England was influenced by Hobbes, John Stuart Mill and Jeremy Bentham. This liberal democratic state has abolished the class structure of the eighteenth century, but it never intended to promote the full participation of and integration into social and economic life of the proletariat. Economic and social equality has not yet been developed to its possible and necessary limits. The peoples' democracies, under the influence of the philosophy of Hegel and the economic philosophy of Marx, have promoted the integration of all classes in society, but have restricted the political freedom of the individual.[43]

41. A more comprehensive treatment of the principle under discussion appears in Fabricius, *Mitbestimmung in der Wirtschaft – Ein gesellschafts-, wirtschafts- und rechtspolitisches Problem,* Frankfurt/M. 1970, p. 57 et seq. and further in Fabricius, "A Theory of Co-determination" in *The Harmonisation of European Company Law,* ed. by Clive M. Schmitthoff, U.K. Comparative Law Series, London 1973, p. 138 et seq.

42. See Toynbee, *Change and Habit,* op. cit. note 25, p. 174.

43. See further *Mitbestimmung in der Wirtschaft,* op. cit. note 38, p. 33 et seq.

e. Human rights and the principle of equality as the central problem

The central problem of the development of a world economic law and a world trade law in the future is the furthering of economic human rights and of the principle of human equality in the economic, social and political sphere.

If we recognise that freedom and equality presuppose each other, as Kant rightly states in his legal philosophy, then it appears that an optimum of freedom will be reached in the world, i.e. freedom for all, if the principle of equality becomes reality. It is difficult to define the ambit of the principle of equality, as we have to decide on what conditions they must be obtained before equal treatment exists. The problem of defining the content of an obligation of equal treatment has arisen in international law. Such definition may become possible as a result of the development of the principle of equality, and giving a substantive content to it. In the beginning it was conceived of as the sovereign equality of states, the "central idea of the world", and as an "alternative to despotism", then in the eighteenth century the decisive step was taken, namely to apply the principle of equality also to individuals. The first result of this was the abolition of slavery and serfdom and in the long run, formal equality under the law and later, political equality were achieved. The task of the twentieth century is now to realise social and economic equality.[44] Such a realisation will mark the progress of democracy in the world, since freedom and equality are the foundation stones of the democratic idea. This development is by no means restricted to the Western world. As J. W. Burton [45] of University College London quite rightly states, the modern welfare state, be it capitalist or communist, is marked by a high degree of democratisation of the process of decision, which comes about as a result of increasing education and of the activities of the mass media, increased communication, as well as of ideological

44. For the principle of equality in its economic aspects see Myrdal, *The Challenge of World Poverty,* op.cit. note 28, p. 63 et seq.; for its historical development Mitrany, *The Progress of International Government,* op. cit. note 21, p. 53 et seq.; in the area of Workers Co-determination Fabricius, *Mitbestimmung in der Wirtschaft,* op. cit. note 38, p. 32 et seq. *A Theory of Co-Determination,* op. cit. note 38, p. 145 et seq.

45. See his article "Conflicts as Function of Change" in *Because we want to survive,* op. cit. note 5, p. 348 and 352.

and other influences which have their effect on the highest echelons of power in society in the present century. Further, J. W. Burton states that this tendency toward democratisation explains the different development of Communism and Socialism, the existence of the capitalist welfare state and the liberation of the colonial peoples.

It is not possible to go more deeply into the question of equality here and to develop its consequences more concretely. The problem can only be touched upon. Adam Smith, whose theses have had a decisive influence on the Western world, recognised in agreement with Kant, four causes which invest a person with authority over others, i.e. which may justify inequality. These causes were:

> "Superiority of personal qualities, superiority of age, superiority of property, superiority of birth".[46]

It is apparent that, given the state of public opinion at present, all these factors cannot be regarded as a justification of human inequality.

F. Final conclusions

1. If international trade law and international economic law can be harmonised on a universal basis, this would contribute greatly to world peace.
2. Regional systems of economic and trade law may help to fulfil this latter function, especially if they can assist developing regions towards an appropriate degree of economic, social and political parity with the rest of the world.
3. Regional systems of economic and trade law may also be of value insofar as they may lead to the realisation of the principles of a democratic welfare state.

G. Some prospects for the future

1. The creation of a world economic law and a world trade law may well be possible if we begin to harmonise and unify those areas which

46. See Wagner, *Die preußischen Reformer und die zeitgenössische Philosophie*, Köln 1956 p. 68.

particularly lend themselves to it. International trade law appears to lend itself especially to these processes, as we have to deal in this area mainly with technical law concerning the formation of business contracts, in respect of which world opinions supports such harmonisation and unification. UNCITRAL has chosen this direction.
2. We should also make a valiant attempt to develop international economic law. International currency conferences, UNCTAD, GATT and other institutions are working in individual areas in this large field, but their plans have not yet fully materialised on a global basis, and cannot be expected to succeed in the near future.

In addition to this, however, there are other possibilities. The prestige of the United Nations would be considerably enhanced if this world organisation were to become the trustee of a world development fund, which would guarantee the distribution of goods as part of an assistance to be given to developing countries. Furthermore, common safety regulations concerning industrial goods as well as minimum standards concerning pollution and pharmaceutical products and qualifications as to hygiene could be developed. The obligation to offer surplus produce which would otherwise be destroyed by the producing countries to a United Nations authority may be implemented, in order to enable the United Nations to buy this produce at the lowest possible price, and to offer it to countries suffering from crop failure and similar problems. A world patent office might also be set up, as well as a world register for multinational enterprises, which are sometimes accused of provoking or exacerbating international currency crises and suspected of stirring up political conflicts.[47]

H. Scientific speculation and reality

During the last twenty years scientific disciplines of all quarters have dealt most intensively with the problem of maintaining peace. I have

47. In this connection, see "Implications of Multinational Firms for World Trade and Investment and for U.S. Trade and Labor, Report to the Committee on Finance of the United States Senate," *U.S. Government Printing Office,* Washington 1973.

tried to contribute to these efforts from the point of view of international economic and trade law. It was an attempt based on reason. The value of such scientific investigations might be questioned. Professor Letiche quoted Goethe who said: *"Die Welt, durch die Vernunft dividiert, geht nicht auf"*. That might be interpreted by a word of Morley in his brilliant essay on Machiavelli: "It is events which make history". Hegel [48] seemed to be more pessimistic. His description of a scientist, who for him was the same as a philosopher, is apparent from his famous statement:

> "If Philosophy paints her grey with grey, then a figure of life has grown old, for with grey in grey you cannot make younger, you can only recognise; the owl of Minerva does not begin its flight until dusk falls".

This image of the scientist only being able to carry out a post-mortem examination does, however, not apply to our present times. In our modern technical world with its pluralistic social structure scientists are expected to predict possible alternative courses of development. The scientist, alas, is not a hero bringing about changes in things. Do we then require strong men modelled on Carlyle's heroic historical figures to effect changes? Or do the great men only give their names to the movements of the nameless masses who make history, as Leo Tolstoi says in his work *War and Peace*. Tolstoi denied the importance of even the most influential and most powerful individuals. Truth appears to lie midway between these two views.

Finally, we may ask if a system, because of its inner contradiction, can be changed only by violence, as the classical authors, especially Karl Marx, thought, or if, as is held by the modern sociology of organisation, consent and integration will suffice.[49] The preferable latter path will be hard to walk and will resemble the form of a spiral, the movement of which is tortuous in detail but always upwards, in a never ending progression.

48. See his work, *Grundlinien der Philosophie des Rechts*, II, ed. Berlin p. 20.

49. See J. A. A. van Doorn, "Der Konflikt in formalen Organisationen" in *Weil wir überleben wollen*, op.cit. note 5, p. 116 et seq.

INDEX OF AUTHORS AND EDITORS

SUBJECT INDEX